Orientation to Higher

Drs Marion Stuart-Hoyle and J. Wiles
Canterbury Christ Church University

ALWAYS LEARNING

PEARSON

Harlow, England • London • New York • Boston • San Francisco • Toronto • Sydney • Auckland • Singapore • Hong Kong
Tokyo • Seoul • Taipei • New Delhi • Cape Town • Sao Paulo • Mexico City • Madrid • Amsterdam • Munich • Paris • Milan

Pearson Education Limited
Edinburgh Gate
Harlow
Essex CM20 2JE
England

and Associated Companies throughout the world

Visit us on the World Wide Web at:
www.pearsoned.co.uk

This Custom Book Edition © 2012 published by Pearson Education Limited

ISBN 978 1 78236 667 6

Printed and bound by Bell and Bain Ltd, Glasgow.

Contents

Preface

This reader has been designed for the use of first year students in the Department of Sport Science, Tourism and Leisure at Canterbury Christ Church University, studying the 'Orientation to Higher Education' module in the first term. Each workshop that students participate in as part of the module has a corresponding chapter in the reader, that can be read before and/or after the workshop, to help them better understand the particular topic at hand. The reader should also serve as a valuable source of study skills information throughout the three years of the degree programme.

Whilst the reader is intended primarily for those undergraduates studying the Orientation module within the Department of Sport Science, Tourism and Leisure, it is equally relevant to all first year undergraduates who are seeking to get to grips with the demands of University life and the skills that need to be developed from the outset of an undergraduate's time at University.

Please note that the references to other pages/chapters within this book may not relate to material in this book as it is a collection of chapters from a range of different books. If you do need to refer to work that cannot be found in this book, the full book details from which chapters have been selected can be found in the contents page.

Dr Marion Stuart-Hoyle and Dr Jim Wiles

Preparing for university

What you and your family need to consider

If you want to get off to a flying start at university, there are several aspects of student life that you should think about beforehand. This chapter prompts you to reflect on possible changes in your study methods, financial situation, accommodation and personal life.

Key topics:
- → Goal setting at university
- → Academic aspects
- → Financial matters
- → Accommodation choices
- → Self-maintenance

Key term
Reflect

Going to university is a life-changing event. It will be an experience that is exhilarating and mind-expanding, but perhaps a little daunting at first. In this book, we aim to peel away some of the myths and mysteries of academic study and help you to make the most of your university years.

Self-orientation and decision-making are themes of this chapter, with the aim of ensuring that your start is as positive as possible. This reflective process is one you may wish to return to from time to time as you progress through university, both to assess your progress and reset your targets (see also Ch 7). The checklists presented here are designed to focus your thoughts, rather than feed you answers; your responses will depend on your own situation and personality. Like much at university, success in turning these thoughts into action will depend on *you* rather than anyone else.

→ Goal setting at university

Your goals at university may vary according to whether you are planning your next move after school or college or whether you are returning to study after doing other things. For both types of student, a good question to ask yourself is: 'Where do I want to be in five years' time and then in ten years' time?'

To help you answer these fundamental questions, run through the 'goal-setting exercise' on page 6. You may not have answers to all the questions right now, but they will help you to start thinking about deeper issues in your life and how you might tackle the challenges of university.

Whether you have just left school or college or are returning to study after time away from a learning environment, the challenges of university life remain broadly similar. It's your responses to them that will possibly be quite different.

Coming to university – a goal-setting exercise

The answers to these questions should help you define your life and study goals:

- What are your life goals?
- What career path do you have as your aim?
- If you haven't chosen a career, will going to university help you choose one?
- What subject(s) do you need to study to achieve your career goals?
- What combination of subjects will best keep your options open?
- How might university limit your options?
- Apart from a qualification, what do you want to get out of your time as a university student?

→ Academic aspects

A large portion of this book deals with the skills required for study at university level, many of which will be quite different from those required at school or college. Before embarking on your course you may benefit from carrying out a mental 'audit' of your current abilities to allow you to focus on areas where you can gain maximum benefit from improvement.

You might start this process by considering the questions below. If you find the final question rather open-ended, a scan through the list of chapters in this book (pages v-vii) will provide a sense of the range of skills you will be expected to have mastered by the time you graduate. Ch 6 includes further information.

Coming to university – a reality check

How much do you really know about what studying at university involves?
  ❏ a lot   ❏ a fair amount   ❏ a little   ❏ not a lot

What level of experience do you bring to university learning?
  ❏ a lot   ❏ a fair amount   ❏ a little   ❏ not a lot

How much effort are you prepared to make in order to graduate successfully?
  ❏ a lot   ❏ a fair amount   ❏ a little   ❏ not a lot

How much support will be necessary from others?
  ❏ a lot   ❏ a fair amount   ❏ a little   ❏ not a lot

What skills do you think you will need to develop?

There is much you can do personally to improve your academic skills levels:

- sign up for appropriate skills-related courses and workshops (for example, those for IT skills, effective writing);
- read textbooks, including this one, that provide relevant guidance and advice;
- search for web-based resources that fit your needs;
- seek help from tutors and support staff - they will provide an impartial, confidential and free service;
- absorb and act upon the feedback you receive on assessed work.

→ Financial matters

For many people, the decision to enter university has important financial implications. No matter what your personal circumstances, it is probably helpful to work out, in broad terms, how much your university education will cost. Figure 2.1 gives some broad

Questions to ask yourself about financing your university studies

- Have I got a good idea of what my university education will cost me?
- How much will my partner or family be helping me?
- How much debt am I prepared to take on?
- How will I control my expenditure?
- Will I need to take on part-time work to finance myself?
- Will I need to get a summer job to help finance myself?
- How will I balance the time and energy needed to work with the time and energy required for study, especially close to exams?

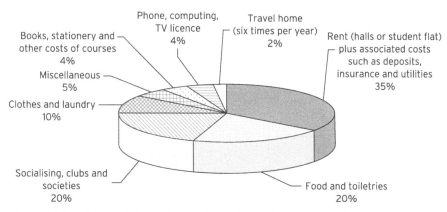

Figure 2.1 **Breakdown of the costs of being a student (per annum).** These proportions are approximate and assume that the student is living in self-catering accommodation. Depending on location, the total costs may amount to £6000-9000 (2008-9 figures) and in some cities the proportional cost of accommodation may be greater. A student living at home might have reduced accommodation costs, but possibly higher travel spending. Mature students may have a different pattern of spending related to pre-existing responsibilities.

Table 2.1 **Expected and unexpected costs of being at university.** This list is not exhaustive, but is designed to help you anticipate your main categories of expenditure (see also Figure 2.1). Table Z.1 (page 544) is a spreadsheet to help you manage your budget as a student (see also Ch 9).

Category of expenditure	Examples	Comments
Fees	• Tuition fees	These vary according to where you come from and where you are studying (see text)
Accommodation costs	• Hall fees • Rent/mortgage • Insurance • Utilities (gas, electricity, phone)	At the present time, students do not have to pay council tax. Insurance and utility costs are inclusive in some types of accommodation
Living and social costs	• Food • Drink • Entertainment • Clubs and societies	Even if living in catered accommodation, you will incur additional food costs, e.g. at lunchtime or in the evening. Entertainment costs will depend on what sort of 'social animal' you intend to be
Travel costs	• Fares or season tickets • Car maintenance and fuel • Parking • Tolls • Visits home	These are greatly dependent on the distance between your accommodation and the campus site(s) you need to visit
Study costs	• Books, stationery • Equipment • Lab deposits • Field trips • Computing • Photocopying and printing	Equipment costs, lab deposits and costs of field trips will only apply in certain subjects
Personal costs	• Mobile phone • Laundry • Toiletries • Haircuts • Clothing • Presents	These are dependent on lifestyle and how fashion conscious you may be
Other	• Childminding/babysitting • Holidays • TV licence	A TV licence is required for all persons in shared accommodation unless it is a group let

categories of expenditure for a typical student and shows what proportion of the total costs each is estimated to take up, and Table 2.1 provides a listing of potential costs to take into account, some of which may be unexpected. The questions on page 7 will also help you define your responses to the financial challenges of university life. Ch 9 covers other issues that will help you to create a working budget to manage your finances.

The university fee system is complex because the fee and loan amounts and terminologies depend on your nationality and where in the UK you are studying.

Precise amounts of fees and loan arrangements may vary year on year. Consult the Universities UK website (**www.universitiesuk.ac.uk/paymentbydegrees**) for up-to-date and detailed information. UK students with low household income may have part or all of their fees paid for them. Visit the Department for Education and Skills website (**www.dfes.gov.uk/studentsupport/students**) for details of the different arrangements that apply to part-time students.

Many institutions have advisory personnel who offer advice and information on money matters. Often there is a student hardship fund, which can be used in cases of extreme financial difficulty. Note that, as a student, you may be entitled to preferential treatment, such as exemptions from payment of taxes such as council tax, cheap travel and concession pricing in stores and entertainment venues.

→ Accommodation choices

Student accommodation is a real concern – you will need to live somewhere that is relatively comfortable, warm and secure. To help focus your thoughts on the choices available, Table 2.2 summarises the pros and cons of different types of accommodation. The main options available to you are:

- **Living away from home.** This can be a big step for some, but most students settle in within a few weeks. You can live in university accommodation, or rent within the private sector. Accommodation in university halls is a safe option and may be guaranteed for first-year students unless they enter through UCAS 'clearing'. While the quality of privately rented rooms is more variable, some universities will have inspected and graded such accommodation. For rented accommodation, you will have to sign a lease or contract for a fixed period. You may have to pay a deposit, for example, the equivalent of one month's rent, which will be refundable on departure. Any charges for damages would be deducted from this deposit.

smart tip

Legal aspects of accommodation

Different legislation governs furnished and unfurnished accommodation. You can gain advice on this and other matters relating to renting property from Citizens' Advice Bureaux and also from student services in your institution.

- **Living in the family home.** This provides a familiar environment, but both the student and the family members should recognise that it involves changes for the whole family, whether you are living in the parental home or in your own home with a partner and possibly children.

Whatever your accommodation, you will need time, space and peace to study. Ideally, this zone should be for your sole use, with good facilities, such as a network connection and storage for your books and files.

Whether you live at home or not, going to university often involves new or altered relationships. The questions on page 11 will help you reflect on the adjustments you and your friends and family may need to make.

Table 2.2 **Factors to consider when selecting accommodation for university**

	Living in university accommodation (student halls and flats)	Living in rented accommodation (private sector)	Living at home with your family
Potential advantages and benefits	• Costs reasonable • Facilities clean, warm and safe • Ready-made social network • Halls may have a good social calendar • Meals provided (at a cost) • Rent inclusive of some services* • Facilities like kitchen and laundry on hand • Support of hall warden(s) • Good complaints procedures	• Wide range of choice • More privacy • Less disturbance and noise (but not always) • Freedom to select those you live with • Your choice of food and meal times • Fewer restrictions	• Familiar environment • Support of family members • Potentially cheaper option • Easy to keep up existing social contacts • Home cooking • Help with services* and laundry • No contracts and no deposits
Potential disadvantages and problems	• Facilities possibly basic • Lengthy contract period • Can be noisy and lacking in privacy • No or little choice of neighbours or flatmates • You might not like the food • Restricted opening/curfews • Financial penalties for damage caused by others • You may have to share a room • Less easy to escape from campus confines	• Can be a costly option • Need to pay a refundable deposit • Additional costs of services* • Potential to be isolated and lonely • Conditions and furnishing may not be ideal • May need to sign up for a lengthy period • Shopping, cooking and cleaning required • Extra travel costs and loss of time commuting	• May be difficult to focus on studies • IT connections may be required • Travel costs and loss of time commuting • Lack of university-based social life • Your desire for personal freedom may conflict with the wishes and lifestyle of your family • Lack of academic and social contact with peers on campus

*'Services' include cleaning, heating, lighting, electricity and/or gas, telephone, internet connection.

→ Self-maintenance

Especially if you are leaving the family home for the first prolonged period, being a student can mean quite a large readjustment to your way of life. You will have to take responsibility for yourself and live with the decisions you make.

Questions to ask yourself about living with others as a student

How well do you think you will get on with others (not your family)?

- ❑ brilliantly
- ❑ it'll be fine
- ❑ I've some reservations
- ❑ don't like the idea at all

How well do you think others (not your family) will like living with you?

- ❑ I'm easy-going
- ❑ I like my own space
- ❑ I'm not good in the mornings or late at night – I need my sleep
- ❑ I don't tolerate fools gladly

How do you think your family will adjust to you becoming a university student?

- ❑ I think they'll be very supportive
- ❑ I think they'll understand that I need some space and time to myself
- ❑ I think they'll miss me

What compromises might you need to make if you share accommodation with people:

- – in a university residence?
- – in a student flat?

If you are a student living at home, what adjustments will need to be made:

- – by you?
- – by other family members?

'Self-maintenance' encompasses a wide range of matters, including feeding yourself, doing your laundry, time management and companionship. Some new skills you may need to consider are:

- shopping for yourself;
- learning to cook;
- learning how to use a washing machine;
- remembering to use a washing machine;
- time management;
- meeting deadlines;
- operating on a limited budget;
- looking after your own health.

If you are living with others, there are other issues to resolve together:

- keeping shared accommodation clean;
- sharing chores fairly;

- working out an equitable way of splitting communal living costs;
- avoiding cliques and creating outcasts;
- being considerate when others need to study or work on an assignment;
- likes and dislikes regarding food and drink.

Practical tips to help you prepare for university

Prepare mentally for your new independence. Many new students fail to realise that no one will be telling them what to do or when to study - or even what to study. Especially in the first months, there's a risk of drifting aimlessly. You will need to set your own rules to help you achieve your goals.

Prepare mentally for the new working regime. The change from school, college or employment or unemployment can involve radical changes to your pattern and level of activity. One option is to act as if you were taking on a nine-to-five job, in that you leave home in the morning and spend your day 'working' in lectures, tutorials, practicals or private study until you return in the evening. That way you can make the most of your non-lecture time during the day. If you have work, social or sporting commitments, the need to plan your activities is even more important (see Ch 8).

Research your loan, grant and bursary entitlements. Check all the literature that has been sent to you and make sure you have sent off all necessary forms in good time. Look at your university's website to see whether you qualify for any grants or bursaries.

Work out a draft budget. Using the tables in this chapter and Table Z.1 on page 544, estimate as best you can what your likely costs will be and decide how to match your expected income and borrowing to these sums. This may involve making decisions about the amount of debt you are willing to incur by the end of your studies.

Research rented accommodation options thoroughly. Look especially carefully at:

- rental cost;
- room size and study facilities;
- distance from campus and lecture halls;
- whether meals are included;
- whether you might need to share a room;
- whether others of similar background to you will be housed nearby;
- whether you will have an en-suite bathroom or will have to share;
- what charges there are for an internet connection.

Decide which aspects are important to you and which are not, and select accommodation appropriately, recognising that some compromise will almost certainly be necessary.

Look into the legal situation regarding multiple occupation. If the accommodation you intend to rent has more than three unrelated people sharing, you should make sure that it has a Houses in Multiple Occupation (HMO) licence. Without this, the accommodation may not meet legal requirements and you may be at risk. Seek advice from the university support service that deals with issues related to leases and other aspects of letting contracts.

Visit the university accommodation if you can. This will help you get a feel for the options and you may be able to talk to existing students who know about specific features that you may not have thought about.

Read the small print of your accommodation contract. When choosing accommodation, read the contracts very carefully. There may be unpleasant or expensive consequences if you fail to deliver what is specified in the small print. For example, you may be penalised if you damage contents or do not clean properly (in the view of the landlord).

Act quickly to reserve accommodation. Once you have made up your mind, make contact or send back the relevant forms as quickly as possible or you may miss out because others have registered their interest first.

Check your inventory. If living in furnished rented accommodation, you should ensure that you are given (and have checked) an inventory of the equipment and furniture present at the outset. On the inventory you should note (date and sign) any broken or damaged items so that you are not charged for these when you leave.

Involve your family. Perhaps you can do this by inviting them to accompany you on a campus visit. This will give them the chance to see your new 'working' environment and it will help them to understand your university life better.

Plan to personalise your accommodation. This will help you avoid feeling homesick. Rented rooms and flats will feel very strange and impersonal at first, so arrange to bring along some favourite objects, such as posters, mascots and family photos.

GO And now . . .

2.1 **Plan your new regime.** If you've thought about your goals for your time at university (page 5), think about what sort of study regime will be required to achieve them; what new societies and sports clubs you may wish to join; how you intend to balance study, employment and social life; and how you will keep in contact with your family. Mature students need to plan equally carefully to achieve a balance between family and study responsibilities. Using a planner such as *The Smarter Student Planner* will help you to allocate your time and keep track of academic and personal commitments.

2.2 **Think about all the new skills you might need to acquire.** If you are leaving home for the first time, list the things you will need to do for yourself for the first time. These might include laundry, cooking, time-keeping and other 'self-maintenance' skills, as well as opening a bank account, dealing with a landlord and registering with a doctor. Enlist the help of your family and other contacts to help you learn about these things before entering university.

2.3 Make a list of items you will require at university. If you are leaving home to go to university, you'll need a good packing list so you avoid returning to collect items or having to buy duplicates. Don't forget:

- clothing for all likely weather conditions;
- fancy dress or ball/party gear;
- sports equipment;
- computers and calculators;
- CD player and TV;
- musical instruments;
- identification and documentation (for example, National Insurance number, details of bank accounts, passport, driving licence) and a secure filing cabinet;
- books;
- stationery;
- bicycle.

Learning, skills and employment

In deciding to study, you have taken a major investment decision – to invest in yourself. This chapter looks at the market in which you will be operating as a graduate, and at what you can do to maximise the return on your investment by developing 'transferable skills'. These are the skills that will help you do well both as a student and as a manager.

Learning outcomes

By the end of this chapter you should:

- understand what is meant by 'transferable skills'
- be starting to plan how you can develop these skills during your studies
- appreciate the ways in which organisations have changed in recent years
- understand the implications of these changes for graduate employment
- appreciate what 'graduate recruitment' means to employers and what they seek when recruiting
- be beginning to consider what you might want from a job.

If you are at the start of your university studies, it can be enlightening to work out just how much investment you are making in yourself: in the time you are committing, the income you are forgoing and the fees you are paying. Presumably you are hoping that this will lead to an enjoyable and well paid career. The bad news is that this is by no means certain. I know some graduates currently facing their thirtieth birthdays in jobs that frustrate and bore them, and pay very little. Although the UK graduate employment situation improved dramatically from a low point in 1983, and was still improving at the time of writing, the job market may have changed significantly by the time you graduate. The good news is that if you start *now* to manage your learning, to think about the sort of job you want, and to develop the skills you need to be attractive as an employee, you can greatly increase your chances of a profitable and fulfilling career. The even better news is that most of the skills that employers value will help you get a better class of degree.

So, although looking at employment skills may seem slightly bizarre at this stage, when your career may seem impossibly far in the future, it makes a lot of sense. This chapter looks at the employment context to clarify *what* you need to learn, suggests ways of starting to develop your learning skills, starts you on the process of thinking about the sort of career you would like, and shows you how you can start to *use* this book to become a successful learner.

As you may already be discovering, learning at university (like learning at work) is likely to be very different from learning at school: the main responsibility will be yours, and you will be learning a much wider range of skills. You need to be able to *manage* your own learning: planning and time management skills are essential for this. You will need to learn with others: team working and communication skills will be important. You will need to locate and use a wide range of information sources: this will require knowledge management skills. But above all you need to understand what learning *means* at this level, why it is so important and how to do it well.

WHAT EMPLOYERS LOOK FOR IN GRADUATES

It is never too soon to consider what you want from your working life, and what employers think they want when recruiting graduates. The job market is highly competitive, and you can greatly increase your chances of a successful career if you start thinking *now*. If this sounds impossible, don't worry. This chapter will give you a clearer idea of what is important to you, and help you clarify your employment goals. The final part of the book will complete the process.

The introduction to Part 1 alerted you to the fact that you will need to *respond* at intervals, rather than merely sit back and read. The process starts *now*: you need to capture your starting position. Then you can return to it at intervals, develop your thoughts further, note how they are changing and check that you have not inadvertently ignored something important.

ACTIVITY 1.1

If you have access to anyone who employs graduates, ask them what they seek in recruits. Look in the recruitments sections of a few newspapers, or visit the websites of companies you might like to work for, and build a list of the qualities mentioned as essential or desirable in interesting graduate vacancies.

_____

_____

_____

Were you more impressed by the similarities between employers, or the differences? Employers are far from agreed on what being a graduate can bring to a job. Variation is not surprising, since recruiters will be seeking to fill widely disparate jobs: there are likely to be as many different views of what constitutes the 'ideal graduate recruit' as there are of the 'ideal husband or wife'. Employers may be looking for people to interact with customers, to solve technical problems, to work with pre-existing teams of various kinds, to 'fit in' and be effective as quickly as possible, or to act as a force for change.

Organisations may be huge or tiny, bureaucratic or flexible and innovative. What they seek from recruits depends on where they sit on these different dimensions. As a graduate this variability may be an asset. Someone, somewhere, is going to see your set of skills as just what they want. Your task while a student is to ensure that the skill set you develop is attractive to the sort of employer for whom you really want to work. This means deciding on the sort of job you want, the sort of organisation you want to work for, identifying those skills, and then making sure that you develop them.

You may also have been struck by similarities in requirements. My own recent and somewhat random trawl of the papers yielded adverts for:

- 'graduates who are ambitious, motivated, good communicators and able to work to deadlines'
- 'a rigorous approach to work matched by highly developed communication and interpersonal skills'
- 'a strategic thinker . . . an excellent communicator with strong networking and negotiating skills'
- 'strong leadership skills, excellent communication and organisation skills, an ability to resolve complex problems and personal resilience and stamina'
- 'competency in a range of business planning issues, excellent writing skills and experience of giving effective presentations'.

Note the similarities. Every advert I found sought good communication skills, and many mentioned other interpersonal skills, planning skills and motivation. The Association of Graduate Recruiters (AGR) survey of summer 2006 suggested that team working, oral communication, flexibility and adaptability, customer focus and problem solving were the qualities most frequently sought by graduate recruiters. You will probably find similar requirements commonly referred to in your own investigations. It is these widely relevant, transferable skills that you need to develop, and which this book seeks to address.

KEY SKILLS AND APPLICATIONS FOR LEARNING AND EMPLOYMENT

Higher education's Quality Assurance Agency (QAA) has specified a set of core skills which it feels all graduates should have, and be able to apply at European and international levels. It has developed a set of benchmark standards for these. You can obtain the full set of benchmarking standards from the QAA website at **www.qaa.ac.uk**. They include:

- Cognitive skills – critical thinking, analysis and synthesis. You need, for example, to be able to identify assumptions, evaluate statements in terms of evidence, check the logic of an argument, define terms and make appropriate generalisations.

- Problem-solving and decision-making skills – quantitative and qualitative. You need to be able to identify, formulate and solve business problems, and generate and evaluate options, applying ideas and knowledge to a range of situations.
- Research and investigative skills – and use to resolve business and management issues, both individually then as part of a team. You need to be able to identify relevant business data and research sources and research methodologies, and for your research to inform your learning.
- Information and communications technology skills – you need to be able to use a range of business applications in any job.
- Numeracy and quantitative skills – data analysis, interpretation and extrapolation. You need to be able to use models of business problems and to draw conclusions from the information you obtain.
- Communication skills – oral and written, using a range of media. You need, for example, to be able to write business reports.
- Interpersonal skills – talking and listening, presentation, persuasion and negotiation. You need to be able to interact effectively with a range of people, including colleagues and customers.
- Team-working skills – leadership, team building, influencing. You need to be able to manage or contribute to team projects.
- Personal management skills – time planning, motivation, initiative – the need for these skills is obvious.
- Learning skills – reflective, adaptive and collaborative. You need to be motivated to learn and able to do so effectively in a range of contexts.
- Self-awareness – sensitivity and openness to others who are different from you. You need to be alert to how others will react to situations – the significance of 'emotional intelligence' is now becoming recognised.

ACTIVITY 1.2

For each of the above categories, think about your current skill level (use any available evidence, including feedback from friends, teachers, past employers and your own feelings). Give yourself a rating on a scale of 1 to 10, where 1 is very low, 10 as high as you can imagine needing. File your responses for future reference, as you will need them for subsequent work. (An electronic proforma is available to make this easy.)

The relevance of these sets of skills to work is fairly obvious – but will be highlighted whenever the skills are addressed in the book. What may be less immediately apparent is the extent to which these 'employment skills' will help you to learn more effectively at university, and to get better marks. Communication is obviously crucial to working with others, for example in group projects. Good communication skills will help you to present information face to face, and to write better assignments. Self-management skills are valuable for improving your own learning and performance and performing your own part of a group's task. Addressing problems involves using information. You can see not only that the skills are relevant in both contexts – they are highly *transferable* – but that they are closely interrelated. Finding a simple classification of something as complex as higher-level human skills is difficult.

There have been many other attempts at providing lists of sets of skills. For example, Harvey *et al.* (1997), drawing on information from a wide range of graduate employers, suggested the importance of looking at skills involved in:

- fitting in – blending into a team and becoming effective quickly
- persuading – whether within the team or in relation to the wider organisation or customers beyond it
- developing ideas – analysing situations rather than merely responding to them, often best done in a team
- transforming – which adds to all the above the ability to apply intellectual skills and leadership skills in order to steer change.

You may find this shorter list helps you think slightly differently about the skills you have and need to develop. Although it covers much of the same ground, the emphasis is slightly different. Finally, you might like to look at the results of a study carried out in the USA (Luthans *et al.*, 1988) into what a wide range of managers actually did. They found that managerial activities could be categorised into the following four sets:

- communication – paperwork and exchanging information
→ Ch 2
- 'traditional management' – planning, decision making and controlling (more on this in the next chapter)
- networking – interacting with outsiders, socialising and politicking
- human resource management – motivating, disciplining, managing conflict, staffing and training.

ACTIVITY 1.3

Look back at your assessment of your own strengths and weaknesses in the light of what you have subsequently read. Amend your earlier list if improvements suggest themselves at this point. Add in any areas where you now feel that your study, as well as your employability, might benefit from development.

As you will now realise, the many activities scattered throughout the book will often be cumulative, and you need a file (paper or electronic) in which to store your responses to these for easy subsequent reference. You will probably find it useful to file your answers and notes by chapter to start with. Once you have accumulated enough material, there will be suggestions as to how you can organise your notes into a more
→ Ch 3
structured *personal development file or ePortfolio.*

CAREERS WITHIN TODAY'S ORGANISATIONS

Earlier I suggested that careers are becoming far more fluid: this means that at regular intervals you will need to think about what you want from work. This will allow you to decide which jobs are most likely to meet your needs, and then to concentrate on the most relevant skills for development.

ACTIVITY 1.4

Log your initial thoughts about working life, both good and bad. Don't agonise about your answer. Just write down the first thing that comes into your head. Aim to write down between 10 and 20 words in response to the following prompts:

The things I am afraid a job might be:

_____

_____

Characteristics of my ideal job would be:

_____

_____

If possible, discuss your answers with four or five other people, to see where their views differ from yours and where they are similar. How many of you are afraid a job will be boring? How many of you want it to offer variety or the chance to meet interesting people? Do you want the chance to learn more, or to travel, or to help other people? Is status important? Were the responses from those who had already had jobs different from those who had not? If the discussion made you aware of things that are important to you but which you had omitted from your list, then construct a revised version and file this as well.

Career – a series of jobs seen in retrospect?

If your 'fears' included boredom, predictability, lack of freedom (the sort of thing that I was worried about most as a student), you were possibly thinking of the traditional 'graduate career' within a large, many-layered organisation, where good behaviour and following the rules would lead to steady progression. Large employers do still recruit graduates, but massive organisational restructuring in recent years has reduced the volume – though at the same time many of these jobs are if anything more interesting.

The 'career' as an organised succession of increasingly senior jobs has probably always been less common in reality than people believed. I can still remember being struck in 1971 by the 'definition' of career as 'a series of jobs seen in retrospect' by Ruth Lancashire, then one of the main researchers in the area, speaking at a conference on careers. Charles Handy (1989) describes how, when starting his first job in the 1950s, he was given an outline of his future career. This was to culminate in a job as chief executive of a particular company in a particular country. He left long before he was in sight of this pinnacle, but already both the projected company and the country had ceased to exist.

Certainly my own subsequent 'career' could not have been planned and seemed at the time to have been driven primarily by external forces. Yet the different jobs I have done have prepared me remarkably well for my present role, one which is more rewarding than any job I could have dreamed of as a student. And careers are becoming ever more 'unplanned' because of the ways in which organisations are changing.

Competitive pressures have driven major restructuring. Organisations have sought to cut costs and increase the speed with which they can respond to competitors and to changes in markets. Developments in information and communications technology have meant that many of the things which managers traditionally did – to do with filtering and funnelling and transmitting information – no longer need so much human intervention.

Organisations are changing

Most large organisations responded to competitive pressures by taking a hard look at their hierarchies and 'delayering', cutting out whole layers of middle management, just the sort of jobs which many graduates have filled in the past. While this decimation of management in itself cut employment costs, many organisations 'downsized' or 'rightsized' (euphemisms in this area abound) more generally, reducing the number of employees at other levels too. They also identified their 'core' business and concentrated on this, looking at ways of contracting out more peripheral activities such as cleaning, catering, warehousing, IT and even graduate recruitment.

The aim was to avoid using full-time permanent staff for non-core work. Such staff are expensive, and it may be slow and expensive to reduce staffing when business is poor. Increasingly, organisations have 'outsourced' non-core activities to specialist suppliers. Flexibility in staffing was also increased by using part-time employees or those on short-term contracts. Also, many large, specialist departments at 'head office' have been reduced by devolving a lot of their responsibilities to line managers.

Cartoon by Neill Cameron, www.planetdumbass.co.uk

IMPLICATIONS FOR GRADUATE EMPLOYMENT

Graduate recruitment prospects at the time of writing are extremely favourable, and the organisational changes outlined above make it clear why the 'thinking' skills developed by means of a degree are so important. The AGR Graduate Recruitment Survey (2006) (www.agr.org.uk) of some of the UK's leading employers showed that the current upward trend is continuing, with more vacancies than at any time since 1995. (Note that in this survey large private sector organisations in the vicinity of London are over-represented, but trends elsewhere may be similar.) Of course, it is impossible to predict what the situation will be by the time you graduate. If you want to track the situation you can find information each year from the Prospects website (www.prospects.ac.uk).

Note, however, that even in the highly favourable 2006 situation, the employers in the survey received an *average* of 28 applications for every vacancy (down from 37.6 in the 2003–04 recruitment year and 42.1 in 2002–03). The most attractive vacancies will receive many more applications than this. So use this book to develop your skills, and make yourself highly attractive to potential employers.

It is worth noting the expansion in opportunities for interesting employment in a wide range of organisations. Some are in smaller enterprises, others at levels which previously would not have attracted graduates, but which now offer precisely the challenges and satisfactions that would have been deemed lacking in the past.

If present trends continue, you can expect to work for a wider range of organisations than did your parents' generation and to change organisations, whether by free choice or necessity, every few years. If you want a higher-level job you may *need* to move: flatter organisations inevitably offer far fewer promotion opportunities than their multi-layered predecessors. So developing a 'career' will require positive action on your part and moves through several organisations.

Alternatively, you may change because you are seeking to develop additional skills or to broaden your experience. This is an important consideration: the wider your skills and experience, the greater your chances of obtaining a higher-level job, or of finding another role or job if your own falls victim to restructuring. It is vital in the current situation to take responsibility for your own development, always considering yourself through the eyes of potential employers. This will maximise your chances of continued satisfying employment, come what may.

Seeing yourself as a product

You will thus need to regard yourself as, in one sense, a *product*, one which you are continually developing with an eye to the *market* for this product, now and in the future. Those responsible for marketing a product find that SWOT analysis is a useful framework for thinking about their strategy. If you have not yet come across this, it is very easy to understand and use. SWOT is shorthand for thinking in terms of:

- Strengths – which you already have, and might build on.
- Weaknesses – which you have but could possibly reduce or otherwise work around.

■ Opportunities – which the market offers and you might be able to exploit better than other people.

■ Threats – again from outside, which you need to be aware of and take action against.

Figure 1.1 shows this framework diagrammatically. To carry out a SWOT analysis on yourself, fill in each of the boxes. Note that you need to be continually alert to likely developments in the employment market, aware of the types of skill and experience that are assuming importance and have a sound assessment of your own skills and experience. You also need to think about how you can *continually* develop these in ways that will open up future employment opportunities. Otherwise you may find you face an ever more restricted range of possible jobs.

Being highly employable means:
■ **seeing yourself as a product**
■ **watching the market**
■ **developing yourself continuously**
■ **being prepared for change.**

Such an approach means taking a much more active, and proactive, approach to your own 'career', seeing it as *your* responsibility rather than that of your employers. Seeking continuous learning and development will be a part of this. You will probably need to make absolutely sure you take advantage of all the training and job moves available in your company. If your employer does not encourage training, you may need to pursue a further qualification in your own time and at your own expense while working. The prospect of taking responsibility for your own development can be somewhat frightening. However, if 'boredom' and 'security' were listed as fears rather than as desiderata in the activity above, the excitement and risk associated with owning your own future should appeal to you.

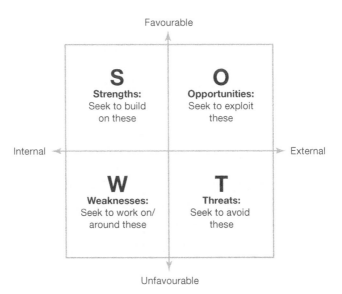

Fig 1.1 **Framework for a SWOT analysis**

The level of competition in the job market means that you need to start *now* to think about the skills that employers need and look for (not always the same thing) and about how to develop these and to *demonstrate* that you have developed them.

Use the SWOT framework, and the work you have already done during this chapter to organise your thinking about your own strengths and weaknesses as they might be seen by future employers. Supplement your research into current employer requirements by thinking about likely trends in the job market that may have altered the situation by the time you graduate. If possible, compare your analysis with those of two or three other people, and modify it if this comparison prompts new ideas. File the final version for future reference. Pay particular attention to your strengths – the developing area of strengths-based coaching suggests that building on your strengths is likely to be far more important in developing your potential for success than trying to bring areas of weakness up to the same level as your strengths You need to address any weaknesses that would stop you from being effective. But once you have achieved an acceptable level of competence in your weaker areas, your focus could usefully move to developing those areas where you are already strong.

What working feels like

If you have not yet had a job, the world of work may seem singularly opaque. Your 'hopes and fears' listed earlier may have been fairly one-dimensional in consequence. And the discussion of structural changes above may have been interesting but not hugely helpful in terms of giving you a clearer picture of what working will really be like. Indeed, given the variety of possible work experiences, it is hard to do this. But the importance of work to your whole future life cannot be overemphasised.

Hating your job is grim. It can even make you physically ill. A huge amount of absence from work is attributed to stress. An experienced and, until then, successful manager told me recently that he had been to see his doctor because he could no longer eat, sleep or think straight. Whenever he heard his manager's voice he felt physically sick. Indeed, when telling his doctor about all this he burst into tears. A stressful job with an over-controlling boss had reduced him to total misery and an inability to function.

→ Ch 2

(Some techniques for managing stress are suggested in Chapter 2, but the best way of managing it is to avoid such situations.)

In contrast, a challenging and worthwhile job can leave you exhilarated and longing to get back to work the next day. The difference between these two extremes is so important that it is worth making every effort to take the challenge posed by this book seriously and do everything you can *now* to ensure that your working experience is positive. This starts with exploring your own views about work, a process that you will need to repeat at intervals throughout the book, and indeed throughout your working life.

ACTIVITY 1.6

List as many words as you can that might be used to describe any of your own experience of work. Ask as many other people as you can to provide up to 10 words which describe their own experience of current, or previous, work.

_____

_____

You may have been surprised at the emotional level of some of the responses you get. Work forms a major part of most people's lives. For some, it is boring, so routine and dehumanising that it is highly stressful and each day becomes something to be endured with difficulty. For others, work is so exciting that they would far rather be working than doing anything else. For some, it is a source of self-esteem; for others, the treatment they receive totally destroys any self-esteem they may have had. Many marriage breakdowns are blamed on the stresses and demands of one partner's job (or both jobs). Some jobs have specific health or physical risks associated with them. More generally, sickness rates correlate to different sorts of work. Studies show that to be without a job at all is highly stressful, destructive of self-esteem and associated with ill health and relationship difficulties.

In evolutionary terms, the centrality of work is perhaps not surprising. Survival has almost always been dependent on wresting food and physical safety from a competitive, if not hostile, environment, normally as part of a social group. And reproductive success, as with other primates, will have depended on status within that group. Without work (whether hunting and gathering or farming or manufacture of some kind), the life expectancy of a person and of any dependants would have been short indeed. Indeed, family members would have been involved in work from a very early age. Survival without work is, in evolutionary terms, very recent.

If you feel it would be helpful to know more about what different types of work offer, there are a number of steps that you can usefully take. The first is to pursue any opportunities for work placements during your course (the learning opportunities offered by such placements are important in a number of different ways). The second is to extend the previous activity and to ask as many people as possible to describe their work experience to you in more detail. Try asking relatives, friends already in employment, fellow students who worked before the course started or who have already been on work placements. The third is to read about the experience of others, and suggested reading is given at the end of this chapter.

If you are asking people about their work experience, which may after all be extensive, it can help to have a framework of questions. If you are working in a group, discuss possible questions, and agree a common list. The following are merely suggestions to get you started:

- What most surprised you on starting work with your present employer?
- What are the most common difficulties you encounter at work?

- What are the most common frustrations?
- What has given you most satisfaction in the past week (or month or year)?
- If you could choose a new job, how would it be different from your present one?
- How would it resemble your present job?
- How much freedom do you have at work?
- How much impact do you feel you have on the way the organisation operates?
- What advice would you give to someone starting out in your organisation?
- What characteristics would the ideal employee have in your organisation?

The answers to such questions will reflect the person answering as much as the job they are doing. The same job could be very satisfactory to one person and hardly bearable to another. Nevertheless, if you can question a number of different people of graduate or equivalent ability about their experience, you should be better informed than before about the characteristics of jobs and possible reactions to them. This should help you become more aware of the nature of the type of job you would like yourself.

ACTIVITY 1.7

Devise a set of questions for asking about work experience, preferably with a group of others, and use this to question a range of people. If working in a group, discuss the results, comparing what those you asked seem to want from work with what *you* think you might want, and using what they say about their work experience to extend your own expectations and awareness. Add any additional 'wants' to your 'ideal job' file entry. You can find a starter questionnaire, based on the questions above, on the website.

STRUCTURE OF THE BOOK

Use the brief overview which follows to help you see how to make best use of the rest of the book. Try to get a feel for how you can use it to develop those skills which you will need, both to succeed as a student, and to be highly desirable to potential employers when you start to apply for jobs.

The first part of the book maps out 'the territory' of employment, management skills and learning. Once you are more familiar with this context, and the more general learning skills that you will need, you will be better able to use the second part of the book, which addresses the specific skills that you will need in order to do well academically: reading critically, and taking effective notes; writing – and arguing – clearly; working with numbers; using computers and the Internet; and doing well in assessment (including exams). You may already be more than expert in some of these areas. If so, it will be good time management to identify and concentrate on those where you are weaker. Although the main aim of this part is to help you do well in your course, most of the skills covered will be also be useful long after you have graduated.

The third part reverses this emphasis. It addresses communication and other aspects of working with other people, either one-to-one or as a member of a team. Although you will need these skills while a student and will have many opportunities to develop them, you have already seen that they are crucial to success at work.

The fourth part addresses skills of equal relevance to study and work: the 'trained mind' that graduates were traditionally deemed to possess. More specifically, it looks at the skills needed to react creatively and appropriately to complicated situations, to investigate them, gather and make sense of relevant information and decide on a way forward. Your course will be addressing problem-solving skills within a specific academic area, but much of the teaching may be implicit. This part of the book aims to make aspects of these skills more explicit and to increase your awareness of them. This should shift slightly your approach to study, so that you are better prepared to tackle problem situations at work.

In the last part, the different areas are brought together in looking at project management, both in general and in the context of any project that is part of your course. Finally, the 'project' of finding a good job is addressed. In this way the circle is completed and you will come back to the issues raised in this chapter, refining your work objectives and developing the skills needed for making a successful job application and doing well in interviews.

The structure of the book in terms of the skills covered can be charted as shown in Figure 1.2. Inevitably, there are many interconnections between the skills covered in different chapters. In particular, the end of the book is designed to draw on almost all that has gone before. You can see that when you are ready to organise your file you will face a considerable challenge. But by then you should have a clearer idea of the skills that are important to you for more effective study, as well as those which are likely to be important to your chosen prospective employers. This will make it easier to design a system well suited to your particular situation.

This chapter has looked mainly at the world of work, arguing that there is a substantial overlap in the skills needed for study and those for employment, and that given the competitive nature of employment you need to start *now* to think about what you want from a job, and what skills you will need to develop it. You will find as you work through the book that each skill addressed will have the added benefit of helping you gain higher grades. This will help you further in your search for a better job. The transferability of most of the skills covered has its roots in two factors. One, obviously, is that if you are studying a course designed to prepare you for employment, then you are likely to be asked to develop those skills that employers value. The second, and less obvious, factor is that the most successful managers are those who continually develop themselves. The ability to learn is vital in a world where organisational contexts are fluid and constantly presenting new challenges. Becoming an effective learner is thus crucial to both contexts. And it is effective learning, along with the equally important ability to display your learning ability, that this book primarily addresses, as the next two chapters make clear.

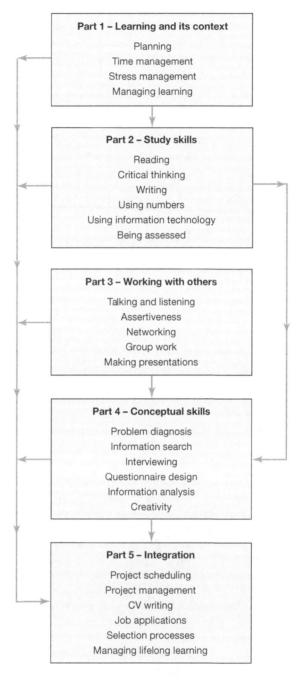

Fig 1.2 A skills framework for the purpose of this book

SUMMARY

This chapter has argued that:

- Studying for a degree represents a major investment: there are opportunity costs as well as direct financial costs.
- To get good grades, and become an attractive employee you need to take responsibility for your own learning.
- Graduate opportunities have improved in the past few years but the situation is still highly competitive. Organisational restructuring has broadened the range of interesting jobs available.
- You can expect to work in several different organisations during your lifetime: managing your own career is important.
- To make yourself attractive to prospective employers you need to develop and demonstrate the skills they seek.
- The transferable skills which this book seeks to develop are relevant to both study and employment.
- These skills are interpersonal as well as intellectual, and include the skill to learn from experience as well as reading, the ability to manage yourself, basic skills in numeracy, literacy and IT, interpersonal, group-working and communication skills, and skills in analysing and solving problems.

Further information

- Fineman, S. and Gabriel, Y. (1996) *Experiencing Organisations*, Sage. An easy-to-read set of stories told by students after their six-month work placements.
- Frost, P.J., Mitchell, V.F. and Nord, W.R. (eds) (1997) *Organisational Reality: Reports from the Firing Line*, 4th edn, Addison Wesley Longman.
- **www.agr.org.uk** – the Association of Graduate Recruiters – for information from the perspective of the employer.
- **www.careers.reading.ac.uk/staff/FullReport.pdf** – this provides an interesting overview of the changes in graduate employment in the ten years to 2006/07.
- **www.prospects.ac.uk** – 'the UK's official graduate careers website' for a range of information on graduate employment.
- **www.qaa.ac.uk** – the Quality Assurance Agency – where you can find information on benchmarking and academic standards.

LOCATING SOURCES

This chapter stresses the importance of searching for sources systematically and invites you to consider the relevance, ready availability, and reliability of materials in relation to your topic. It also provides tips on effective time management as you search the literature in your subject area.

The chapter covers:

- Systematic searching for sources
- The relevance of sources
- The ready availability of sources
- The reliability of sources
- Literature searches
- Using your university library
- Moving from general to specific research.

Using this chapter

From Chapter 3 of *Academic Research,Writing & Referencing*, 1/e. Mary deane.

INTRODUCTION

Chapter 2 offered tips on avoiding plagiarism; Chapter 3 now highlights the need for a system to search for the sources you will use in your writing. It stresses the importance of understanding your purpose for writing and explains how to move from seeking general sources to finding specifically relevant materials.

A SYSTEM FOR SEARCHING

Although your approach will differ based on the purpose of each writing task, you can develop a system for locating potentially useful sources that is adaptable to each assignment (Hacker 2006: 6, Lunsford 2008: 258).

Sources should be:

- Relevant
- Readily available
- Reliable.

Relevance

The relevance of sources depends upon the content, style, author, and intended audience (Lunsford 2008: 252). The clearer you are about the aim, style, and format of your own work, the better equipped you will be to find the right kinds of texts for your purpose. Do not neglect to search for numerical data and images if these are also relevant. Begin your systematic approach to locating the right sources for your task by thinking about these three questions:

1 What is the scope of the source?
2 Is this relevant to my writing?
3 Should I just make a record of this source (using a referencing management system, on paper, or on file) and move on?

Readily available

Once you have learnt how to use the catalogue, databases, and resources readily available via your university library you will not be dependent upon the internet, which is only one way to access materials and will not necessarily yield relevant sources for your purpose (Hacker 2006: 10). The next phase in your systematic approach to searching for sources is to consider these three questions:

1 Is there a paper-based copy in my university library?
2 Do I need to order the source from another library or collection?
3 Is there a digital copy accessible via my university library website using the catalogue, databases, or search engines?

Reliability

Sources are reliable if they are accurate, well designed, and written by authors with the right credentials for your purpose (Hacker 2006: 23). Mostly you will need to refer to scholarly sources for your academic writing, so the material you select should be based on valid research. It is often preferable to consult peer-reviewed sources because they have been verified by experts in the field. The third stage in your systematic approach to searching is to address these questions:

1 Is the information in the source confirmed elsewhere?
2 Is the author qualified to produce the source?
3 Is the source intended for academic use?

Peer review

Peer review is a process designed to ensure the quality, reliability, and originality of published material. Tutors often expect you to locate sources that have been peer-reviewed, which means that expert readers evaluate material and provide feedback on the areas requiring improvement, expansion, or revision. Blind peer review is when feedback is supplied anonymously and this is considered to be a more rigorous form of assessment.

If you are not sure whether sources have been peer-reviewed you can ask for advice at your university library or consult your tutors. The challenge of accessing sources online is that sources distributed via this digital environment do not always undergo peer review, and consequently they can be poorly phrased, badly organised or inaccurate. Therefore, do not rely exclusively on sources you have accessed online and instead research scholarly materials which have been assessed by experts and identified as reliable for academic use (Hacker 2006: 24–6).

RELEVANT SOURCES

When you receive an assignment brief or writing project, one of your first tasks is to analyse the requirements and begin to search for sources to help you fulfil your brief. It is often necessary to do independent research, and most often you will not be able to carry out the task successfully without drawing on existing knowledge. As discussed in the next chapter, your use of sources must be documented fully to avoid unintentional plagiarism.

Researching existing ideas can help you to formulate your own perspective on a subject, which will contribute to making your academic writing original. In most contexts this quality is highly valued, so enhancing the innovative nature of your work could improve your performance. However, originality is an often misunderstood term and is not as demanding as it may appear because, although your tutors expect a fresh engagement with topics from each student, they are aware of the constraints of time and experience. So, in practice and especially at undergraduate level, originality is achieved mainly through original research, which helps writers identify fresh angles on their topics.

Researching existing ideas can also give you the authority to deal with a subject effectively, because the more you know about a topic the more confident your treatment of it will be. Writers who are unclear about important issues are unlikely to organise their material well, which will have a negative impact on the quality of their writing. If you have a strong understanding of a particular topic you will be in the best position to identify the most cogent points to include or debate, which means that you will not include irrelevant data which disrupts the flow of ideas. Effective research will help you to gain clarity about the ideas and information you are discussing – this can improve your written expression to create an impression of professionalism and mastery of your material.

Keep focused on your deadline

Whilst research is usually essential to effective academic writing it is also vital to limit the time you spend locating sources so that you can maximise the time available for assessing, reading critically, and integrating sources into your assignments. The three-stage process outlined below offers tips on being efficient and effective as you gather information before you start to write. However, this is just one approach to research and you should adapt it to suit your own style as a scholar.

Collect together all the guidance you have received from your tutor about producing your piece of writing. This may include the assignment brief, the module handbook, and notes from lectures or seminars. Tutors often put coursework guidelines on the module web, so, if relevant, have a look at this. The earlier you gather these guidelines, the better your chances will be of getting support about issues you do not understand.

Here are five important questions to ask yourself when you are analysing the purpose of your writing in order to locate appropriate sources:

1 Who is the main audience for this piece of writing? (For instance, subject specialists)
2 What information should I assume this readership already knows? (I will not need to explain this in my writing)
3 What do I already know? (From lecture notes, readings, experience)
4 What background information do I need to acquire? (This should be presented in a concise way early in my writing)
5 Which key terms, concepts, or theories do I need to research? (Do I need advice about these?)

Find the right sources for your purpose

Jot down your answers to these five questions and take your notes to the library when you go to research or keep them with you as you go online to find appropriate

30

databases via the library website. The advantage of visiting the library in person is that you may be able to speak to a library specialist on duty, who can help you to locate the best sources for your purpose.

Work with others to find suitable sources

Discuss the kinds of sources you might use with others who are studying your subject, either by chatting in person or corresponding online. Although it would be plagiarism to copy another person's work, it is good practice to search for information together, as long as you generate your own ideas for writing about the sources you find.

You could develop a joint plan for locating sources with a friend and divide the task between you; for example, if you need to investigate several theories you could research one each and report back about your findings at an agreed time, but remember to read key sources for yourself and acknowledge them in your writing. Supporting each other will make the research process more efficient and enjoyable, so collaborate with colleagues to locate information for your projects.

Begin with what you know

The aim of the lectures and other teaching sessions on your course is to prepare you for producing the written assessments, so if you have attended these regularly you should have some relevant knowledge before you begin writing an assignment. Try to take full notes when you attend any kind of class and keep these safe as a starting point for your writing projects. Begin by re-reading your notes and the handouts you received before you start to write, and jot down important points or ideas sparked by reviewing this information. Your tutors will probably provide tips about useful sources, which will be good starting points for your research.

If you find yourself in a situation where your knowledge about a topic is limited or you were unable to attend all the relevant classes, you can take some useful steps to gather together information. First, look on your module web if this is relevant and download any advice that is available about the writing you have to do. Secondly, as soon as possible contact your module tutor to make an appointment to attend at an office hour or at another suitable time. Do some preparation for this meeting, such as reading your assignment brief and making a list of questions about issues you find confusing. You could also attempt to make a plan for your writing and take this along to seek advice, or draw up a shortlist of possible sources and ask whether you have missed anything important. Thirdly, contact a classmate and ask for some tips on understanding the assignment and locating relevant sources. You could offer to help in return by reading your classmate's draft and offering constructive feedback. Or you could offer to report back on sources you locate which could be mutually useful, but be clear that you do not wish to copy or allow your classmate to copy your work.

READILY AVAILABLE SOURCES

With a little effort you can expand the range of sources which are readily available to you by using your university library's catalogue to locate a diversity of online and paper-based resources (Hacker 2006: 9).

Literature searches

Using the tips below and keeping in mind the need to be systematic, learn how to search for the literature you need for your writing. You should consult a range of different types of sources, including books, journal articles, magazines, reference works, and audiovisual sources. Although much of the source material you need is available digitally, it can be helpful to locate paper-based sources, and do not neglect the older materials and seminal works in your field because they can give you a useful grounding in your subject area.

Library catalogue

Library catalogues are gateways to a wealth of sources produced for academic audiences, and without exploiting this access to scholarly materials you cannot fulfil the central requirements of advanced level study to read widely and research independently. Although most library catalogues are intuitive to use you will benefit from attending training sessions, or reading the self-help guides available in your library and usually also downloadable from the library website.

Databases

Databases are repositories of such extensive information that they can be daunting at first, but the time you invest in learning how to use them may yield the best returns of any skill you master at university. Students who avoid databases do themselves an injustice because they shut the door on the richest selection of relevant, reliable, and readily available materials there is (Hacker 2006: 9).

Training in how to navigate around databases and use them efficiently is available at every university library, either as part of an induction programme or on request. The advantage of seeking individual training from a library specialist is that you can ask about the databases most relevant for your discipline or research project. If possible, make an appointment with a subject specialist who will give you inside information on the best places to start your search for information. As you spend time learning how to use databases you will develop your own expertise about their usefulness for different types of writing. Some databases provide access to a broad range of articles and books and these can be helpful as you begin to search, while others focus on discipline-based topics and are invaluable when you narrow down a topic for your writing.

Make sure you are equipped to work online at home by checking at your library to find out if you need a password to access databases off-campus. Whether or not you require a password to authenticate your access, you will benefit from advice about the best way to locate digital sources remotely because the route may differ from the approach you use on university computers.

Searches in catalogues and databases

Ask library specialists to advise you about the protocol for searching for sources within the databases which are most relevant for your studies (Lunsford 2008: 235). Here are some general tips, but be aware that usage can vary, so you also need to familiarise yourself with the relevant system for you:

- Attend the training sessions on using databases, search engines, and catalogues at your library
- Seek individual advice from library specialists and see the guidance on the library website
- Make notes about how to search because databases vary and it is easy to forget the individual systems
- Decide on a broad search topic to start with
- Narrow your search as soon as you can
- Be ready to discard general sources in favour of more relevant materials
- Keep notes or use a reference management system.

Although public access search engines (like Google™) are easy to use and may yield interesting general results, relying on these exclusively does not constitute scholarly practice and will severely limit the type of sources you can access. Experiment with the search engines available via your university library website and you will substantially enrich your options and access to scholarly sources (Hacker 2006: 11, Lunsford 2009: 159).

When searching:

- Decide whether to search for a key word, subject, or author depending on the options available in a database, search engine, or catalogue
- Input a key word or words for your broad search topic
- Use the advanced options to narrow your search
- Use 'and' to extend your search
- Use 'or' to distinguish between key words
- Use 'not' to refine your search
- Use double quotation marks to narrow your search like this: "academic and writing"
- Use brackets to target your search like this: (academic writing)
- Use a star to search for variations of a key word (such as write and writing) like this: write*.

Reference management systems

You can make a paper-based or a digital list of the sources you locate which appear to be appropriate for your writing. Alternatively, you can benefit from tools to help you with this time-consuming task such as RefWorks™ and EndNote™. These reference management systems are usually available via university libraries, which often provide training and support. If you are unfamiliar with these tools you should enquire at your library or ask your tutors, because once you have learnt how to use them reference management systems can save you vast amounts of time.

Special collections

Find out whether your university library has an audiovisual collection or any other specialist holdings and visit these sections to meet the specialists and familiarise yourself with the materials. You can enhance your research or writing by drawing on archives, media, or artwork which may give you a fresh angle on your topic and enable you to undertake innovative work (Lunsford 2009: 163).

Interlibrary loan and document supply

If you find out about a source that is not held in your university library and you have started to search early enough, you can take advantage of the interlibrary loan system which enables you to order material from other collections (Lunsford 2009: 163). Often you are required to complete a form that has been signed by your tutor, so find out about the protocol at your university library and plan ahead with your search for sources. Gaining access to relevant sources your library does not hold can give you an edge as a researcher and boost the quality of your work.

RELIABLE SOURCES

What constitutes reliability may vary depending on your task, but in essence you need to find the right tools for the job each time you undertake a piece of writing (Hacker 2006: 6). You also need to be assured that the content of your sources is accurate, wellfounded, and well expressed, because this will help you draw on the contents for your own work.

Digital media

Select internet sites and other digital media with care because the material may be inaccurate, incomplete, or inappropriate for academic writing (Hacker 2006: 31). Be cautious if you think the material was designed to manipulate readers or favour a particular stance. In certain cases it is useful to discuss this bias in your academic writing, but, while internet sites provide general information to get people thinking about a topic, they are not always relevant as sources for scholarly writing. You can take a number of precautions to improve the likelihood of locating useful sources online by considering the following three points.

Who is the author?

In addition to the corporate author of the website it is often possible to identify the name of a contributor or the person who wrote particular articles. This is a good sign because authors who research their material and take care to present it clearly are most likely to put their name to their work. If you can identify an author you could try using a search engine such as Google™ to check this person's affiliation, such as a university, research group, or professional organisation. This is not always important, but it is a good approach to consider who produced digital material and what the main aim might be (Hacker 2006: 25, Lunsford 2009: 171).

Are the contents attributed or acknowledged?

One sign that a website is valuable for your own writing is clear and consistent acknowledgement of sources. Although it is not always appropriate, most topics demand research and you should avoid using sites which fail to credit the material that is borrowed from elsewhere. If the authors of websites have not acknowledged their sources, you could cite material in the usual way, giving full acknowledgement to the site you have consulted, but still be accused of copying.

This is because a plagiarism detection service such as Turnitin™ can identify the unacknowledged source and may interpret the fact that you have not cited it as an intentional omission of credit. Do not think that you can solve this problem by failing to cite the website you have read because this will also be identified. So, while it can be useful to read websites before you get into more targeted research for a project, you should only borrow material from sites which follow the same scholarly codes of practice you are expected to uphold at university, because otherwise your sources could seriously let you down.

Who is the intended audience?

As you read any website you should assess the intended audience, which might be professionals in a certain field, researchers in a subject area, or scholars. Only borrow material from sites intended for scholarly use unless they happen to be relevant for your project, for example because they contain specialist information or they form part of your research topic (Lunsford 2009: 164).

Always distinguish the informal style used for writing on the internet from the academic language you are required to produce at university. Never emulate the phrasing used on websites, because even brilliant ideas will be obscured by poor written expression. This means that if you borrow ideas from internet sites it may be best to paraphrase or summarise material, so in effect you are translating material from a colloquial style into academic English.

GENERAL SOURCES

Start your research process by locating sources which provide general information about your topic. These may include:

- Dictionaries
- Encyclopaedias
- Textbooks
- Internet sites
- Newspapers
- Magazines.

The kinds of general sources you need depend upon the purpose and audience of your particular project, but every written assessment requires an initial stage of consolidating your knowledge about the topic in general (Lunsford 2009: 156). Consider which of these sources are appropriate for each piece of writing you undertake.

Dictionaries

Although the value of dictionaries is often overlooked in the initial stages of research, you might find it useful to look up key terms used in your assignment brief so that you are clear from the outset about what you are being asked to do. Your assignment brief may contain important instructions that you need to carry out in order to succeed. For example, you may be asked to **discuss** a topic, **analyse** data, or **evaluate** information. These key terms have distinctive meanings, and they imply different kinds of writing in different disciplinary contexts, so you should check with your tutor that you understand their application in your own field.

Encyclopaedias

Many people read encyclopaedias for general interest but omit to consult them for academic writing. They are useful to provide quick access to facts and fill in the basic context to boost your understanding of a general topic. Usually encyclopaedias are accessed online, but use your own judgement to assess the quality of online resources before you borrow material for your academic writing (Hacker 2006: 14).

For instance, the online source Wikipedia is used by many writers to get started on a topic, but if you choose to consult this source remember that anyone can contribute an article and consequently there is a danger that the information is inaccurate. To prevent yourself repeating errors you can check an alternative source, preferably a more scholarly one such as a textbook. If the information is corroborated you can use it for your writing, but it is often preferable to borrow information from the more scholarly source and cite that in accordance with your chosen referencing style.

Some tutors will not consider digital sources such as Wikipedia to be appropriate types of information for advanced level study owing to the lack of quality control. You can ask your tutor about this issue, but avoid using inappropriate sources you have accessed online or elsewhere because they can undermine the quality of your writing. On the other hand, the list of references accompanying the articles in Wikipedia can be very helpful in providing suggestions for general sources to consult.

Textbooks

Textbooks are particularly useful for gathering general information about a subject, and books recommended by your tutors are the best place to start. Use the contents page and the index to decide where to focus your reading so you do not waste time covering material that is not relevant for a particular assignment. Also consult the references and recommended reading lists for more targeted information on particular topics. Although textbooks provide information in an efficient way, they are designed to offer only an introduction, so you should read more advanced sources when you have become familiar with your topic in general.

Newspapers

Reading broadsheets like the *Guardian, The Times*, and the *Independent* is an excellent way to gather general information on current affairs, political debates, and economic issues, and in the course of regular reading you might come across articles about the subjects you are studying at university. Owing to the brevity of newspaper articles they are most likely to provide introductory ideas or give you a new angle on your topic, which can be a useful starting point. However, it is essential to progress to more in-depth information for your writing. You should also be aware that, except for certain assignments, tutors may not consider newspapers appropriate sources and will instead expect you to begin reading recommended readings and then conduct independent research to locate more specific information. Importantly, you should not emulate the journalistic style of newspapers, which is too informal for academic writing.

Magazines

Reading magazines like the *National Geographic* is another good way to gain awareness about general interest topics, and you may find an article dedicated to an issue you are writing about. The journalistic form and style of magazines is not usually appropriate for written assessments at university, so consider your own use of language carefully and try to locate additional, more scholarly, sources to inform your thinking and writing.

SPECIFIC SOURCES

When you have identified some general sources, the next step is to locate specific sources that will provide further insights into the subject about which you are writing. Most written assessments are set to help you gain knowledge and understanding which you can apply in new contexts; for instance, in your future career. So, you should use the process of researching and writing to demonstrate your ability to manage, synthesise, and communicate information. Specific sources may include:

- Journal articles
- Chapters in edited collections
- Chapters in monographs
- Dissertations
- Theses
- Reports.

Journal articles

There are five main reasons for locating scholarly journal articles as sources for your projects:

1 Journal articles focus on a specific topic and they engage with scholarship in that area

2 Journal articles are relatively short, so they offer a quick way to becoming familiar with a subject or debate

3 Journals are often available digitally, so you can access them easily via the databases provided on your university library website

4 Journals are usually produced four times per year, so articles allow you to access the most up-to-date research in your field

5 Journal articles are produced according to the style and format commonly used in academic disciplines, which means that not only the content but also the form is a valuable model for your own academic writing.

Although journal articles may appear to be a bit formal and technical to start with, the more you read the easier they become to understand. It is not usually necessary to read through an entire volume of a journal; instead use a database to select the articles which relate to the topic about which you are writing.

Time spent familiarising yourself with scholarly journal articles is very well invested because they provide excellent exemplars for your own writing. It is often useful to emulate the syntax, terminology, and phrasing of articles from your academic discipline to improve your written expression. Obviously you must cite any material you borrow for your writing, but it is acceptable to keep a notebook and jot down signal phrases, verbs, and terms used by scholarly authors to enhance your own vocabulary. For example, if you are simply re-using transition phrases or terms to integrate research into an argument and you are not borrowing other people's **ideas** then it may not be necessary to cite and reference. If you are unsure, you should acknowledge your source, and remember that the golden rule is that you need to credit the intellectual property of others.

Chapters in edited collections

Although you may not have time to read entire books as you move into researching specifically relevant sources, you should try to locate chapters on your topic. Often edited collections bring together specialists in a particular field, or explore themes relevant to your work. The relatively short length of chapters gives you an easy way into complex subjects, and as chapters in edited collections are self-contained they can offer a stand-alone synopsis or an interesting angle on relevant subjects. Also, the style in which chapters in edited collections are written is usually a good example of academic prose which you might want to emulate in your own writing.

Chapters in monographs

Monographs are whole books usually written by a single author based on research projects or doctoral theses. They are invaluable for providing extensive information on a specific topic and are well worth locating, not only for the content but also for the scholarly style in which they are written and the specialist language employed. However, owing to the constraints of time it is often wise to target particular chapters or to consult the index to find the most relevant passages.

Dissertations

Dissertation is the term used in the UK for research projects produced in the final year of undergraduate study or for the postgraduate degree Master of Arts, Master of Science, MPhil, and other higher qualifications. These degrees take 1 or 2 years to complete and the dissertation explores a research question in some depth.

Dissertations are usually accessible via your university library, and as they are targeted at a specific research question they can be extremely useful as a specific source for your writing. The references may be especially valuable in providing leads for your research, and as the conventions for writing dissertations vary in each subject area, may offer a model for your own work. The quality of dissertations can be variable, so you should use this resource with a particularly critical eye.

Theses

Thesis is the term used in the UK for the extended research project submitted for a PhD, DPhil, or doctorate. The length is usually equivalent to a book, and theses are sometimes revised for publication as monographs to disseminate the research in the public sphere. Many theses are not formally published but, like dissertations, they are accessible via your university library. If you identify an especially interesting thesis, it is also possible to purchase a hard copy via the British Library. You should target individual chapters or sections that are most relevant for your research by consulting the list of contents, and you should examine the references to check for sources which may prove useful for your own writing.

Reports

Reports produced by corporations, industries, organisations, government departments, research groups, and other official bodies can provide invaluable data for your own writing. Reports are often accessible online and can provide unique insights into the issues you are researching. Always apply the criteria outlined in the next section to assess the purpose and intended audience of reports so you can read them with a critical eye. Reports are usually written from a particular viewpoint, so there may be an inherent bias in the presentation of data, findings, and conclusions drawn. Like other public documents, reports are usually written with an agenda, but as long as you can identify a report's main aim and you critique the methodology you will find this kind of specific source helpful in boosting the quality of your work (Lunsford 2009: 172). The style of report writing in professional spheres may be the same as the conventions you are required to adhere to at university, but you might be required to structure your report in an alternative way and use more academic language, so check with your tutor before emulating the organisation and style of reports, especially those you access online.

SUMMARY

This chapter has stressed the value of systematic searching for sources by considering the relevance, ready availability, and reliability of materials. This focused approach to research will help you avoid wasting time because, with these criteria in mind, you are less likely to consult literature that is inappropriate or inadequate for your task.

The main arguments in this chapter:

- Get training and advice on how to use the catalogue and databases provided by your university library
- Get the right tools for the job each time you start a piece of writing by locating relevant sources
- Be prepared to reject irrelevant material at an early stage.

QUIZ

1 Why is it essential to learn how to search for sources via your university library catalogue?

2 To develop a systematic approach to searching for sources, which three Rs should you remember?

3 What is the main benefit of consulting sources which have been peer-reviewed?

4 Should you start by searching for specific or general sources first?

5 What is a monograph?

Critical reading and note taking

As a student you will spend hundreds of hours reading. This chapter suggests steps you can take to cut down on these hours while increasing the benefit gained. There are two parts to this. One is to read more efficiently. This can greatly reduce study time, while improving your understanding and retention of what you read. The other is to think differently while you read, by becoming more critical in your reading. This will deepen your learning and develop the critical skills expected of a graduate. Both skill-sets are useful in the workplace. Taking useful notes is important in a wide range of work contexts.

Learning outcomes

Provided you not only read this chapter but *practise* the skills covered as well, you should be better able to:

- select appropriate reading material
- use techniques appropriate to that material in order to make most effective use of time
- reduce physical causes of inefficiency
- take a critical approach to what you read, questioning evidence, assumptions and reasoning
- take useful notes when reading, in lectures, or when using online material.

Whatever your preferred learning medium, much of the information you obtain as a student is likely to be from words. You may well spend more time reading than doing anything else. Despite twenty or more years' experience, you may be a far less efficient reader than you think. Increasing your skills in reading and note taking is therefore an important part of becoming more effective as a student. Note taking is equally important for lectures, and will be important for other contexts such as when interviewing, perhaps for a research project. Developing your skills in reading and note taking will mean that you spend less time reading yet learn more in the process. Reading skills will probably be important throughout your career. Most managers, and those in other graduate-type jobs, claim that they are 'swamped' with reading material. The ability to deal with this material efficiently and to evaluate its worth will contribute significantly to your likely success at work.

'SIMPLE' READING SKILLS

Gaining information by reading is one of the most sophisticated skills that we possess. Fine-tuned physical skills are required to use our eyes effectively. A wide range of conceptual skills are necessary too. It is not enough for the eye to focus on the word. The 'meaning' of that word must be interpreted and the 'meaning' of the sentence and paragraph and chapter of which it is a part. Your interpretation will depend upon the context, on other things you have read or experienced, and on your judgement of its acceptability and potential usefulness.

Choosing what to read is equally important. Your university library is likely to stock many relevant books and journals, and to offer online access to many more. The Internet gives you access to what feels like an infinity of materials of varying reliability and relevance. A necessary first step is to be able to select sensibly from this overwhelming array of potential reading materials.

Your choice will largely depend upon your purpose. You may need to reply to a letter, to write an essay, to comment on draft proposals for a change at work, to write a briefing document for your superiors based on what you have read about the latest technological developments in your field, or draft a marketing plan based on market research reports. In some cases (such as the letter) there may be no choice over what you read; in others you may have substantial freedom.

Given our reliance on text, it is small wonder that 'read and respond to written materials' is one of the elements in the key skill of 'communication'. And while effective reading is a component of other skills, it depends in turn on a number of conceptual skills exercised at different levels of mental activity, as well as demanding the physical skill of using the eyes.

There is a common (mis)perception that 'speed reading' techniques, which primarily address the physical side of reading, will allow you to perform miracles. (Woody Allen claimed that after such a course he was able 'to go through *War and Peace* in 20 minutes. It's about Russia.') This chapter, however, addresses much broader issues. Sometimes a superficial scanning *will* serve your purpose, and it is a useful skill to develop. But for much of your course reading, and the reading required of you during your career, will need to be far more thorough. The chapter's primary aim is to increase the *effectiveness* of your reading rather than merely its speed. That said, physical techniques for increasing speed are important and make a good place to start.

Using your eyes

It is important that you do the following exercise before reading any further.

READING SPEED TEST

This requires you to time how long it takes to read the next section quickly but carefully, without stopping, aiming to remember any significant information contained in the text. There will be a short test to check how much you have absorbed. Read without a break until you are told to look at your watch again. Look at your watch *now* and note your starting time before reading on.

Most readers are unaware of their eye movements while they read, assuming, if they think about it at all, that their eyes are moving steadily along each line before moving to the next. If this were the case, reading at one line per second (which most people would guess to be a reasonable speed) you would cover 600–700 words per minute. At this pace you would find you could easily cope with the volume of reading materials you are likely to encounter on your course. Eye movements when reading are far more complex, however. The eye makes a series of extremely rapid jumps along a line, with a significant pause, 0.25 to 1.5 seconds, between each jump. Furthermore, many readers do not move straight along a line, even in this jerky fashion. Instead, as Figure 4.1 shows, they indulge in frequent backward eye jumps, fixating for a second or even a third time on a previous word, and at intervals their eye may wander off the page altogether. With erratic eye movements like this and forward jumps from word to adjacent word, many readers achieve reading speeds of only 100 words per minute. At this rate of reading, the volume of work for your course, or that found in many jobs, is likely to prove an impossible task.

At the purely technical level, it is possible to achieve reading speeds of up to 1000 words per minute by:

- reducing the number of fixations per line, stopping every three to six words rather than every one
- eliminating backward movement and wandering
- reducing the duration of each fixation.

If you wish to reach this sort of speed, you will need to work at it. It will require concentration and considerable practice. But as well as improving your ability to get through your course materials and lessening eye fatigue in the process, such a reduction in eye movements will enable you to deal with reading material at work more quickly. This is important when time is at a premium. Any investment in developing your skills will therefore pay off handsomely. Furthermore, although you might expect comprehension to be reduced by more rapid reading, the reverse may well be the case. The pattern of a sentence and its meaning may emerge much more clearly and be more readily absorbed if the sentence is read in phrases rather than one word at a time. Your interest is more likely to be maintained if ideas are coming at you

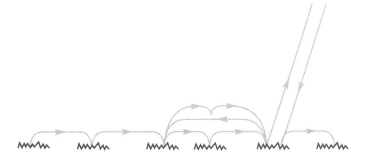

Fig 4.1 **Typical eye movements while reading**

more quickly and your motivation will be higher if you feel you are making rapid progress, so the rewards of improved reading techniques are many.

→ Ch 3

If practice is all that is needed, you may wonder why we are all reading so slowly. Surely we have been practising reading most of our lives. But remember that learning requires a change of behaviour, usually in the light of feedback. If there is no feedback which suggests the need for improvement, we are likely to establish bad habits more firmly, rather than to develop rapid reading techniques. Breaking such habits is extremely difficult. It takes considerable effort, at least at first, to read at an increased speed. Improvement will be made only through the practice of exercises specifically designed for that purpose. Even when you have developed efficient reading techniques, you may still find that you have to make a point of consciously practising them at intervals, to prevent yourself from falling back into less efficient habits.

READING SPEED CALCULATION

Look at your watch again and note the time _____ . Note how long it is since you last noted the time _____ . There were approximately 590 words in that piece of text. Divide that figure by the number of minutes elapsed in order to find your reading speed in words per minute. Write this down _____ .

TEST EXERCISE 4.1

The activities you have carried out so far have not had 'right' answers, although sometimes the text which followed may have suggested the sort of thing that you might have written. The quiz which follows is the first exercise where your answers can be checked. Answers to test exercises are given at the end of the book.

Now check your comprehension and retention by answering the following questions, saying whether each statement is true or false according to the preceding text. Do not glance back at the text! Cover it so that you cannot. This is a check on what you have understood and can remember. Do the whole quiz before checking any of your answers. Remember, the information is for your use. It will tell you whether or not you need to do subsequent exercises. If you look back (or forward) before answering, you will lose this information.

True/false

1 Poor readers fixate once per word. ☐

2 With practice a poor reader can increase from a speed of 100 to 1000 words per minute. ☐

3 A speed reader will fixate only once per line. ☐

4 Once you have mastered speed reading techniques they will become second nature. ☐

5 The only drawback to rapid reading is that it tends to reduce comprehension. ☐

6 The duration of each fixation can range from as little as 0.25 of a second to as much as 1.5 seconds. ☐

The two exercises you have just done will have given you some idea of how well you are reading at present, in terms of both speed and comprehension/retention. If you got more than one of the above questions wrong, you should be aiming to improve your retention while you read. You were specifically directed to remember any significant information in the passage. If all your answers were right and you were reading at 250 words or more (even with a diagram), you may not need to work on your reading skills. This will become a priority only if you are studying a course, or are in a job, with an overwhelming volume of material to be read. If you found your speed to be less than this, or your retention needs to be improved, the following exercises will be extremely helpful in both study and subsequent employment.

Increasing reading speed

The following practice activities have been developed from those suggested by Tony Buzan (2003b). They will enable you to make significant improvements in your reading speed, provided you are prepared to invest the time and effort needed for practice: 20–30 minutes daily for several weeks will probably be required to reach the full speed of which you are capable.

ACTIVITY 4.1

If the speed and comprehension test above suggested that your reading skills need to be developed, the project can provide an excellent portfolio exhibit demonstrating your learning skills. You will need to include your diagnostic information from the previous exercises, as part of your justification for targeting this skill, to set targets for improvement and to keep a record of your progress. Comments in the following text will give pointers to how you can do this, rather than being cast as specific exercises.

Feedback is essential to keep up your motivation and to enable you to see when your rate of improvement is starting to level off. Keep a graph of your progress. Select a single book (not a set of readings) to control for ease of reading – material varies enormously in difficulty. When you start, and every week thereafter, time yourself for five minutes, noting start and finish points in the text. Aim to remember significant content – you can jot down the main points from memory at the end of the five minutes. Check this and give yourself a mark out of 10 to reflect how much you remembered. Count the words you covered. Log both scores in your file.

Many of the following practice activities require you to pace yourself. A metronome is ideal for this, as you can vary the speed of its movement. Failing that, you might be able to find a clock with a loud tick or set your PC to emit beeps at intervals. You will also need to measure intervals – a kitchen timer will be invaluable here.

You need to find suitable practice materials of different text densities. A light novel would be low density. An advanced specialist textbook would be heavy density. The informative parts of a serious Sunday paper, or a periodical like *The Economist* or *New Scientist*, would lie somewhere between. You can vary your practice materials. It is only your test 'feedback' text that must stay the same.

Your final resource will be an 'eye guide'. You need this in order to coax your eyes to fixate less often and more rapidly. Point with it to where you wish to fixate and move it after the duration of fixation required. A finger will do or some other pointer. Perhaps best when you are studying is a highlighter, as it allows you also to highlight key points of the text as you go along. You need to be careful when merely pointing to keep it just *above* the page to avoid spots before the eyes.

Reading practice activities

1 Muscle exercise
Fixate alternately between the top left-hand and right-hand corners of the page, moving your eyes between them as quickly as possible. Then alternate between top and bottom and between diagonals. Aim to speed up slightly at each session. (If using a metronome, note your speed each time.)

2 Page turning
Practise rapid page turning. Turn pages at a rate of three seconds per page, increasing to two seconds per page after about ten sessions. Move your eyes rapidly down each page, aiming to absorb *something*, though it will not be much at first. Do this for about two minutes at a stretch.

3 Reducing fixations
Practise fixating less often. Start by pointing at every third word, or every second one if you find three too difficult, and moving your pointer every 1.5 seconds. After a few sessions, gradually increase both the speed at which you move the pointer and the distance you move it, until you eventually fixate only once per line, for one second only. It will take a while to achieve this. You might then experiment with more than one line per fixation, but this is unlikely to be possible with the density of materials you need for study.

4 Speed reading
Still using your eye guide, practise reading as fast as you can for one minute, regardless of comprehension. Mark start and finish points. Then read for a further minute, aiming for comprehension of significant points, noting your end point. Count and record words per minute. Do this exercise several times per session, using different density materials each time.

5 Progressive acceleration
Using light- to medium-density material, and starting with your fastest comfortable 'reading with comprehension' speed, increase your speed by about 100 words per minute and read for one minute, then by a further 100 words per minute for a further minute, until after four minutes you are reading for a minute at approximately 500 words per minute faster than your starting speed. Calculate the speed at which your eye guide must move to achieve these speeds. Then read for a further minute, aiming for the fastest 'with comprehension' speed you can achieve. It should be higher than in the previous exercise.

6 Pre-scanning

Using fairly light-density material, start at the beginning of a chapter. Estimate approximately where 10 000 words will take you and insert a marker. Scan read to the marker, taking 2–4 seconds per page. Then go back to the beginning and read aiming for *some* comprehension, at a minimum of 1500 words per minute. As you get better, increase both the speed and the density of material scanned.

If you practise the above activities regularly, your speed of reading should increase significantly without loss, perhaps even with some gain, of comprehension. But reading effectiveness depends on more than this. You need at the same time to develop study strategies that will help you to choose appropriate things to read, to select appropriate speeds at which to read them, to think about what they contain while you read and to take good notes to supplement recall. It can also be helpful to index these notes for later reference.

SELECTING MATERIALS AND CHOOSING READING SPEEDS

Knowing what to read can be extremely difficult. Some lecturers may present you with a long list of books and articles, none of which is easy to track down. If you do manage to find them they may be dated or of little use. I did hear of one lecturer who had not updated his reading list in 25 years. I hope the story was a campus myth. But even in less extreme cases you may face a problem in knowing what you need to read for an essay, and an even greater one when doing a literature search for a dissertation.

→ Ch 12

→ Ch 2

→ Ch 13

Sometimes you will not know where to start. Sometimes the list may be impossibly long. In this chapter there is a brief introduction to selecting material. It is a variant of the systematic approach to problem solving covered in detail in Chapter 12, and used in short form in Chapter 2 as the basis for self-management. You will find much more detail on how to search for and select information in Chapter 13.

Define your objectives

→ Ch 13

What are you trying to achieve? Why do you want to read something on this topic? What do you really need to know? Are you seeking facts, ideas, theories or frameworks to help you develop your understanding? (More of this in the next section.) Are you looking for appropriate techniques or background information? Is the information something you may need for an examination? Is it necessary or potentially useful for a written assignment or clarification of something totally obscure from lectures? Is it merely for your own interest? Until you are clear what you want, you cannot start to look for it (though Chapter 13 explores some ways in which you may need to start with a vague idea and, through looking, find out enough to clarify your objectives).

Identify options

What sources exist? How easily can you access them? What does the library have, both hard copy and accessible electronically? Until you are comfortable exploring by yourself, staff will usually be happy to help. Is a text sufficiently important to be worth buying? If so, is there a second-hand source? What does a bookshop have on the topic? While the extreme case described above is rare, some lecturers do not update their lists as often as they ought. There might be something newer and cheaper than a suggested text, though you would need to check that it was as good or better. Ask teaching staff and other students for guidance, particularly before buying your own copy. If you are generating your own source list, look at references at the end of recent or key papers on the topic. See whether there are copies of relevant theses or dissertations in the library – they often have good bibliographies. Search key words. Check whether there are relevant government publications – these tend to be available free of charge online. If relying on a library, do remember that others are likely to want the same books as you do, and at the same time. The early student gets the book!

Identify selection criteria

Obviously it is important that the book or paper covers the topic you are interested in. But other factors need to be considered too. Is the text recent (or a classic)? By a reputable author? Pitched at the right level? Is it in a reputable, refereed journal? If it is on the web, how reliable is it? Is it based on evidence or opinion? How relevant/adequate is the evidence to your purpose? Are there any other factors which are important to your choice in this instance?

Selection itself

Selection is difficult unless you have access to the possible materials and can scan them briefly. Otherwise you will need to accept advice from tutors, librarians or others with knowledge on the subject. In North America in particular, academic tenure depends largely on the length of an academic's publication list, so there is enormous pressure to publish regardless of the density of the ideas or the information contained in the book or article. It pays to be sceptical when selecting. It is all too easy to think that everything in print is worthy of your attention. An important graduate skill is to know how to separate that which has value from that which is flawed, whether in terms of logic or in terms of evidence used.

Choosing your reading speed

Sometimes you will be looking for a highly specific piece of information. Did this research use a particular technique? What sample was used? What does the author have to say on a particular point? If your purpose is to answer such questions, a full reading of the selected text is unnecessary. Instead, use the index, plus rapid scanning of the material to identify the part you need to read in detail. Just as you can hear your name being mentioned at the other side of a crowded room, so you can bring selective attention to bear on written materials. While scanning the page too rapidly to read it, you can still notice the word or phrase you need. This will require serious concentration, however, and a refusal to be side-tracked. Of course, interesting digressions are what true education is all about, so indulge in them whenever you have the time.

The next fastest type of reading after scanning is aimed at getting a picture of the overall pattern of a book, chapter or article. For this, focus first on any contents list, then introductions and summaries, main headings and subheadings. Diagrams and tables of results are useful too. Several rapid passes may help you map the material better than a single slower one.

Slightly slower still is speed reading at your fastest speed. This may be suitable for lengthy materials, where the level of relevance is fairly low, or for background reading. Your aim will be to absorb the main arguments and assess the extent to which these are based on relevant and reliable evidence.

Much of your study will require a slower rate. The exercises you did earlier will still have been useful in eliminating inefficient habits, but where almost every word is relevant and you need to think really hard about the concepts and arguments contained, there will be a limit to how quickly you can work. You will probably need to take notes, both to aid comprehension and for later recall. You may sometimes need to stop reading, think and perhaps consult other sources before proceeding.

Slowest of all is reading to learn by heart. If you need to be able to reproduce an equation, a diagram, an argument or a set of categories, then you will need to spend time on every detail, committing these to memory. If you need not only to reproduce but also to apply what you are learning, you will need to practise this, preferably across a range of applications. There is not much to be gained (except possibly marks in a simple test) from learning something if you do not also learn how and when to use it.

You may find that once you have devoted time to understanding all the details, relationships and possible uses of material, you have in the process learned it. If not, try to devise a mnemonic, this is, something which is easier to remember than the thing itself. Acronyms or rhymes are good for this. You can probably already remember the requirements for objectives because SMART is so easy to remember and it is easy to go from that to what the letters stand for. The stages of group formation introduced in → Ch 10 Chapter 10 are easily remembered as 'form, storm, norm, perform'. Sometimes rote learning may be more efficient, particularly if frequent fast recall is needed. This is the way multiplication tables were once taught, involving going over and over something until it sticks. Rote learning can decay rather more quickly than rhyme or acronym, so it needs refreshing if it is used for something you will need only occasionally.

READING CRITICALLY

→ Ch 3 The idea of questioning the material you read was introduce in the previous chapter in the context of reflection on what you learned from reading. There, the focus was very much on how what you read related to your existing mental models, and whether it suggested that you might be able to enhance or improve them. This is closely related to the process of reading critically, and indeed depends upon it. But here I want to look in rather more detail at the 'critical' element, with a focus shifted towards the material read and its author.

Critical thinking is a key graduate skill, and one increasingly emphasised in learning outcomes for courses. So it is important to get a clear idea of what is meant. 'Critical' is not used in the sense of saying disparaging things about an author. Rather, it means engaging with the materials at a 'deep' level, making sure that you understand the claims that are being made and the arguments and evidence that the author is using to support these claims. It means understanding how these claims relate to those made by other authors, and understanding, too, the context within which the author is writing. There may be cultural, discipline-based or other assumptions which are never made explicit but which underpin the claims made. (As a one-time psychologist I have always had immense difficulty coming to terms with papers written by those with a sociology background: the agendas and the vocabulary and the assumptions made seem to me to differ radically from those with which I am familiar.) When you read critically you need to be alert to these assumptions, and prepared to question them. It is also helpful to know when the author was writing. Some older books and papers offer splendid insights, but it is important to be aware of possible differences in organisations and their contexts at the time of writing, and of the implications of these if drawing conclusions about the present.

The nature of claims

Having established the context in which something was written, the next step to becoming a critical reader is to understand the sorts of claims being made. By claim I mean any idea which someone says is true. Usually they give reasons for this claim. The claim and its associated reasons constitute an argument. Before looking at arguments and how they are constructed, it is helpful to understand some of the terms used. In particular I should like to look at possible differences between concept, model, metaphor, framework and theory. I say 'possible' because these terms are used in different ways by different authors. Even though these words are distinguished differently on occasion, the distinctions themselves are worth noting.

A *concept* is any abstract idea. 'Motivation' is a concept. 'Learning' is a concept. 'Hidden agenda' is a concept. Such concepts can be helpful in making you aware of an aspect of a situation and helping you to understand it. I can still remember my excitement when I first came upon the idea of hidden agendas and started to look for the *real* objectives of people in meetings, something it had never occurred to me to consider before. In the previous chapter I mentioned 'cognitive housekeeping': adding a new concept is one of the ways you can improve your 'cognitive house'. When you are reading something, it is important to understand any concepts which the author uses and with which you are not familiar. Be particularly alert to 'everyday' words or phrases that seem to be being used in a non-everyday manner. ('Critical' is one such example in this chapter.) If you do not understand the specialist sense in which the word is being used then your reading will be of little benefit.

A *model* in everyday language is a simplified representation of something. Thus the map of the London Underground is a model of one aspect of the system itself, namely the relationship between lines and stations on a line. An architect's 3D representation of a building he has designed is another sort of model. When you are diagramming a situation you are creating a model of it, often concentrating on only one aspect of the situation. It is important to remember this uni-dimensionality when dealing with models, and not to confuse them with the reality: 'the map is not the territory'.

A *metaphor* is the use of a familiar term to describe something probably less familiar. It carries with it the suggestion that understanding the former will help you understand the latter. Examples include talking about an organisation as a 'well oiled machine', or 'a tight ship'. Metaphors can usefully highlight key features of a situation. Morgan (1986) uses the spider plant as a striking metaphor for one form of organisational structure. But they are only as useful as the similarities contained. The comforting feeling of understanding that they give can be a dangerous illusion if you draw too many conclusions. As with models, you need to remember that metaphors only partially resemble the thing you are applying them to. Metaphors can, however, be a great aid to creativity, as discussed in Chapter 15.

→ Ch 15

Framework tends to be used to indicate a rather more organised abstraction. Frameworks are extremely common in management 'theory'. Thus you may well encounter the 4 (or 7) Ps in your marketing studies, and you have seen the SWOT framework in this book. Such frameworks tend to provide useful checklists for analysing a situation. If you wanted to look at the environment in which you were operating you might use STEEPLE (and look at sociological, technological, environmental (in the physical sense), economic, political, legal and ethical factors surrounding the organisation). You have already tried SWOT and SMART as frameworks for examining yourself and formulating your objectives.

'Management theory' is often used as a loose collective term to refer to any of the above, but it is more useful to think of *theory* as being an organised set of assumptions which allow you to make predictions about a situation. The STEEPLE framework alerts you to a lot of things to look for, but does not in itself allow you to predict anything; expectancy *theory*, however, allows you to make a number of predictions. For example, it suggests that if you reduce the value of outcomes, or link them less closely to performance, or make it appear less likely that effort will produce performance, then less effort is likely to be made. Management theories in this sense are rather less common than frameworks.

Management writing varies greatly. Sometimes the author may be proposing a new theory or a new framework, or may be critiquing some other theory. Or they might be describing a case study, or (in the case of some of the less academic publications) proposing the answer to life, the universe, and everything. When you are reading critically it is helpful to be clear whether the author is proposing – or drawing on – a theory or framework, or using metaphor. Some of the questions you would ask while reading will depend upon the nature of the claim.

Analysing the argument

In most papers you read, the author will be claiming that one or more statements are justified/true/useful, and providing arguments from evidence (which might be other theories, or research data or even armchair observations) to support this case. So before going further you need to work out the main claim that the author is making, and indeed any secondary claims. As an example of this sort of thinking I'll take another classic motivation theory, Herzberg's (1966) 'motivation–hygiene' theory: you are likely to encounter this at some point in your studies and we have already introduced two other theories of motivation so it allows comparison. I shall abbreviate the argument here, for simplicity.

Herzberg claims that man has two sets of needs: one set concerns the need to avoid pain and the other concerns the specifically human need to grow psychologically. This claim is supported by the results of interviews with 200 engineers and accountants 'who represented a cross-section of Pittsburgh industry'. Interviewees were asked to think of a time when they had felt especially good about their jobs, and then to answer questions about why they had felt like that, and its impact on their performance, personal relationships and well-being. This process was then repeated for a time when they had negative feelings about their job. Five factors stood out as strong determinants of job satisfaction: achievement, recognition (for achievement), work itself, responsibility and advancement. Dissatisfaction was associated with company policy and administration, supervision, salary, interpersonal relations and working conditions. Thus satisfaction was associated with the person's relationship to what they do, dissatisfaction with the context within which they do it. A chart showing how responses are distributed is included, which broadly supports the 'two-factor' idea: although most things are cited in the context of both satisfaction and dissatisfaction, mentions in the 'wrong' category are much less frequent than those in the 'right' one.

Remember the original claim: there are two categories of human need operating. The evidence to support it appears plausible. Different circumstances seemed to cause feeling good about your job, and feeling bad. But consider the evidence: is it actually adequate? No detail is given about whether the 'theory' was already known to the person categorising the responses, or whether the experiment was done blind. There is room for subconscious bias in any subjective judgements: the paper I was reading (an extract from a book) did not make this clear, so I would need to go back to the original research paper to check the method. (At this point you would make an action note to do this.) Then what about the sample of people interviewed? You could argue that two professional groups in a single US city is not really a representative sample. Would blue-collar workers respond in the same fashion? Would poor people in other countries be similarly unmoved by money?

Then what about the reasoning? Is the conclusion inevitable from this evidence? Would you get these results *only* if people had two different sets of needs? There is quite a lot of evidence to suggest that in other contexts we tend to take personal credit for good things that happen to us, and blame others for the bad. Herzberg's results could be explained equally well by this human tendency. Alternatively, as indeed Herzberg points out, the 'motivators' tend to be associated with performing the task, the dissatisfiers with the context in which it is performed. Would not expectancy theory, which was being developed at around the same time, predict exactly this? And in a way that enabled further predictions to be made about ways in which strengthening the effort–outcome link could increase motivation?

The next question is the 'so what' one. At the time, Herzberg's theory had a profound influence on organisations. It proposed a whole new approach to improving employee motivation. Instead of pay rises, organisations found ways of increasing responsibility. A whole 'job enrichment' industry grew up, following a very prescriptive approach which Herzberg developed. (Indeed, this is still the thrust of many job redesign exercises today, although because the underpinning theory is less simplistic, the chances of success are arguably higher.)

Did it work? Sometimes. But in other cases the effort–performance link was already weak because the staff concerned did not have the skills to do even what was required of them before the intervention. As expectancy theory would have predicted, the effects of job enrichment in such cases was catastrophic. It might have saved a lot of money in some of the organisations concerned if a more critical reading of Herzberg had been undertaken before job enrichment was embarked upon.

Mapping the argument

In looking at this particular, much quoted and, at the time, highly influential piece of writing, I was trying to do three things:

- identify the claim being made
- evaluate the evidence being used in support of the claim
- evaluate the reasoning used to link the evidence to the claim.

It can be helpful to approach this graphically. You can use the form of a mind map (described later in this chapter) where each branch represents a single 'reason' with the twigs being the pieces of evidence that together form that reason. Figure 4.2 shows an example of an argument map, Figure 4.3 (on page 96) a spray diagram on note taking.

Branches might be in the form of different logical links. Thus one set of twigs might 'prove' something, make it fairly likely to be the case, be consistent with it, be inconsistent with it, or actually disprove it. You could write this on the branch. When

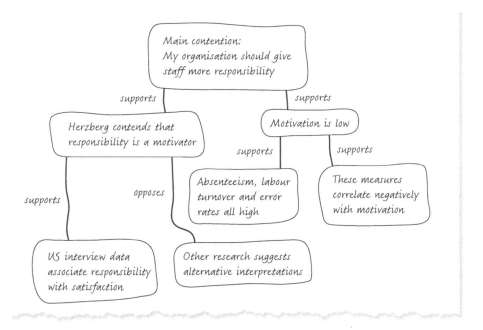

Fig 4.2 **Example of an argument map**

you have a complex argument, unless there is actual proof – rare in management research – you will be faced with working out how much weight to give to the different reasons. This will depend upon the strength of the evidence itself, its consistency, and the strength of the evidence–claim links.

Although we have been talking about mapping other people's arguments, the technique is valuable for mapping your own reasoning when you are planning an essay answer. If you are planning a research project or dissertation it can also be invaluable to think about your potential evidence before you finalise your research design, and consider how → Ch 8, 16 – however it comes out – it relates to claims you might hope to make in your report.

Software packages which allow you to map arguments can be really useful if the argument is complex. And arguments can be *very* complex, with many reasons operating on several levels. In these cases each twig is in itself a claim, and has supporting reasons (premises), objections to reasons (rejoinders) and objections to objections (rebuttals). By teasing them apart it is possible to evaluate each chain of claim-supporting claims-evidence, by looking both at the logic involved and the evidence (and assumptions) to which this logic is applied. As in the example above, you may find that both the evidence and the reasoning leave something to be desired. If you are interested in this, you can find material online. It may be designed to support – and sell – a particular product, but in the process may provide more detailed teaching than there is room for here (try **www.austhink.com/reason/tutorials**).

ACTIVITY 4.2

Select an article from a business or management journal or professional magazine. Try to identify: the principle claim and any secondary claims. If applicable, it may help to decide whether theory, framework and/or metaphor is involved. Define any new concepts. Ask 'so what'? If the claim is true, what does it imply? If the implications are important enough to justify the effort, try to tease apart the arguments involved. What claims and/or evidence are used to support the claim(s) and what, if any, evidence is used to support any intermediate claims? What are the logical links used? Do they add up to a valid argument provided the evidence is sound (i.e. is the conclusion drawn the only possible one)? Is the evidence adequate? Are there any hidden assumptions being made? If so, how valid are these assumptions?

Hidden assumptions are difficult to identify but may be critical to an argument. There was a hidden assumption in the Herzberg case which you may have seen once the alternative explanation was pointed out. This was that 'no other explanation is possible'. Once this assumption was queried, other possible explanations were looked for, and some found. So when a reason is offered it is always worth asking whether this reason is sufficient in itself to support the claim.

The other difficulty in business research is the complexity of most of the issues addressed, and the variety of contexts in which these issues arise. This makes it very difficult both to obtain convincing evidence and to know how far to generalise from it. Even if the evidence and argument were adequate in their context, would it be reasonable, for example, to draw conclusions about all employees from two professional groupings in one city? It was clear in the example above how difficult it was to interpret the subjective responses given by the professionals concerned. There is a real dilemma faced by many authors between seemingly 'scientific' quantitative data and the richer, but harder to interpret, qualitiative information. More of this in Chapter 13.

→ Ch 13

There are many other useful questions to ask when reading critically. A basic selection, including those already covered, is given in Box 4.1.

BOX 4.1

Useful questions when reading critically

- When/where was this written and what was the author's purpose?
- What claims is the author making?
- What new concepts are introduced, and what do they mean?
- Are they really new or merely a 're-badging' of existing ideas?
- How/when might they be useful?
- What new frameworks are introduced?
- What do they add to existing frameworks?
- How/when might the new frameworks be useful? Are there limitations to their application?
- Is there any new theory introduced?
- Do the 'organised assumptions' that make up the theory hang together logically?
- Does it extend an existing theory? (Sometimes quite small additions can be surprisingly useful)
- Is it consistent with other theories that you already know? If not, what are the inconsistencies? Are they explained/justified?
- How/when might the new theory be useful? Are there limitations to its application?
- Are there ways in which this new theory might usefully be amended?
- Was the author arguing a case to which s/he was personally committed? (This can indicate potential for bias)
- How good is the argument supporting the claim? Are there any shortcomings in the evidence or the logic, or any hidden assumptions which might be questioned?
- If there are inadequacies, is this because the paper is a shortened version of something else? If so, could you find more of the evidence by looking at other sources?

NOTES AND ANNOTATIONS USING WORDS AND DIAGRAMS

Take notes for:
- concentration
- understanding
- retention
- reference
- revision.

Note taking is a crucial study skill, but also invaluable at work. You have probably often taken notes to help you remember something afterwards. But note taking is far more than merely a way to extend your memory. It is a key component in active learning. And if you are one of those who learns best by writing, it will be one of your best 'aids'.

In writing notes you are – or should be – *organising* material, and therefore organising your thoughts. By extracting themes and key points, and jotting them down in a way that *makes sense* to you, you are interacting with the material. This interaction engages your mind. It stops your attention drifting off. It is *interesting*. It means that you will *absorb* the key points you have extracted, almost without effort. And good notes are likely to be far more useful to you in essay writing or revision than the original material.

'Good notes' are clearly more than a verbatim record of a lecturer's words or a section of text. Of course there will be times when a diagram or piece of text is so important that you will want to copy (or photocopy) the whole thing, or save it from the Internet. Even if you do, it will normally be helpful to take notes on it as well. When your notes do include direct quotes it is important to make this very clear, so that when you come back to them you know which parts are the author's words and which your own. There are two reasons for this. First, you may want to quote exactly what someone said when you are writing an essay or dissertation, so you need to know which words are a direct quotation. (With this in mind it is always a good idea to note beside it the page number from which the quote is taken – you may be asked to give this when quoting.) Second, and possibly even more important, if you quote without giving credit to an author, this is the deadly (in academic terms) sin of

→ Ch 8 plagiarism (see Chapter 8). If your notes do not make make clear what is a direct quotation you are in danger of accidental plagiarism when you come to use these notes in writing.

As suggested earlier, the active process of organising material into notes can maintain your concentration and help you sort out the structure of what the author is saying (you might try mapping their arguments). Thus you learn at a deeper level, understand more and remember more than if you merely read passively.

Not only that, good notes can often be far more useful than the original material. They will be easier for you to understand, as you will have organised the material into a form which makes sense to you. You can also include cross-references to relevant material from other sources or other courses. If working on paper, you can use colour to emphasise structure and aid memory. Notes which are briefer than the originals are likely to be much easier to refer to and to revise from. This is particularly the case if you devise an indexing system which allows you to find related topics easily.

As with everything else, you need to be clear about *why* you are keeping notes. If you are working with borrowed materials which will be crucial for a major project later, you will need to keep more detailed notes and to copy quotations and key diagrams as well as any useful references that you may need to explore and/or quote. When accessing materials on the Internet there is a strong temptation merely to copy huge chunks. While such copies may have their uses, remember the advantages of notes just mentioned. Without active 'digestion', condensing and restructuring you are likely to miss major benefits. Keep a full copy for reference, but make brief notes to supplement this. The same applies to photocopying. Apart from the potential expense, copies of papers and chapters will not help you merely by sitting on your shelves. Indeed, if they give you a false sense of achievement they can be a hindrance. They are only any good when you *interact* with them. So how can you do this effectively?

Annotation

If you are working with your own copy of materials, the most basic form of note taking is annotation, highlighting key points or concepts and making brief marginal notes or inserted comments. This will ensure that you are *thinking* as you read, searching for the key ideas, and that you stay awake. When you return to the materials you will be able to extract key points from the highlighting, and the brief notes you have added will remind you of relevant examples from elsewhere or how you finally sorted out a point in the text that was confusing.

Précis

When you cannot annotate materials, or if you want more condensed notes, it can be helpful to make a précis or summary, where you write down key points made. If working from annotated materials, you may merely jot down your highlighted words plus marginal comments. But ideally you are aiming to say something more concise than the original *and in your own words*. The translation process will go far to making the meaning sink in. Normally you will want your summary to be organised point by point, even if the original is less clear.

Diagrammatic notes

In taking notes you will often be looking for *relationships* – between ideas in a text or lecture, or between this material and some other. Diagrams are a particularly useful technique for representing relationships, with huge advantages over linear text for this purpose. A number of diagramming techniques are introduced at different points in the book: you have already encountered argument mapping. This is part of the same 'family' of diagrams as the more general mind-mapping technique, sometimes called brain patterns, described by Tony and Barry Buzan (2003). Variants of this basic form will appear in a variety of contexts and with different names. It is extremely versatile; note taking is just one of its applications.

In drawing a mind map, you start in the centre of the page, with a word or phrase indicating the main idea or central theme, then branch out from this, giving each sub-theme a separate branch. These branches divide further into sub-sub-themes. If you are exploring your own thoughts in this way it is called a mind map. If you are teasing out the content of something else, then it is often called a spray diagram. Figure 4.3 shows an example of a spray diagram on note taking. In the next chapter you will see how a similar diagram can be used to plan the structure of something that you are going to write. Software is readily available for drawing mind maps, and many students find this useful. Computer-drawn mind maps look much neater but they may be less memorable and can sometimes feel more constrained.

Buzan highlights the following advantages of this type of diagram over linear notes:

- The central idea is more clearly defined.
- Position indicates relative importance – items near the centre are more significant than those nearer the periphery.
- Proximity and connections show links between key concepts.

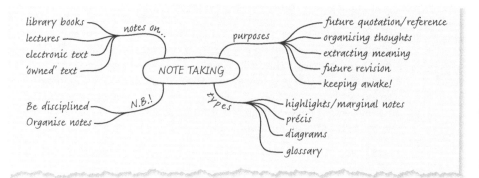

Fig 4.3 **Diagrammatic notes on note taking**

- Recall and review will be more rapid and more effective.
- The structure allows for easy addition of new information.
- Patterns will differ from each other, making them easier to remember.
- (For divergent, creative use – covered later) the open-ended nature of the pattern helps the brain make new connections.

Thus you can see how mind maps help you with both the digesting and structuring of material you are studying and its later recall.

ACTIVITY 4.3

Return to whatever notes you took on Chapter 3 (or to the chapter itself if you did not take notes). Draw a mind map of the main points. Reflect on the extent to which this helped to make the structure clearer. If working with others, compare diagrams and discuss both your diagrams and the extent to which they helped. Draw mind maps for the next five serious chapters or articles that you read. You should be hooked on the technique by then!

ACTIVITY 4.4

Prepare an exhibit showing that you can select, read and summarise in note form an appropriate chapter or paper. Your exhibit will need to document your objectives, the selection process used, the full reference of the text selected and your summary.

Lecture notes

Lecture notes present a particular challenge, as you have to go at the speed of the lecturer and cannot usually ask for a point to be repeated until you have grasped it. A few lecturers make things easy by providing handouts with the slides they use, so that you can make notes against these. More commonly you will simply need to do the best you can at the time and remedy any deficits later. While you do not need to become proficient at shorthand, working out your own abbreviations for frequently repeated words is a great help. If you are taking notes on a lecture, you may eventually become good enough to rely on mind maps, but at first it is better to keep more narrative notes on one page, perhaps trying to build up a mind map in quiet moments on the facing page.

Some lecturers distribute their notes in hard copy. Does this mean you do not need to take notes during the lecture? It does rather depend upon your preferred learning mode. Some people who are strongly auditory may find that taking notes gets in the way, and if notes are to be provided it is best not to make their own. Most people, however, will find that note taking has the same benefits in lectures as it does when reading in terms of maintaining their concentration and forcing them to engage with the key points being made and the relationships between them.

As well as drawing mind maps, try using sketch diagrams. These can sometimes clarify meaning more quickly than words. Space is useful too – leave gaps for things you missed. Leave space, too, for things which will need expansion if they are ever to make sense to you three months later. Indicate as you go along all the points where your notes are not adequate. Then discipline yourself to make good the deficits *as soon as possible*. You will be able to do this relatively easily within 24 hours, while the event is still fresh in your mind. Check with others whose notes, memories or comprehension may be better than yours. If you wait more than a day, the task will be far more difficult, if not impossible.

Discipline and organisation

However you take your notes, whether you use notebooks, loose-leaf files, PDA or laptop, it is vital that you are disciplined about organising your notes. Well organised notes can be invaluable. Dozens of scruffy pieces of paper scattered around your flat, or cryptically labelled documents distributed seemingly randomly between equally cryptically labelled folders, or left unsorted with hundreds of other things in 'My Documents' have little use at all. (Google desktop may provide some sort of rescue in the latter case, but is far from a total solution.) Part of this organisation should include a good index to your materials, so that you know what notes you have on which topics and can easily access them, and related materials, if an assignment or project requires it. A page numbering system is important for paper notes – you need to be able to

For good note taking:
- use words and diagrams
- 'organise' content
- 'improve' within 24 hours
- file systematically.

reorder them if you drop them in a gale or lend them to a friend who mixes them up. If you are keeping electronic notes it is essential to make back-up copies at regular intervals. It can be heartbreaking to lose all your notes, especially if this happens shortly before you need to start your revision. PDAs are particularly prone to being lost, stolen or dropped, so you need to copy your notes to PC at frequent intervals. Hard disks on PCs can fail. So back-up frequently, and keep your back-up copy separate and safe.

Discipline is also important when it comes to references to any materials you do not own. Keeping a full reference list (use the format in the list of references at the end of this book if you have not been told to use something different) with your notes will save hours of searching perhaps months or even years later, when you need to use it for a paper or dissertation. It may seem a bother at the time, but it is more of a bother to resurrect an elusive reference when everything you can remember about it is insufficient to identify it.

Organised and disciplined notes will have potential uses beyond the particular course to which they relate. They may be a useful resource for a subsequent dissertation or project, or indeed help in a situation at work. Unless you are very pressed for space, it is therefore worth retaining them. It can be infuriating to need something and then realise you threw it away a year ago.

Similarly, you will have many occasions after your degree when you will need to take notes. Whether you are interviewing potential employees, listening to a speaker at a professional association, reading a lengthy report or sitting in a meeting, you will need similar skills so it is worth developing the skills – and the discipline – to take notes that will be of use after the event.

SUMMARY

This chapter has argued the following:

- Improving your reading skills can make you a far more effective learner, and aid career success.
- Practice can significantly improve reading speeds.
- It is possible to increase your reading speed without loss of comprehension.
- Efficient reading requires you to think more clearly about what you need to read, and why, and about where to find it.
- Lecturers, library staff and other students can help you find and select appropriate reading material.
- Different reading speeds are appropriate for different purposes.
- When reading it is important to adopt a critical approach, asking a range of questions as you read.
- It is important to identify the claims the author is making and to evaluate their internal consistency and the strength of the evidence and reasoning given in support of these claims.
- Mapping the arguments can be a useful approach when evaluating a case.
- It is important to relate your reading to other materials on the same subject, to the author's purpose and to the context in which it was written.
- Taking notes will increase the effectiveness of your understanding and learning and give you something for future reference.
- Mind maps can form a useful part of your notes.
- It is essential to be disciplined in organising and storing your notes.

Further information

- Buzan, T. (2003) *The Speed Reading Book*, BBC Publications.
- Buzan, T. (2003) *Use Your Head*, BBC Publications.

- Buzan, T. and Buzan, B. (2003) *The Mind Map Book: Radiant Thinking – Major Evolution in Human Thought*, BBC Publications.
- Morris, S. and Smith, J. (1998) *Understanding Mind Maps in a Week,* Institute of Management.
- Rose, C. and Nicholl, M.J. (1997) *Accelerated Learning for the 21st Century*, Piatkus.
- Russell, L. (1999) *The Accelerated Learning Field Book*, Jossey-Bass/Pfeiffer.

AVOIDING PLAGIARISM

This chapter suggests ways of maintaining academic integrity, including the KnACK strategy for avoiding plagiarism. This strategy entails **Kn**owing what you are doing, **A**cknowledging your sources, **C**reating your own perspectives, and being prepared to **K**eep revising your position to strengthen the originality of your work. This chapter highlights the importance of effective time management and suggests why some students plagiarise so you can avoid common pitfalls and improve your own chances of academic success.

The chapter covers:

- Defining plagiarism
- Avoiding plagiarism
- Time management
- A positive approach to citing and referencing
- Penalties for plagiarism.

Using this chapter

From Chapter 2 of *Academic Research,Writing & Referencing,* 1/e. Mary deane.

INTRODUCTION

Having introduced the concept of academic integrity, this chapter defines plagiarism and provides tips on avoiding unintentional plagiarism.

WHAT IS PLAGIARISM?

Plagiarism is the omission of acknowledgements when you borrow ideas, images, statistics, or other data from sources, or the attempt to present the intellectual property of another person as your own (Neville 2007: 28). Marsh (2004) offers the following comment about definitions of plagiarism as a negative act:

> Most generic plagiarism definitions – drawing on the Latin *plagium* ('net to entangle game') – stress that plagiarism is stealing, kidnapping, or theft of intellectual property.
>
> (Marsh 2004: 428)

Although plagiarism is penalised at university, learning how to avoid it also represents a chance to learn ways of improving your research and writing so, rather than focusing on problems you might encounter, try concentrating on the opportunity to learn new strategies for generating and disseminating knowledge in a scholarly fashion (Howard 2007: 13).

A positive approach

Many writers worry about plagiarism and find that this stress has a negative impact on their experience of university or their academic performance. While it is important to adopt the codes of academic practice outlined in the introduction, the more you enjoy discovering information and generating your own ideas, the less likely you are to plagiarise unintentionally.

Although you may not be aware of it, you make decisions about whether or not to plagiarise all the time; for instance, by reading this book you are choosing to learn about scholarly practice to prevent plagiarism in your work. So, you can relax to some extent because you are raising your game academically by seeking this guidance. Build upon this excellent start by thinking about your written assessments for yourself and acknowledging all the ideas, information, images, statistics, and other data from which you borrow for your own writing.

DEVELOPING A KnACK FOR AVOIDING PLAGIARISM

Learning how to avoid plagiarism takes patience and perseverance, especially if this approach to research and writing is new to you. The opposite of plagiarising is generating new knowledge, and the tips below help you to make this your priority. The simple way to avoid plagiarism is to produce your own work and credit the work of others using an appropriate system for citing and referencing sources. More specifically, you can avoid accidental plagiarism by focusing on what you know or think about the subject you are discussing in your writing.

Here are four tips to help you get the KnACK for generating ideas of your own:

1 **Kn**ow what you are doing for each written assessment
2 **A**cknowledge your sources
3 **C**reate your own perspective based upon research
4 **K**eep revising your position to strengthen the originality of your work.

Often, the difference between a writer who plagiarises accidentally and one who does not, is the evidence of the latter's thought processes, which reveal to readers that the work is original. Following the KnACK approach to generating ideas will help you deepen your knowledge so you can make this learning apparent in your writing and receive the credit you are due when examiners give you feedback (Neville 2007: 12).

Know what you are doing for each written assessment

Unless you understand the task you have been set or the steps involved in completing your research project, it is impossible to carry it out successfully. Knowing what you need to do is therefore the first step to success and this is where you need to start generating ideas. Read any guidance you have been given and take time to brainstorm about the various ways you could tackle your task. Seek further advice if necessary, and, if appropriate, you could put together an initial plan and ask your tutor for comments.

Acknowledge your sources

At an advanced level it is unusual to receive a written assessment or to undertake work that does not draw on existing research, ideas, images, data, or information. Although it is not possible to generalise, tutors usually expect to see evidence of your research and acknowledgements within your writing each time you borrow material.

Create your own perspective based upon research

The advantage of taking this scholarly approach is that it enables you to isolate the intellectual property of others from your own thinking. As readers and examiners are mostly interested in your assessment of the subject, developing a knack for building on what others have argued is one route to academic success. So, whenever it is appropriate, try to use your acknowledgement of sources as a stepping stone to positing your own ideas.

Keep revising your position to strengthen the originality of your work

The generation of new perspectives and insights takes time, and unless you allow yourself the opportunity to refine your thinking you can undermine your chances of success. Talking about and jotting down your ideas are essential to finding ways of articulating them clearly and organising them for the highest impact upon readers. Therefore, revising your position about a subject is an important part of generating new ideas and this may allow you to make a contribution to knowledge in your field.

TIME MANAGEMENT

Effective time management is essential to avoiding plagiarism (DeVoss and Rosati 2002: 194). Do not make the mistake of ignoring your project if it is unclear from the start, and do not expect your tutors to respond to last minute queries. You can take advantage of your tutor's office hours or ask questions during classes if you need clarification about the purpose of your task, but remember that academics are extremely busy and may not receive your message in time to respond before the deadline. Moreover, advanced level study requires you to take responsibility for your own study and to plan ahead, so be aware that if you delay in getting started with your work it is not your tutor's role to accommodate this lack of organisation.

On the other hand, there are structures in place at every institution to support students who require advice about study skills, welfare, and any issues that affect their chances of academic success. Find out about the systems in place at your own university by enquiring at the library, the Students' Union, or other units such as the Disabilities Office, the Welfare Office, and the Academic Office. If you take steps to help yourself you will be well supported, but it is up to you to seek the advice you need to work effectively.

Tutors expect you to locate the sources they recommend on reading lists and in other documents, so you need to plan ahead to access books and journals at the earliest opportunity. This is especially true if colleagues may be seeking the same texts as you, and if you leave your research to the last minute you could be disadvantaged from the outset by a lack of relevant material.

However, if you do find yourself in this situation, try finding an electronic version of the books you need to read. Although search engines (such as Google™, for instance) can be problematic because they provide access to inaccurate, misleading, and unscholarly material, they also give you access to scholarly sources. Search for books you have been recommended via an online forum (for example, Amazon) and you can probably read useful extracts for your writing. Remember to record all the information you need to acknowledge the source in your chosen referencing style, including the page numbers. Record e-books in the appropriate format with the website address and the date you accessed the source.

Penalties for plagiarism

The two main categories of plagiarism are intentional and unintentional, and there are serious penalties for both kinds. A distinction is not necessarily made between these two categories because students are responsible for adopting scholarly practice and are expected to produce their own work to gain qualifications.

The penalties for plagiarism are set by individual institutions and these are usually outlined in the appropriate place on the university website and in the documentation distributed to students when they start a course. If you are unfamiliar with the penalties at your institution it is up to you to find out what they are, because they apply to you whether or not you know them in detail.

Depending on the extent and nature of a case of plagiarism, the penalties might include a mark of zero for an assignment, the outcome of fail for a course, or exclusion from the university. There are procedures in place at every university to give students who are suspected of plagiarism a fair hearing, and you can usually find this information listed under 'academic integrity', 'academic conduct', 'plagiarism', or related terms on your institution's website.

The main forms of plagiarism are shown in the box below (Neville 2007: 28).

Forms of plagiarism

Intentional plagiarism

- Omitting in-text citations in your writing
- Omitting sources in your list of references
- Omitting the list of references
- Taking material written by another person and submitting it as your own work
- Collusion, or co-writing an assignment with another person and submitting it as your own work
- Cheating in exams
- Purchasing an assignment on the internet and submitting it as your own work
- Attempting to gain credit for the same work twice by re-submitting all or part of a written assessment.

Unintentional plagiarism

- Inaccurate or incomplete in-text citations
- Inaccurate or incomplete list of references
- Poor quoting
- Poor paraphrasing
- Poor summarising.

Why study?

What is your main purpose for undertaking a degree? Is it to enhance your intellectual development generally, to learn about a new field specifically, to improve your chances of success professionally, or to enjoy the university environment? If you plagiarise either on purpose or by accident you are likely to undermine your purpose for studying, and you could also mar your academic record for the future. Howard (2007) asserts the importance of learning and points out that plagiarism undermines this activity:

> [P]lagiarism in the academy matters so dearly because writing assignments are intended to help students learn course materials and gain communication and thinking skills. If those assignments are undermined through plagiarism, none of that learning takes place, and the academic enterprise is itself endangered.
>
> (Howard 2007: 11)

The requirement to document sources explicitly and accurately is usually a feature of assessment criteria because tutors expect to see evidence of independent research. When critical thinking is a required part of an assessment, critiquing clearly documented sources is also valued. So, remember to incorporate acknowledged sources into your writing because this is the foundation upon which academic work is built.

WHY DO SOME WRITERS PLAGIARISE?

Reasons for unintentional plagiarism

There are many reasons why writers plagiarise by accident; for instance, they may lack confidence when it comes to documenting sources fully, or they may be unfamiliar with the conventions of research writing in their field (Neville 2007: 30).

Incomplete records

A common reason why writers plagiarise unintentionally is that they forget to record all the details necessary to cite and reference properly. It is much easier to keep notes as you go along than to hunt for sources at the last minute, so be organised and keep a record of the details you will need (Williams and Carroll 2009: 22).

Learn how to cite and reference the main types of sources you use and keep a manual or guide handy for the less common types of sources. Remember that documenting sources in your academic writing requires you to use your common sense when you encounter a source that you do not know how to reference. In this situation ask yourself whether it could be a variant on the format for a book, journal article, or website, and reference it in a clear and consistent manner.

Lacking confidence

Some writers plagiarise unintentionally because they are not sure how to cite and reference properly. If you are not clear about what to do, you are more likely to make unintentional errors, and the way to avoid this is to dedicate time to practising, and to take every opportunity to gain feedback from your tutors. You can also avoid accidental plagiarism by working with a friend and swapping texts to help each other spot omissions and errors. Often we cannot see our own mistakes, but we can easily identify problems in other people's work, so it can be invaluable to find a colleague and help each other out. Remember that collusion, or co-writing a piece of work that you submit as your own, is a form of plagiarism so only include your own ideas in your written assessments and credit the intellectual property you borrow from sources.

A different approach

Writers who travel to an English-speaking nation for their higher education may encounter a different approach to research and writing than that to which they are accustomed (Lunsford 2008: 284). Remember that acknowledging sources allows writers to build upon research to articulate their own ideas, which is valued very highly at English-speaking higher education institutions. If you need some tips, read the instructions you receive from your tutors and take advantage of training courses offered by the library, for instance, and if you have specific questions you should ask your tutor.

Similarly, writers who have recently started a higher education degree may find the conventions different from their previous experience. Not all schools and colleges require students to use referencing systems, and it can be very confusing at first. The best way to become more familiar with the conventions you should adopt at university is to read journal articles in your field. The added advantage is that journal articles show you how to present a scholarly argument based on evidence. Scholarly articles are superb examples of how to organise the shape and contents of advanced level writing, and in addition you will learn about your topic as you read.

Reasons for intentional plagiarism

There are also many reasons why writers plagiarise on purpose; for example, they may have poor time management skills or they might lack commitment to a course.

Time

Writers who are under the pressure of time sometimes choose to cheat by copying material without crediting the sources. There is no excuse for this, especially as the situation can be avoided by planning ahead. Although some people think that no one will notice, academics are expert at tracing the line of argument and analysing the style of texts so it is very easy for them to spot irregularities, differences in tone, and material taken from elsewhere. Plagiarism detection services such as Turnitin[TM] can identify use of unacknowledged material by scanning the contents and checking this against a comprehensive database of sources and academic assignments. For an informative critique of such services, see Marsh (2004).

Lacking commitment

Some writers do not appreciate the need to engage with the culture of scholarly writing and attributing ideas to authors. However, these are essential abilities to cultivate, and without learning how to research and reference effectively writers are un-likely to pass their courses. Some students do not realise that, in addition to the formal penalties for plagiarism, other consequences stem from not acknowledging sources:

- It obscures your efforts to search for relevant sources
- It hides the time you spend selecting sources
- It undermines your efforts to read and understand sources.

AVOIDING UNINTENTIONAL PLAGIARISM

You can avoid plagiarising unintentionally by displaying academic integrity as you research, write, and reference written assessments, reports, studies, and other kinds of academic work. Here are some tips to help you adopt a scholarly approach throughout your studies:

Tips on avoiding plagiarism

Research

- Do not forget to take full notes recording the details necessary to document your sources properly
- Jot down the page numbers for passages you may quote, paraphrase, or summarise
- Also note the page numbers for images, statistics, or other data you might borrow.

Writing

- Always introduce the ideas, images, data, and words you have borrowed from sources
- When appropriate, comment on the sources you integrate into your own writing
- Give page numbers as appropriate (when you refer to a specific page)
- Check your paraphrasing of passages is accurate
- Check your summarising of passages is accurate.

Referencing

- Learn how to use a reference management system such as EndNote or RefWorks
- Cite sources as you are writing in accordance with the recommended referencing style
- Give full details for each source you have cited in the list of references at the end of your work in accordance with the recommended referencing style
- Ask a friend to check your in-text citations and list of references.

WHAT DOES *NOT* REQUIRE REFERENCING?

There is an element of judgement involved in deciding when you need to acknowledge sources in your academic writing and when you do not (Neville 2007: 20). If you are unsure it is preferable to include an in-text citation rather than omit one in case you accidentally plagiarise a source. The conventions are distinct within disciplinary contents and, to help you learn about the practice in your field, you should read the texts your tutors have recommended. Notice in particular how authors do not document common knowledge or generally accepted facts (Lunsford 2009: 190). Here is a list of the types of material you do not usually need to cite and reference:

- **Your own ideas**
- **Your own work**
- **General knowledge.**

Your own ideas

You do not usually need to document your own ideas because they are your intellectual property. However, if you are unsure you should check this with your tutor because there may be exceptions. For instance, if you refer to work you have published or submitted for assessment already, it could be important for examiners to know this because an attempt to gain credit for the same piece of work twice is viewed as plagiarism.

Your own work

If you undertake research involving experimentation, data collection, or the generation of results you do not usually need to document your findings, providing the material is your own intellectual property. If you report the views or ideas of others, for instance through interviews or focus groups, you should acknowledge their contributions although this can be done anonymously. Follow the guidelines for ethical research practices at your institution and seek specific advice from tutors or expert researchers in your field.

General knowledge

If you refer to common knowledge, such as the dates of world wars, well known myths, or well established facts, you do not usually need to document the source because general knowledge implies a general holding of the intellectual property. On the other hand, if you refer to an author or artist's interpretation of a story or event, this is the intellectual property of another person and it must be acknowledged with accurate citation and referencing.

SUMMARY

This chapter has suggested ways of maintaining academic integrity, including the KnACK strategy for avoiding plagiarism which entails **Kn**owing what you are doing, **A**cknowledging your sources, **C**reating your own perspective, and being prepared to **K**eep revising your position to strengthen the originality of your work. The chapter has highlighted the importance of effective time management and outlined potential reasons for plagiarising so you can avoid these pitfalls and improve your own chances of academic success.

The main arguments in this chapter:

■ You can take a positive and practical approach to avoiding plagiarism

■ This takes time and forward planning

■ It requires you to learn how to cite and reference

■ It also takes practice.

QUIZ

1 Here is an extract from an article by Lawson et al. (2009) called 'Does the Multi-lateral Matter?' Is this passage missing any in-text citations?

Does the Multilateral Matter?

The International Monetary Fund (IMF), the World Bank and the World Trade Organization (WTO) have a common origin in the conference held in Bretton Woods, New Hampshire during July 1944 and share a focus on multilateral cooperation. But each addresses a different aspect of international economic interaction. The IMF and World Bank were created to address international monetary cooperation and development issues respectively.

(Lawson et al. 2009: 2)

2 Read the examples below and decide whether the writers were correct to document this information.

Example 1

As part of her study, the author took the photograph in Figure 1 to illustrate the behaviour of cats.

Figure 1: Cats' involvement in human activities
(Long 2010).

Example 2

An increased consumption of calories with no additional exercise results in weight gain (Edwards 2010).

Example 3

The story of Cinderella is a well known fairytale (Grimm and Grimm 1812) which has long been popular.

Example 4

Scholars have argued that leadership is a quality possessed by everyone, and external conditions determine whether or not individuals fulfil their potential (Potterson 2008, Zinger 2010).

THE HARVARD STYLE

This chapter demonstrates how to use the Harvard style and provides a wide range of examples. The chapter stresses the importance of clear and consistent acknowledgement of sources, and points out that you need to use your own judgement when you are acknowledging unusual sources.

The chapter covers:

- Variations of the Harvard style
- In-text citations
- The list of references
- Written sources
- Secondary sources
- Numerical sources
- Audiovisual sources
- Digital formats.

Using this chapter

From Chapter 10 of *Academic Research, Writing & Referencing*, 1/e. Mary deane.

INTRODUCTION

This chapter explains how to cite and reference using the Harvard style. However, before adopting any referencing system you must consult the guidance given to you by your tutors and follow their advice. Course handbooks and assignment briefs usually specify which style you should use, and if in doubt you should ask your tutors or seek advice at your university library.

VARIATIONS OF THE HARVARD STYLE

There is no single version of the Harvard style because there is no official publication providing instructions on how to use this referencing system. Instead, you will find many different websites and manuals which all give slightly different advice. The existence of different versions of the Harvard style can create confusion because each version recommends slightly different use of punctuation, and sometimes different ways of formatting the pieces of information required for list of reference entries. For example, you may be advised to insert a comma after the author's surname, or write 'p.' instead of a colon before giving page numbers.

Do not let the existence of different variations of the Harvard style confuse you, but choose a version in consultation with your tutors and stick with it. The main aim of referencing is to show readers **where you have borrowed material from sources**, and, as long as this information is *clear and consistently formatted* you will be successful as a scholar and researcher.

TWO ELEMENTS

Whichever version of the Harvard style you use, there are two elements you need to master (Williams and Carron 2009: 7). The two elements are:

1 *In-text citations* every time you borrow material from a source
2 A *list of references* at the end of your work.

Your academic writing must contain both in-text citations and a list of references. In-text citations are acknowledgements of the author, date, and when appropriate the page number each time you borrow from a source. You should place in-text citations within brackets and insert a colon before the page number like this:

> Academic writing involves 'careful citation and critical thinking' (McArthur 2010: 5).

It is a serious omission not to cite the sources you refer to in your writing, and this omission constitutes *plagiarism* because it is a failure to acknowledge authors' intellectual property.

There are various ways of integrating sources into your own writing. When you borrow numerical data or images you should introduce these clearly, and if appropriate label them as figures or tables. When borrowing words and ideas, you can quote, paraphrase, summarise, and critique sources (Neville 2007: 36). Whichever method you choose to integrate sources into your own writing, you must give *an in-text citation* to acknowledge the material you borrow.

As mentioned above, in addition to your in-text citations you must make a list recording more information for each source you have cited. The most challenging aspect of referencing is to **learn the formula** for formatting different types of sources such as books, journal articles, and websites, but with practice this becomes increasingly easy.

IN-TEXT CITATIONS

As previously mentioned, the term 'in-text citation' means an acknowledgement of your sources each time you borrow material for your writing. The Harvard style is easy to use because you simply cite the author's surname, the date, and when appropriate the page numbers in brackets. When you borrow images or statistics, and when you quote, paraphrase, or summarise a short passage, you should usually give the page number. Here is an example:

Give the author's surname and the date, then insert a colon and give the page number enclosed within brackets

(Jones 2010: 34)

Here is another example:

The role of academic writing in assessment at university

Accuracy and agility as a writer are essential to obtain good grades at university (Smith 2010: 4). According to Shah (2009: 7) strong written communication is one of the determining factors in success at this advanced level.

This example shows that each time you borrow from a source you should give the author's surname and date, plus the **page number if you refer to a specific page**. You can either name the authors in your own sentence, or give their surnames within your in-text citations, and you can vary this depending on the emphasis you want to give.

How to cite

You need to gather three pieces of information when you are making notes to produce accurate in-text citations. Ask yourself:

1 Who is the *author*?

If there are multiple authors, write them all down in your notes. If the author is an organisation or group of people this is known as the **corporate author**.

2 In which *year* was the source published?

If the source is digital, when was it last updated?

3 Do you need to give *page numbers*?

You usually do if you quote, paraphrase, summarise an extract from a specific page, borrow data, or use images from printed sources. Ask your tutor if you are unsure.

CITING WRITTEN SOURCES

You should also take note of the ways authors cite material in journal articles because these often provide models for academic writing in your own discipline. In particular, notice how authors integrate quotes, paraphrases, summaries, and critiques of sources as they develop their own ideas.

Multiple authors

It can be disruptive for readers if you cite a source with many authors because this interrupts the flow of your own writing. To avoid this, the convention when one source has many authors is to give the first author's surname, then use the Latin term 'et al.' which is an abbreviation of et alii meaning 'and others'. Note that you must insert a full stop after 'et al.' because it is an abbreviated term. Here is an example:

> Gillett et al. argue that writing is a core capability at university (2009: 54).

Remember that although you are writing one author's surname you are actually referring to multiple authors, so your own sentence must agree grammatically. It is inaccurate to write 'Gillett et al. argue<u>s</u>' because you are referring to authors in the plural, so your own verb must agree.

Variations of the Harvard style give different recommendations about when to use 'et al.' and how to format this term. A common approach is to use et al. when there are more than *two* authors. However, some variations of the Harvard style recommend using et al. when there are more than three authors. Similarly, some variations of the Harvard style require you to italicise *et al.* thus because it is a Latin term and foreign phrases are often italicised in academic writing.

The examples below offer further advice on using in-text citations in the Harvard style.

Mentioning authors at the start of sentences

You can refer to an author directly and cite the source near the start of your sentence like this:

> McCutcheon (2010: 43) argues that academic writing cannot be taught generically, but must be explored as an 'integral part' of disciplinary studies.

Mentioning authors at the end of sentences

Alternatively, you can refer to an author directly and cite the source near the end of your sentence so it does not disrupt the flow of your argument, like this:

> McCutcheon argues that academic writing cannot be taught generically, but must be explored as an 'integral part' of disciplinary studies (2010: 43).

Giving authors within in-text citations

You can give the author's name in your in-text citation rather than in your own sentence like this:

> Academic writing cannot be taught generically, but must be explored as an 'integral part' of disciplinary studies (McCutcheon 2010: 43).

As you will see when you read scholarly journal articles, authors tend to use all three approaches in their writing. Notice the most common way of citing in your subject area and adopt this, but also feel free to vary these three techniques to suit your own written style.

Citing more than one source

Be careful if you refer to more than one source in a single sentence because you must ensure that your readers can identify which author has made which point. Look at the two examples of citing below. Which is clearer?

Example 1: many citations in a list

> Recent research into road safety recommends a revised approach to teaching children how to cross roads through national education programmes and local initiatives (Anderson 2000: 3, Potter 2001: 54, Scott 2003: 6, Jones and Sharma 2009: 87).

In the example above, the writer has cited four sources in one sentence so the reader is unclear what each source is about.

Example 2: many citations clearly distinguished

> Recent research into road safety recommends a revised approach to teaching children how to cross roads through national education programmes (Potter 2001: 54, Scott 2003: 6) and local initiatives (Anderson 2000: 3, Jones and Sharma 2009: 87).

In the second example the writer has listed only two sources in each in-text citation so that readers are much clearer which authors made which points. When you are citing sources try to make it clear who made which point and avoid listing many texts at once because this can confuse readers. If your in-text citations are precise they are more helpful for readers who are interested in your topic.

The order for listing citations

When you list a number of citations in one sentence you should think about the order. Check the guidelines in your chosen referencing style and be consistent. Notice that in the example above, the citations are given in chronological order with the oldest first. Some referencing styles recommend listing the most recent source first, so check with your tutor if you are unsure.

Page numbers and in-text citations

Every time you quote, paraphrase, or summarise a short section you should usually give the page number, unless you are using a digital source that does not contain page numbers.

The same applies when you borrow *images* or *numerical data*. Basically, whenever you borrow from a particular page your readers may need to know the page number to locate that page for themselves. However, check with your tutor as practice can vary in different disciplines.

There are three main reasons for giving page numbers. First, it demonstrates your professionalism and conveys your ability to make notes in a scholarly way. Secondly, it helps readers track down the passages, images, and data you have borrowed and consult this information themselves. Thirdly, examiners may want to check you have understood a source, and they will not be impressed if you do not leave a clear account of exactly where in your source you have referenced. In general, omitting page numbers gives an impression of laziness, so avoid this by jotting down the page numbers when you are making notes, and include them in your in-text citations whenever you quote, paraphrase or refer to a specific page.

Why give page numbers?

1 To show professionalism

2 To help readers track down the passages, images, and data you have borrowed

3 To meet marking criteria and show examiners you can cite in a scholarly fashion.

Page numbers and paraphrasing

Most versions of the Harvard style advise you to give page numbers when you paraphrase a passage from a source. This is because, although when you paraphrase you put an author's ideas into your own words, borrowing material in this way is not very different from quoting.

Page numbers and summarising

There are two different ways of summarising material; one of which is to summarise the whole source, and the other is to summarise a short section of a source. If you summarise an entire book or journal article you do not need to provide the page numbers in your in-text citations. However, if you summarise a specific passage you should give the page number in case readers wish to locate the passage. You will need to use your judgement when deciding whether or not to give page numbers, but it is better to give pages unnecessarily than to omit them when they are required. In particular, some examiners may penalise writers who quote without giving the page numbers.

CITING SECONDARY SOURCES

Secondary sources are sources cited in the texts you read. They are 'secondary' because you have not seen them yourself. If you can locate the original sources and cite them as usual this demonstrates your research skills. As secondary sources are sometimes reported inaccurately, locating them for yourself helps you avoid bringing errors into your work.

However, if you are unable to locate the original source, you must make it clear to readers that you are citing a source you have not seen. To cite a secondary source, give the author of the secondary source and the date, then write 'cited in' and give the author, date and page number of the source you have read. Here is an example of citing a secondary source:

> Academic writing demands time, planning, and commitment (Adams 2007 cited in Downs 2010: 34).

CITING NUMERICAL SOURCES

Give an in-text citation acknowledging the author or statistician each time you borrow statistics, graphs or other numerical data from sources. Follow the same basic practice for citing numerical data as you would for citing written sources. You will often have to make a judgement about who to cite as the author, and this will depend on the purpose of your writing. Here is an example of citing statistics:

> A recent survey indicates that 24% of pet owners rescued their animals from homes or charities (Pets Research 2010: 32).

When you borrow numerical data from a specific page in a printed source you should give the *page number* so readers can locate the same place in the source with ease.

Depending on the nature of your writing, it may be useful to put numerical data into a table. This is particularly appropriate if you are writing a substantial piece of work such as a report, dissertation or thesis. If you do this you should give the figure a title and produce a contents page for your document, including a list of figures. Remember to discuss the significance of the data (see Figure 10.1).

CITING AUDIOVISUAL SOURCES

Just as you integrate written sources into your writing using different techniques such as quoting, paraphrasing, summarising, and critiquing, you should also integrate audiovisual sources into your writing in a scholarly fashion. Figure 10.1 shows how to cite numerical data.

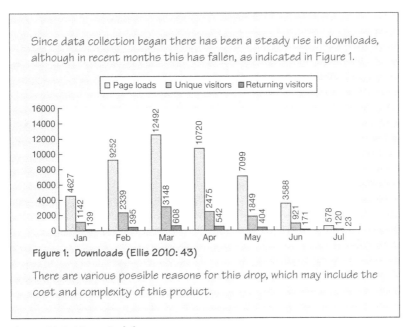

Since data collection began there has been a steady rise in downloads, although in recent months this has fallen, as indicated in Figure 1.

Figure 1: Downloads (Ellis 2010: 43)

There are various possible reasons for this drop, which may include the cost and complexity of this product.

Figure 10.1 **Numerical data**

Always assess the value of sources before borrowing from them for your work and be clear about the purpose they serve. Remember to give the page number when you borrow data and images from printed sources.

Introduce each audiovisual source as you introduce it into your writing and comment on it as appropriate. If you are writing a substantial document such as a report, dissertation, or thesis you should label the images as figures and include a list of figures in your list of contents. Figure 10.2 shows how to cite visual sources.

Citing films, videos, and DVDs (not downloaded)

For this type of source you need to decide who to cite as the author, and most commonly it is appropriate to cite the director or producer. Here is an example of citing a DVD:

In *Cold Mountain*, Kidman brings the American Civil War to life (Minghella 2004).

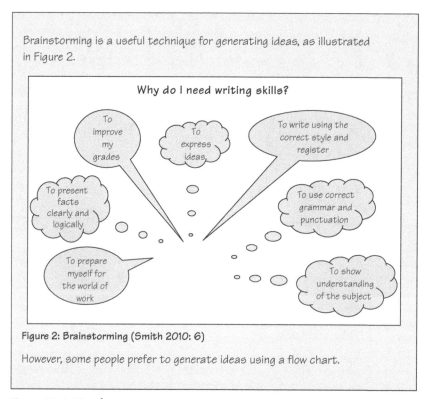

Figure 10.2 **Visual sources**

CITING DIGITAL FORMATS

Many different types of sources are available digitally, so the best way to support you in documenting your digital sources is to provide some general guidelines for you to adopt as appropriate for your different writing projects.

Quality control and online sources

Websites can be very useful as leads for future research; for example, the website Wikipedia is not subject to scholarly review so anyone could make an inaccurate contribution and it would be unfortunate to repeat errors in your own work. On the other hand, the references supplied within Wikipedia articles are potentially valuable if you follow them up and assess their value for your own use.

It is vital to analyse the quality of online sources before you draw on material for your academic writing (Hacker 2006: 31). Some online sources are unreliable or inaccurate and therefore inappropriate for use in academic writing. Be aware, for instance, that translations may not be accurate. The danger of citing unreliable sources is that this can undermine the quality of your own work, so before using online sources, consider whether it is worth consulting more scholarly sources instead.

Corporate authors

If a source is not written by people, but instead is produced by an organisation or professional body, this is known as a 'corporate author'. When citing from sources created by an organisation you should cite the corporate author.

It is not always easy to identify the author of a website, but as long as you give the same details in your in-text citations as in your list of references your readers will be able to locate the source for themselves. This is because your list of references entry will contain the full website address (URL) (see Figure 10.3).

Figure 10.3 **Corporate authors**

To locate the author of online sources, check the bottom of a webpage to see if there is an acknowledgement or any copyright information. In Figure 10.3, although it is not visible, on this website it says at the bottom of the page:

> © The Economics Network of the Higher Education Academy, University of Bristol.
>
> Supported by the Royal Economic Society.

The corporate author here is the Economics Network because the copyright symbol © signals that the intellectual property rights belong to this group. To cite this corporate author you would write:

(Economics Network 2009)

Notice that you do *not* give the website address (URL) within in-text citations because it would disrupt the flow of your own writing. Instead the website address is recorded in your list of references.

Dates and online sources

It is often difficult to find a date within online sources. Check the information at the bottom of the webpage if you cannot see the date at first, and you might find the date when the site was last updated, which you can use for your in-text citations. If no date is given, you can either estimate and give the year you are viewing if recently updated, or write 'n.d.', meaning 'no date', like this:

> (Economics Network n.d.)

Page numbers and online sources

Online sources do not have page numbers, so it is usual practice to omit page numbers for in-text citations of online sources. This is acceptable because readers who wish to locate these sources can use the website address (URL) given in your list of references.

Downloads

Digital media are often available as podcasts and in other formats which allow you to listen to programmes again. To acknowledge these sources when you borrow material for your own writing, you should cite the author and date in brackets. You are the best person to decide which author to cite as you acknowledge your sources, and as long as you link the in-text citations to entries in your list of references your readers will be able to locate the sources for themselves. Below are some examples.

Citing the speaker as author

You can refer directly to the speaker as the author like this:

> As part of the BBC programme *In our time with Melvyn Bragg*, John Haldane discussed the life of St Thomas Aquinas (2009).

Citing the organisation as corporate author

Or, you can refer to the corporate author like this:

> As part of the programme *In our time with Melvyn Bragg*, John Haldane discussed the life of St Thomas Aquinas (BBC Radio 4 2009).

Citing personal communications

To cite a personal communication, quote, paraphrase, or summarise and give the author's surname and the date. Either mention the author in your own writing or in your in-text citation. Here is an example in which the author is mentioned directly:

> In a personal communication Professor Saunders explained his theory in depth (2009).

Citing blogs

To cite a blog, quote, paraphrase, or summarise and give the author's surname and the date. Either mention the author directly, or in your in-text citation. Here is an example in which the author is mentioned in the in-text citation:

> 'This week something great happened: two of my former students connected with me' (Dwyer 2009).

Citing online discussion fora and mailing lists

To cite an online discussion list or listserv, quote, paraphrase, or summarise and give the author's surname and the date. Here is an example in which the author is mentioned in the in-text citation:

> 'Interrogating our approach is essential' (Harris 2009).

Decisions about citing

This section of Chapter 10 has explained how to cite using the Harvard style. It has covered the main points you need to know and recommended that you seek advice from your tutors when you are unsure about any aspect of citing and referencing. It has stressed that there are times when you have to make **decisions** about how to cite sources in your writing. Base these decisions on the following three rules:

1 Be *clear* about where in your writing you have borrowed from sources

2 Be *consistent* as you make choices about which information to cite as the author and date

3 Be *comprehensive* in giving the author, date, and page numbers (when appropriate).

THE LIST OF REFERENCES

A list of references is a full record of all the sources you have cited in your writing. The purpose of this list is to provide all the details readers require to locate your sources for themselves. The example below demonstrates how to produce a list of references.

List of References

Abrahams, B. (2010) *Academic Writing in the United Kingdom*. London: Routledge

Carr, S. (2009) Writing for success: Assessment in higher education. Maidstone: HarperCollins

Potter, H. (2005) An *Introduction to Human Anatomy* . 4th edn. London: Adam Arnold available from <http://anatomy/introduction/human/htm> [27th March 2006]

There is a specific format for referencing each different type of source. For printed sources you should record the publication details, and for online sources you should provide the website address and the date you accessed the data.

THE LINK BETWEEN IN-TEXT CITATIONS AND THE LIST OF REFERENCES

As previously mentioned, every source that is given in your in-text citations must be fully recorded in your list of references.

The most efficient way to ensure that all the sources you cite are recorded in your list of references is to compile both elements as you are drafting your work. You should work hard to develop a method that works for you. Many scholars find reference management systems such as EndNote and RefWorks effective for this task (Neville 2007: 23, Williams and Carroll 2009: 78). Ask about these tools at your university library because they can save you lots of time.

How to construct a list of references

The list of references goes at the end of your document and the sources are listed in alphabetical order according to the authors. You should not subdivide this list into types of sources, but you do need to learn how to format the entries for different types of sources. The three main types of source you need to learn about are:

- Books
- Journal articles
- Websites.

Once you have mastered how to reference these three types of sources you will have enough knowledge to reference other source types because they are mostly variations of these three formats.

Use your judgement

Referencing requires you to exercise your **judgement**, especially when you need to document uncommon or unusual types of sources. When choosing a format, do not be afraid to adapt the formula for referencing a book, journal article, or website, depending on which is most appropriate for the source you want to cite and reference. The information below contains tips on referencing these three main types of sources and adapting the formats for less common types of sources.

REFERENCING BOOKS AND SIMILAR TYPES OF SOURCES

You usually require six pieces of information to reference a book. It can be difficult to find these six details but, with practice, you will become an expert. The tips below will help you to grow in confidence in finding and recording this information:

1 Author

2 Date

3 Title

4 Edition, if relevant

5 Place of publication

6 Publisher.

Books

Here is a book entry for the list of references with some explanation:

Give the author's surname and initial, then the date in brackets and the title in italics, followed by a full stop. Give the edition, if relevant, then the place of publication followed by a colon and the publisher

Jones, P. (2010) *Enhancing Academic Practice*. 2nd edn. Harlow: Pearson Education

E-books

If you are using an electronic book (e-book) or a digital format you need to add two more pieces of information. These are:

7 The full website address (URL)

8 The date of access (when you viewed the source).

The reason for giving the website address is so that readers can access the e-book for themselves. The reason for giving the date you accessed it online is that internet sites are regularly updated, so readers need to know when you viewed the book in case the interface has changed since then.

Here is an example of how to reference an e-book:

Give the author's surname and initial, then the date in brackets and the title in italics, followed by a full stop. Give the edition, if relevant, then the place of publication, followed by a colon and the publisher. Write 'available from' and give the full website address within chevrons (< >), followed by the date of access in square brackets

Potter, H. (2005) *An Introduction to Human Anatomy*. 4th edn. London: Adam Arnold available from <http://anatomy/introduction/human/htm> [27th March 2006]

Authors

On a book's cover (see below) you should find the name of the authors and the title. If there is more than one author you must record the names in the order you find them written on the book cover. This is because the order may signal the amount of work each author has done, with the person who produced the most material listed first. However, most often authors are listed alphabetically and you should reproduce this order as you document their work.

Figure 10.4 **Book authors and titles**

Editors

If a book has an editor instead of an author you should write (ed.) after the name and before the date like this:

Give the editor's surname and initial, then write 'ed.' in brackets, followed by the date in brackets. Give the title in italics followed by a full stop. Give the edition, if relevant, then the place of publication followed by a colon and the publisher

Long, H. (ed.) (2010) *Adventures in Sound*. 2nd edn. Oxford: Oxford University Press

If a book has both an editor and an author, you should give the author first and then the date followed by the editor like this:

Give the author's surname and initial, then the date in brackets. Write 'ed. by' and give the editor's surname and initial, then the title in italics followed by a full stop. Give the edition, if relevant, then the place of publication followed by a colon and the publisher

Smart, K. (2010) ed. by Knowles, G. *Scholarly Writing*. 2nd edn. Oxford: Oxford University Press

Translators

If the author is the translator you should give the author as usual, then acknowledge the translator after the title like this:

Give the author's surname and initial, then the date in brackets and the title in italics, followed by a full stop. Write 'Trans. by' then give the translator's surname and initial then the place of publication followed by a colon and the publisher

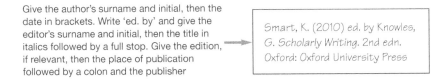

Hatter, P. (2010) *Social Welfare*. Trans. by Hatter, P. Oxford: Oxford University Press

If the translator is not the author as well you should give the author first then the translator.

Dates of publication

Dates can be confusing, but the most important year to record is usually the date a book was first published. This is given inside the cover with all the information about the printer and publishing house. In the example below, the year to cite and reference is 2006:

First published 2006

Reprinted 2007, 2008 (twice), 2010

Dates when a book was just **reprinted** are not relevant, so in the example above you would ignore the dates after 2006. Reprinted simply means that another set of copies was made and the contents of the book remain identical, so the convention is to continue to cite the date the book was first published.

Editions

However, if the book you are using is a new or revised *edition*, you should not record the first date given, but instead record the 2nd, 3rd, or revised edition date depending which one you read. A revised edition is usually indicated on the book's cover as well as inside in the initial pages, where you will usually find information like this:

First published 2006

Second edition published 2010

When a new edition of a book is produced, the author re-writes sections and often adds material to update the publication, so the page numbers change and readers need to know which edition you have read. In the example above you would cite and reference the date as 2010, the year the second edition was published. You must also indicate this fact in your list of references entry like this:

Harrison, M. (2010) *Academic Writing: Tips and Tricks.* 2nd edn. Harlow: Pearson Education

Titles

If there is a subtitle you must include this detail in your list of references entry and add a colon before the subtitle like this:

Academic Writing: Tips and Tricks.

Capitalisation when referencing books

Always consult the guidance your tutors provide on capitalisation when referencing books. Usually in the UK, significant words in book titles are capitalised, but check the instructions in your recommended referencing style.

Note that prepositions and conjunctions are not normally capitalised.

Place of publication

The place of publication is usually a city, and this information is given inside the book cover and usually also on the title page. If you see a list of several cities you should just record the first one, so London is the place to document from this list:

> London, New York, Paris, Milan.

You may come across the full address of the publisher like this:

> Edinburgh Gate
> Harlow
> Essex CM20 2JE
> England.

In this case you need to identify the city, which is Harlow in the example above. Essex is a county and England is a country, so you do not document these in your list of references.

Publisher

The publisher is relatively easy to identify because there is usually a logo or indication of who published a book on the front cover, and often on the spine of the book. The publisher is usually written inside the book cover in the initial pages, for example, like this:

> Pearson Education Limited.

In the example above you would not include the word 'Limited' but simply write 'Pearson Education' as the publisher.

So, if you put all five pieces of information together, your entry in the list of references for a book should be as shown in Table 10.1.

Table 10.1 **Books**

Author's surname and initial	Date	Book title	Edition	Place of publication	Publisher
Jones, B.	(2010)	*Academic Writing: Tips and Tricks.*	2nd edn.	Harlow:	Pearson Education

Other types of books

Edited collections

Edited collections are books containing chapters written by different authors. You will usually need to cite material from a specific chapter, so record the name of the chapter author, the chapter title, and the first and last page numbers for the chapter. In addition, document the same information you usually need to reference a book.

Here is an example of how to reference a chapter:

Give the surname and initial of the chapter author, then the date in brackets and the chapter title followed by a full stop. Write 'In', then the title of the edited collection in italics, followed by a full stop. Write 'Ed. by' then the editor's surname and initial followed by the place of publication followed by a colon and the publisher, then a colon and the page numbers of the article	*Skillen, J. (2006) Teaching Academic Writing from the 'Centre' in Australian Universities.* In *Teaching Academic Writing in UK Higher Education: Theories, Practices and Models.* Ed. by Ganobcsik-Williams, L. Houndmills: Palgrave Macmillan: 140–53

A note about referencing chapters in edited collections

Some referencing styles instruct you to put single quote marks around chapter titles. Follow your recommended guidelines and if unsure, check with your tutor.

So, your entry in the list of references for a chapter from an edited collection should be as shown in Table 10.2.

Table 10.2 **Edited collections**

Author's surname and initial	Date	Chapter title	Write 'In' then the title of the edited collection	Edition	Write 'Ed. by' then the editor's surname and initial	Place	Publisher	Page numbers of chapter
Skillen, J.	(2006)	Teaching Academic Writing from the 'Centre' in Australian Universities.	In *Teaching Academic Writing in UK Higher Education: Theories, Practices and Models.*		Ed. by Ganobcsik-Williams, L.	Houndmills:	Palgrave Macmillan:	140–53

Reports

The formula for referencing reports is similar to the method for referencing books. Here is an example of how to reference a report:

Give the author or corporate author and the date in brackets, then the title in italics followed by the number of the report and a full stop. Give the place the report was produced, and a colon, then the organisation or publisher

> Dietetics Committee (2009) Department of Health Report on Dietary Health no. 41. London: Stationery Office

Pamphlets

The formula for referencing pamphlets, leaflets, and brochures is similar to the method for referencing books. Here is an example of how to reference a pamphlet:

Give the author or corporate author and the date in brackets, then the title in italics, followed by a full stop. Give the place the pamphlet was produced, and a colon, then the organisation or publisher

> National Health Service (2009) Catch it, Bin it, Kill it. Coventry: University Hospital

Unpublished booklets, manuals, guides, and handbooks

The formula for referencing any unpublished source is similar to the method for referencing books. Here is an example of how to reference an unpublished booklet:

Give the author and the date in brackets, then the title, followed by a full stop. Give the place the source was produced, and a colon, then the organisation

> Dawson, E. (2010) Guide to Writing Reports. Coventry: Coventry University

REFERENCING SECONDARY SOURCES

Secondary sources are sources cited in materials you have read, but you have not seen them yourself. To reference a secondary source, give the publication details for the secondary source, followed by the publication details for the source that you have read.

Here is an example of how to reference a secondary source:

For the secondary source, give the author's surname and initial, then the date in brackets and the title in italics, followed by a full stop. Give the place of publication followed by a colon and the publisher then a full stop. Write 'Cited in' then do the same for the source you have read

> Adams, K. (2007) Researching and Writing. Harlow: Pearson Education. Cited in Downs, E. (2010) Strategies for Success. Harlow: Pearson Education

REFERENCING JOURNAL ARTICLES AND SIMILAR TYPES OF SOURCES

Journal articles

You usually need seven pieces of information to reference a journal article. These are:

1 Author

2 Date

3 Article title

4 Journal title

5 Volume number

6 Part or issue number (if there is one)

7 Page numbers of the article.

Here is an example with more information about the formula for referencing a journal article:

Give the author's surname and initial, the date in brackets, and the title of the article followed by a full stop. Give the title of the journal in italics, the volume number, the part (or issue) number in brackets, then the page numbers of the article

→

Elston, C. (2009) Making Group-work Work: An Overview. *Journal of Learning Development in Higher Education* 1 (1): 1–7

A note about referencing articles in journals

Some referencing styles instruct you to put single quote marks around article titles. Follow your recommended guidelines and if unsure, check with your tutor.

Accessing journal articles online

If you download an online journal article and your version is exactly the same as the hard copy in the journal, including the page numbers, you should reference the article as if you were using the hard copy. However, if the page numbers in your version are not the same as the hard copy in the journal you need to add two pieces of information. These are:

■ The full website address (URL)

■ The date of access.

Here is an example of how to reference an article you have accessed online when the page numbers are different to the hard copy in the journal:

If you are supplying the URL, write 'available from' and give the full website address within chevrons ($<$ $>$), followed by the date of access in square brackets

→

> Elston, C. (2009) Making Group-work Work: An Overview. *Journal of Learning Development in Higher Education* 1 (1): 1–8 available from <http://www.aldinhe. ac.uk/ojs/index.php?journal=jldhe& page=article&op=view&path%5B%5D= 36&path%5B%5D=17> [1st October 2009]

So, your entry in the list of references for a journal article you have accessed online should be as shown in Table 10.3:

Table 10.3 **Journal articles**

Author's surname and initial	Date	Article title	Journal title	Volume no.	Part or issue no.	Page numbers of article	Full website address (URL)	Date of access
Elston, C.	(2009)	Making Group-work Work: An Overview.	Journal of Learning Development in Higher Education	1	(1):	1–8	available from <http://www. aldinhe.ac. uk/ojs/index. php?journal= jldhe&page= article&op= view&path%5 B%5D= 36&path% 5B%5D=17>	[1st October 2009]

Newspapers and magazines

The formula for referencing articles in newspapers and magazines is similar to the method for referencing journal articles, and if you access a newspaper online you should include the website address in the same way. Here is an example of how to reference a newspaper article you have accessed online:

Give the surname and initials of the authors, the date in brackets, and the title of the article followed by a full stop

→

Give the name of the newspaper in italics, then the day it was printed. If you are supplying the URL, write 'available from' and give the full website address within chevrons ($<$ $>$) followed by the date of access in square brackets

→

> Clark, D., O'Connor, M., Bangay, R. and Roche, R. (2009) Guardian's Quick Carbon Calculator. *Guardian* 21st October 2009, available from <http://www.guardian.co.uk/environment/ interactive/2009/oct/20/guardian- quick-carbon-calculator> [25th October 2009]

A note about referencing articles

Some referencing styles instruct you to put single quote marks around article titles. Follow your recommended guidelines and if unsure, check with your tutor.

REFERENCING WEBSITES AND SIMILAR TYPES OF SOURCES

You usually need five pieces of information to reference a journal article. These are:

1 Author

2 Date

3 Webpage title

4 The full website address (URL)

5 The date of access.

Here is an example of how to reference a website:

Give the author or corporate author, the date in brackets, then the title of the webpage in italics. Write 'available from' and give the full website address within chevrons (< >) followed by the date of access in square brackets	*Economics Network (2009) Effective Writing and Referencing* available from <http://studyingeconomics.ac. uk/effective-writing/> [1st October 2009]

So, your entry for the list of references for a website should be as shown in Table 10.4:

Table 10.4 **Websites**

Corporate author	Date	Webpage title	Full website address (URL)	Date of access
Economics Network	(2009)	*Effective Writing and Referencing*	available from <http://studyingeconomics. ac.uk/effective-writing/>	[1st October 2009]

Audiovisual recordings as downloads

Downloaded sources are referenced in a similar way to a website. As there is such a range of different digital sources, the best advice to give is that you should adapt the formula for referencing websites using your own judgement, and as long as you are clear and consistent you will do a good job. If you have any concerns about referencing more unusual digital sources, ask your tutor for advice or seek guidance at your university library. Here is an example of how to reference a down-loaded audio source:

Give the corporate author, the date in brackets, then the title of the download in italics followed by a full stop, then the day and time it was broadcast. Write 'available from' and give the full website address within chevrons (< >) followed by the date of access in square brackets

> BBC Radio 4 (2009) *St Thomas Aquinas. In Our Time with Melvyn Bragg.* 17th September 2009 9.00am, available from <http:// www.bbc.co.uk/podcasts/series/iot> [23rd September 2009]

Audiovisual recordings (not downloaded)

Give the same author as you gave in your in-text citations and supply enough information for readers to find the source for themselves. Here is an example of how to reference a DVD giving the director as the author:

Give the surname and initial of the author, the date in brackets, then the title of the DVD in italics followed a full stop. Give the name of the company who produced the DVD

> Minghella, A. (2004) *Cold Mountain.* Buena Vista Home Entertainment

Blogs

The formula for referencing blogs is similar to the method for referencing websites. Here is an example:

Give the surname and initial of the author, the date in brackets, then the title of the entry in italics, followed by a full stop, then the day and time it was added. Write 'available from' and give the full website address within chevrons (< >) followed by the date of access in square brackets

> Dwyer, J. (2009) *Back to School: Tips for Teachers.* 18th September 2009 8.01pm available from <http://blog.facebook.com/> [22nd September 2009]

Online discussion fora and mailing lists

The formula for referencing discussion lists is similar to the method for referencing websites. Here is an example:

Give the surname and initial of the author, the date in brackets, then the title of the discussion thread in italics, followed by a full stop, then the day and time the comment was added. Write 'available from' and give the full website address within chevrons (< >) followed by the date of access in square brackets

> Harris, O. (2009) *Teaching Practice.* 1st September 2009 5.30pm available from <eataw-conf@lists.hum. ku.dk> [22nd September 2009]

Personal communications

The formula for referencing personal communications is similar to the method for referencing websites. Here is an example of how to reference an email:

Give the surname and initial of the author, the date in brackets, then the subject of the email in italics, followed by a full stop, then the day and time it was added. Write 'available from' and give the full website address within chevrons (< >) followed by the date of access in square brackets

Simms, P. (2010) *Enquiry re Invoice.* 5th January 2010 1.10pm available from <http://mail.live.com/default.aspx?&n=1011776457> [10th January 2010]

Lectures

The formula for referencing lectures is similar to the method for referencing a website, especially if you downloaded notes from your module web.

Should you borrow material from lectures?

It is not necessarily appropriate to cite and reference lectures in your academic writing because lecturers usually expect you to conduct independent research based on the ideas they share and the reading lists they distribute at lectures.

Here is an example of how to reference a lecture:

Give the surname and initial of the lecturer as author, the date in brackets, then the title of the lecture in italics followed by a full stop. Give the course code, a comma, then the day the lecture was delivered. Add a full stop then the university. Write 'available from' and give the full website address within chevrons (< >), followed by the date of access in square brackets (omit the URL and date of access if you did not download the lecture notes)

Hobbs, R. (2010) *Case Law and Legal Writing.* Module 102 Law, 10th February 2010. Coventry University available from <http://legalwriting.ac.uk/caselaw-module102/> [1st February 2010]

Decisions about referencing

This section of Chapter 10 has explained how to reference using the Harvard style. It has covered the main points you need to know and recommended that you seek advice from your tutors or library specialists when you are unsure about any aspect of citing and referencing. It has indicated that there are times when you have to make decisions about how to reference sources. Base these decisions on the three following rules:

1 Be *clear* about where you have accessed sources

2 Be *consistent* in documenting sources in your list of references

3 Be *comprehensive* in giving all the details readers require to find sources for themselves.

SUMMARY

This chapter has explained how to use the Harvard style and has provided a wide range of examples (Deane 2009b). It has stressed the need to be clear and consistent as you acknowledge all the sources you use in your academic writing. It has emphasised that as you cite and reference unusual sources you need to use your own judgement and make decisions based on the advice of your tutors, library specialists, and your recommended referencing guidelines.

The main arguments in this chapter:

- To cite sources you should give the author, date, and page number when appropriate
- To reference sources you should learn the format for each type of source in your recommended referencing guidelines.

Academic writing style

How to adopt the appropriate language conventions

Writing for academic purposes is a vital skill, yet the stylistic codes you need to follow are rarely comprehensively defined. This chapter will help you understand what it means to write in an academic style and outlines some forms of language to avoid.

Key topics:

→ What is academic style?
→ Being objective
→ Appropriate use of tense
→ Appropriate use of vocabulary
→ Appropriate use of punctuation
→ Transforming non-academic to academic language

Key words
Acronym   Colloquial   Idiom   Noun   Phrasal verb   Pronoun   Register   Rhetorical question   Verb

The format, the content and the presentation of projects and dissertations differ according to discipline. One thing that is common to all these types of writing is that they need to follow academic style. While it is possible to identify differences between 'scientific' and 'humanities' styles in the finer detail, this chapter covers the common features of all types of academic writing.

→ What is academic style?

Academic style involves the use of precise and objective language to express ideas. It must be grammatically correct, and is more formal than the style used in novels, newspapers, informal correspondence

From Chapter 22 of *How to Write Dissertations and Project Reports*. Kathleen McMillan. Jonathan Weyers. © Pearson Education Limited 2008, 2010.

and everyday conversation. This should mean that the language is clear and simple. It does not imply that it is complex, pompous and dry. Above all, academic style is *objective*, using language techniques that generally maintain an impersonal tone and a vocabulary that is more succinct, rather than involving personal, colloquial, or idiomatic expressions.

British English (BE) versus American English (AE)

Academic writing in the UK nearly always adopts BE. The differences are most evident in spelling; for example, 'colour' (BE) and 'color' (AE). However, there are also differences in vocabulary, so that in AE people talk of 'professor' for 'lecturer'; and in language use, so that in AE someone might write 'we have gotten results', rather than 'we have obtained results'. In some disciplines, there is an attempt at standardisation, for example, in chemistry the spelling of 'sulphur' (BE) has become 'sulfur' (AE) as the international standard.

→ Being objective

In academic writing, it is important that your personal involvement with your topic does not overshadow the importance of what you are commenting on or reporting. Generally, the main way of demonstrating this objectivity and lack of bias is by using impersonal language. This means:

- Avoiding personal pronouns – try not to use the following words:

  I/me/one

  you (singular and plural)

  we/us.

- Using the passive rather than active voice – try to write about the action and not about the actor (the person who performed the action).

You can use other strategies to maintain an impersonal style in your writing. For general statements, you could use a structure such as 'it is . . .', 'there is . . .' or 'there are . . .' to introduce sentences. For more specific points relating to statements you have already made, you could use the structures 'this is . . .' or 'these are . . .'; 'that is . . .' or 'those are . . .' with appropriate tense changes according to the context. Don't forget that when you use words like 'it', 'this', 'these', 'that' or 'those', there should be no ambiguity over the word or phrase to which they refer.

Another way in which you can maintain objectivity by writing impersonally is to change the verb in the sentence to a noun and then reframe the sentence in a less personal way, for example:

> We **applied** pressure to the wound to stem bleeding (*verb in bold*).
> The **application** of pressure stemmed bleeding (*noun in bold*).

This kind of text-juggling will become second nature as you tackle more and more assignments.

Passive and active voice

This is best explained from examples:

- Pressure was applied to the wound to stem bleeding (passive).
- We applied pressure to the wound to stem bleeding (active).

Some would argue that the second example is clearer, but their opponents would counter-argue that the use of 'we' takes attention away from the action.

You may find that the grammar checkers in some word-processing packages suggest that passive expressions should be changed to active. However, if you follow this guidance, you will find yourself having to use a personal pronoun, which is inconsistent with impersonal academic style. If in doubt, ask your tutors for their preference.

→ Appropriate use of tense

The past tense is used in academic writing to describe or comment on things that have already happened. However, there are times when the present tense is appropriate. For example, in a report you might write 'Figure 5 shows . . .', rather than 'Figure 5 showed . . .', when describing your results. A material and methods section, on the other hand, will always be in the past tense, because it describes what you *did*.

In colloquial English, there is often a tendency to misuse tenses. This can creep into academic writing, especially where the author is narrating a sequence of events. This can be seen by contrasting:

> Napoleon *orders* his troops to advance on Moscow. The severe
> winter *closes* in on them and they *come back* a ragbag of an army.
> (Present tense in bold.)

and:

> Napoleon *ordered* his troops to advance on Moscow. The severe
> winter *closed* in on them and they *came back* a ragbag of an army.
> (Simple past tense in bold.)

While the first of these examples might work with the soundtrack of a
documentary on Napoleon's Russian campaign, it is too colloquial for
academic written formats.

Plain English

There has been a growing movement in recent times that advocates
the use of 'Plain English', and it has been very successful in persuading
government departments and large commercial organisations to
simplify written material for public reference. This has been achieved
by introducing a less formal style of language that uses simpler, more
active sentence structures, and a simpler range of vocabulary avoiding
jargon. This is an admirable development. However, academic writing
style needs to be precise, professional and unambiguous, and the
strategies of 'Plain English' campaigners may not be entirely appropriate
to the style expected of you as an academic author. For the same
reasons, some of the suggestions offered by software packages may
be inappropriate to your subject and academic conventions.

→ Appropriate use of vocabulary

Good academic writers think carefully about their choice of words. The
'Plain English' movement (see above) recommends that words of Latin
origin should be replaced by their Anglo-Saxon, or spoken, alternatives.
However, this does not always contribute to the style and precision
appropriate to academic authorship. For example, compare:

> If we *turn down* the volume, then there will be no feedback.

and

> If we *turn down* the offer from the World Bank, then interest rates
> will rise.

Both sentences make sense, but they use the two-word verb 'turn down' in different senses. These verbs are properly called phrasal verbs and they often have more than a single meaning. Furthermore, they are also used more in speech than in formal writing. Therefore, it would be better to write:

If we **reduce** the volume, then there will be no feedback.

and

If we **reject** the offer from the World Bank, then interest rates will rise.

By using 'reduce' and 'reject' the respective meanings are clear, concise and unambiguous. If you are restricted to a word limit on your work, using the one-word verb has additional obvious advantages.

→ Appropriate use of punctuation

In formal academic writing good punctuation is vital to convey meaning. However, punctuation standards are being eroded as corporate logos and design practice seek to attract the eye with unconventional print forms that ignore the correct use of capitals, apostrophes, commas and other punctuation marks. Consider the following:

1. visitors car park   (meaningless – simply a list of words)

2. Visitor's car park   (car park for a single visitor)

3. Visitors' car park   (car park for more than one visitor)

4. Visitor's car, park!   (instructing a single visitor to park)

5. Visitors, Car Park   (greeting many visitors and, rather oddly, inviting them to park or it could be a sign (a) giving directions for visitors to follow and (b) directions to a car park)

Either versions 2 or 3 could be valid and the remainder are likely to be nonsensical. This example serves to demonstrates how clear punctuation avoids ambiguity. Without punctuation or with inappropriate punctuation, sentences become meaningless or, worse still, confusing and/or impenetrable. Table 22.1 illustrates some of the more common errors that appear regularly in student writing, models the correction and explains the error.

Table 22.1 **Common punctuation errors and their corrections.** The following common errors with their corrections should help you to find an answer to most punctuation dilemmas.

Punctuation mark	Error	Correction	Explanation
1.1 Apostrophes: singular	The Principals' Committee will meet at noon today.	Principal's	There is only one Principal, therefore the apostrophe goes immediately after the word 'Principal'. Then add the s to make it correctly possessive.
1.2 Apostrophes: plural	The womens' team beat the mens' team by 15 points and the childrens' team beat them both. The boy's team won the prize.	women's men's children's boys'	The words 'women', 'men' and 'children' are plural words. To make them possessive, just add an apostrophe after the plural word and add 's'. The word 'boys' is a plural and is a regularly formed plural, thus, the apostrophe comes after the 's'.
1.3 Apostrophes: contractions	Its not a good time to sell a property. Its been up for sale for ages. Well need to lower the price.	It's = it is It's = it has We'll = we shall	'It's' is a contracted form of the words 'it is' or 'it has'. In this case, the sentence means: 'It is not a good time to sell a property'.
1.4 Apostrophes: not needed	The tomatoes' cost 60 pence a kilo.	tomatoes	The word 'tomatoes' is a plural. No apostrophe is needed to make words plural.
1.5 Apostrophes: not needed	The Charter includes human rights in it's terms.	its	No apostrophe needed to show possession.
2.1 Capital letters: sentences	the first day of the term is tomorrow.	The	The first letter of the first word of a sentence in English always needs a capital letter.
2.2 Capital letters: proper names	The prime minister is the first lord of the treasury. The north atlantic treaty organisation is a regional organisation. Pearls found in the river tay are of considerable value.	Prime Minister; First Lord of the Treasury North Atlantic Treaty Organisation River Tay	Proper nouns for roles, names of organisations, rivers, mountains, lochs, lakes and place names. These all require a capital for all parts of the name.

3 Colon	A number of aspects will be covered, **including** • Energy conservation • Pollution limitation • Cost control	... including: • energy conservation; • pollution limitation; • cost control.	A colon to introduce the list. Each item, except the last one, should be finished with a semicolon. No capital is necessary at each bullet if the list follows from an incomplete sentence introducing the list.
4.1 Commas	**The leader of the group Dr Joan Jones** was not available for comment.	The leader of the group, Dr Joan Jones, was not available for comment.	This is a common error. The name of the person gives more information about the leader; thus, the person's name needs to be inserted with commas before and after.
4.2 Commas	There are several member-states that do not support this view. They are **Britain France Germany Portugal and Greece.**	There are several member-states that do not support this view. They are Britain, France, Germany, Portugal, and Greece.	Strictly speaking, when making a list such as in the example, a comma should come before 'and'. This is called the 'Oxford comma' and its use has caused much debate. However, increasingly, the comma is being omitted before the word 'and' in lists such as this one.
4.3 Commas	**However** we have no evidence to support this statement.	However, we have no evidence to support this statement.	The 'signposting' words often used at the beginning of sentences are followed by a comma. Some of the more common of these words are: however, therefore, thus, hence, nevertheless, moreover, in addition.
4.4 Commas	**Although we have had significant** rainfall the reservoirs are low.	Although we have had significant rainfall, the reservoirs are low.	When a sentence begins with 'although', then the sentence has two parts. The part that gives the idea of concession in this sentence is 'Although we have had significant rainfall'. The second part gives us the impact of that concession, in this case, that 'the reservoirs are low'. A comma is used to divide these parts.
4.5 Commas	**To demonstrate competence** it is important to be able to face challenges.	To demonstrate competence, it is important to be able to face challenges.	Another way to write this sentence would be: 'It is important to be able to face challenges to demonstrate competence'. By putting the phrase 'to demonstrate competence' at the beginning of the sentence, it places emphasis on the idea of competence and, in order to make that word-order distinction, a comma is needed.
5 Ellipsis	There is a deficit in the budget...... brought on by mismanagement at the highest level.	There is a deficit in the budget ... brought on by mismanagement at the highest level.	Ellipsis marks always consist of three dots, no more.

→ Transforming non-academic to academic language

Thinking about the style of your writing should be a feature of any review you make of drafts of your written work Table 22.2 gives a specific example of text conversion from informal to formal style. Table 22.3 provides several pointers to help you achieve a more academic style.

Table 22.2 Example of converting a piece of 'non-academic' writing into academic style. Note that the conversion results in a slightly longer piece of text (47 versus 37 words): this emphasises the point that while you should aim for concise writing, precise wording may be more important.

Original text (non-academic style)	'Corrected' text (academic style)
In this country, we have changed the law so that the King or Queen is less powerful since the Great War. But he or she can still advise, encourage or warn the Prime Minister if they want.	In the United Kingdom, legislation has been a factor in the decline of the role of the monarchy in the period since the Great War. Nevertheless, the monarchy has survived and, thus, the monarch continues to exercise the right to advise, encourage and warn the Prime Minister.
Points needing correction	**Corrected points**
• Non-specific wording (*this country*)	• Specific wording (country specified: *in the United Kingdom*)
• Personal pronoun (*we*)	• Impersonal language (*legislation has*)
• Weak grammar (*but* is a connecting word and should not be used to start a sentence).	• Appropriate signpost word (*nevertheless*)
• Word with several meanings (*law*)	• Generic, yet well-defined term (*legislation*)
• Duplication of nouns (*king or queen*)	• Singular abstract term (*monarch*)
• Inconsistent and potentially misleading pronoun use (*he or she, they*)	• Repeated subject (*monarch*) and reconstructed sentence
• Informal style (*can still*)	• More formal style (*continues to exercise*)

Table 22.3 **Fundamentals of academic writing.** These elements of academic writing are laid out in alphabetical order. Being aware of these elements and training yourself to follow them will help you to develop as an academic author and will ensure that you don't lose marks by making some basic errors of usage or expression.

Abbreviations and acronyms
It is acceptable to use abbreviations in academic writing to express units, for example, SI units. Otherwise, abbreviations are generally reserved for note-taking. Thus, avoid: e.g. (for example), i.e. (that is), viz. (namely) in formal work.

Acronyms are a kind of abbreviation formed by taking the initial letters of a name of an organisation, a procedure or an apparatus, and then using these letters instead of writing out the title in full. Thus, World Health Organisation becomes WHO. The academic convention is that the first time that you use a title with an acronym alternative, then you should write it in full with the acronym in brackets immediately after the full title. Thereafter, within that document you can use the acronym. For example:

The European Free Trade Association (EFTA) has close links with the European Community (EC). Both EFTA and the EC require new members to have membership of the Council of Europe as a prerequisite for admission to their organisations.

In some forms of academic writing, for example, formal reports, you may be expected to include a list of abbreviations in addition to these first-time-of-use explanations.

'Absolute' terms
In academic writing, it is important to be cautious about using absolute terms such as:

  always and **never; most** and **all; least** and **none.**

This does not prevent you from using these words; it simply means that they should be used with caution, that is, when you are absolutely certain of your ground (see p. 149).

Clichés
Living languages change and develop over time. This means that some expressions come into such frequent usage that they lose their meaning; indeed, they can often be replaced with a much less long-winded expression. For example:

  First and foremost (first); **last but not least** (finally); **at this point in time** (now).

  This procedure is the **gold standard** of hip replacement methods.
  (This procedure is the best hip replacement method.)

In the second example, 'gold standard' is completely inappropriate; correctly used, it should refer to monetary units, but it has been misused by being introduced into other contexts.

Table 22.3 continued

Colloquial language
This term encompasses informal language that is common in speech. Colloquialisms and idiomatic language should not be used in academic writing. This example shows how colloquial language involving cliché and idiom has been misused: **Not to beat about the bush,** increasing income tax did the Chancellor **no good at the end of the day** and he **was ditched** at the next Cabinet reshuffle. (Increasing income tax did not help the Chancellor and he was replaced at the next Cabinet reshuffle.)
'Hedging' language
For academic purposes, it is often impossible to state categorically that something is or is not the case. There are verbs that allow you to 'hedge your bets' by not coming down on one side or another of an argument, or which allow you to present a variety of different scenarios without committing yourself to any single position, for example: **seems that   looks as if   suggests that   appears that.** This involves using a language construction that leaves the reader with the sense that the evidence presented is simply supporting a hypothetical, or imaginary, case. To emphasise this sense of 'hedging', the use of a special kind of verb is introduced. These are: **can/cannot   could/could not   may/may not   might/might not.** These can be used with a variety of other verbs to increase the sense of tentativeness. For example: These results **suggest** that there has been a decline in herring stocks in the North Sea. Even more tentatively, this could be: These results **could suggest** that there has been a decline in herring stocks in the North Sea.
Jargon and specialist terms
Most subjects make use of language in a way that is exclusive to that discipline. It is important, therefore, to explain terms that a general reader might not understand. It is always good practice to define specialist terms or 'regular' words that are being used in a very specific way.
Rhetorical questions
Some writers use direct rhetorical questions as a stylistic vehicle to introduce the topic addressed by the question. This is a good strategy if you are making a speech and it can have some power in academic writing, although it should be used sparingly. Example: **How do plants survive in dry weather?** This might be a question starting a chapter. It could be rephrased as: **It is important to understand how plants survive in dry weather.** (Note: no question mark needed.)

Table 22.3 continued

Split infinitives
The most commonly quoted split infinitive comes from the TV series *Star Trek* where Captain James T. Kirk states that the aim of the Star Ship Enterprise is 'to boldly go where no man has gone before'. This means that an adverb (boldly) has split the infinitive (to go). It should read as 'to go boldly'. Many traditionalists consider that the split infinitive is poor English, although modern usage increasingly ignores the rule. Nevertheless, it is probably better to avoid the split infinitive in academic writing, which tends to be particularly traditional.
Value judgements
These are defined as statements in which the author or speaker is imposing their views or values on to the reader. For example, a writer who states that 'Louis XIV was a rabid nationalist' without giving supporting evidence for this statement is not making an objective comment in a professional manner. Rewording this statement to: 'Louis XIV was regarded as a rabid nationalist. This is evident in the nature of his foreign policy where he ...' offers the reader some evidence that explains the claim (see p. 148).

 ## Practical tips for ensuring that you write in an academic style

Think about your audience. Your readers should direct the style you adopt for any writing you do. For example, if you were writing to your bank manager asking for a loan, you would not use text-messaging or informal language. For academic writing, you should take into account that your reader(s) will probably be assessing your work and, in addition to knowledge and content, they will be looking for evidence of awareness and correct use of specialist terms and structures.

Avoid contractions. In spoken English, shortened forms such as, don't, can't, isn't, it's, I'd and we'll are used all the time. However, in academic written English, they should not be used. Texting contractions are also inappropriate.

Avoid personal pronouns. Experiment with other language structures so that you avoid the personal pronouns, I/me/one, you and we/us, and their possessive forms, my, your and our.

Take care with style in reflective writing. Some subjects, such as Nursing, Education and Social Work, involve student practitioners in a process of reflection on professional contexts and their roles within them. When this type of requirement is part of a written assessment, then moderate use of the first person (I or we) is expected. If your subject requires this approach, then balance your use of personal identification with the more neutral style expected more generally in academic circles. In other words, don't overuse the words 'I' or 'we'.

Avoid sexist language. The Council of Europe recommends that, where possible, gender-specific language be avoided. Thus: 'S/he will provide specimens for her/his exam'. This is rather clumsy, but, by transforming the sentence into the plural, this is avoided: 'They will provide specimens for their exams'. Alternatively, 'you' and 'your' could be used.

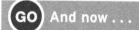

GO And now . . .

22.1 **Take steps to improve your grammar.** You may be able to find repeated errors that your supervisor or other lecturers may have identified in your work. Highlight points that you do not know how to rectify at present and resolve to find further information. You can do this by consulting a grammar book - for example, Foley and Hall (2003) - to find out more about the relevant grammar point. You can consolidate your understanding by doing the exercises provided in such books.

22.2 **Ask a friend to work with you on your writing style.** Swap a piece of writing and check over your friend's writing and ask them to do the same for yours. When you have done this, compare the points you have found. Try to explain what you think could be improved. Together, you may be able to clarify some aspects that you were unaware were problematic. Afterwards, follow the suggestion in point 22.1 above.

22.3 **Learn from published academic writing in your discipline.** Look at a textbook or journal article - especially in the area that discusses results or evidence or recommendations. Try to find examples of the use of 'hedging' language (Table 22.3) and note what else authors do with language in order to ensure that they avoid implying absolute judgements.

Essay writing

 ## Introduction

During your course of study, you may be asked to write an essay about a particular topic. Few people, especially students, write essays for pleasure. Essays are usually written as part of coursework (or examinations) to enable the tutor to assess your understanding and appreciation of a topic. This will require you to research the topic thoroughly in order to formulate your ideas before writing the essay.

An academic essay is not just an ordered presentation of relevant information about the topic, but is an argument (*thesis*) for which you should adopt a particular stance and in support of which you present evidence. The objective when writing an essay is to convince your reader that your particular standpoint is valid by presenting reasoned argument, based on evidence from authoritative sources.

The art of good essay writing lies in having something interesting to say and saying it clearly, concisely and with conviction. Writing an essay can be an arduous and time-consuming task to tackle, but when you are able to write essays with confidence, other types of assessment will seem relatively easy. If you have not had much experience (or success) with essay writing in the past, sitting down to write the first one at college or university can seem a daunting experience, but there are really only five basic stages in producing a good essay:

1 Analyse the essay title.

2 Find and organise the relevant material, making appropriate notes.

3 Make a plan.

4 Produce a rough draft.

5 Write the essay.

Each of these stages will be explored in a little more detail in the following sections. This will help you to understand why each stage is necessary.

Activity 15.1

Identifying difficulties

If you have written an essay before, list any difficulties that you have already experienced with writing essays.

→ Analysing the essay title

Sometimes you may be given a list of topics or titles from which you may select the one(s) you are going to tackle. Before making your choice, read all the titles carefully and consider the following:

- *Your interest in the topic.* There is little point in writing an essay on a topic in which you have no interest (unless, of course, none of the titles holds any interest for you, but you have to complete one).

- *Your understanding of the topic area and the title itself.* Choose one that you have some understanding of, rather than something new and unfamiliar. This will help to save time.

- *The resources that are available.* You need to be sure that the information required is easily accessible in the time available.

If the subject of the essay is new to you, read about the topic to gain some understanding before beginning to plan the essay or make notes for it. Understanding the topic before writing about it is crucial for you to be able to select appropriate material for inclusion or to develop logical arguments around the material.

Once you have chosen the essay title, examine the title of the essay again and consider its meaning carefully. The essay title should be interpreted as literally as possible. It will have been very carefully thought out and phrased to be as clear as possible.

Content (what is the essay about?)

A useful starting point is to break the question up phrase by phrase, word by word if necessary, and highlight (by underlining or making a list) all of the *key words* or phrases. The key words indicate the subject matter to be dealt with in the essay. A dictionary or thesaurus can be helpful for definitions of the key words or concepts, but be careful not to lose the context of the words. It is not a good idea to go off at a tangent when learning to write good essays. When you are an experienced essay writer, you may be able to justify taking a novel or idiosyncratic approach, and this may lead to very high marks.

Table 15.1 **Common instructional words and their definitions**

Instructional word	Meaning
Account for	Give reasons for; provide evidence to support (do not confuse with 'give an account of', which is asking for a description)
Analyse	Break down into the component parts and explain how they relate to each other
Appraise	Assess; evaluate; find the value of
Assess	Estimate the importance or value of; judge
Compare	Examine similarities and differences – perhaps reach a conclusion about which is preferable
Consider	Take into account; weigh up the advantages/disadvantages
Contrast	Examine the differences between and provide explanations
Criticise	Give your judgement about the merit or demerit of theories or opinions or about the truth or falsehood of facts; support your judgement by a discussion of evidence or reasoning involved
Define	Give the precise meaning of a word or phrase. In some cases it may be necessary or desirable to examine different possible or often-used definitions
Demonstrate	Prove with examples; show
Describe	Give a detailed account; provide the main characteristics
Differentiate	Explain the difference; distinguish between
Discuss	Investigate and/or examine in detail; sift the arguments and debate; give reasons for and against; examine the implications
Distinguish between	Describe the important aspects, pointing out pros and cons
Evaluate	Appraise the merit or worth of something; judge the impact, importance or success of; include your personal opinion and evidence to support your evaluation
Examine	Investigate, scrutinise and question all the evidence
Explain	Provide details about how something happens/ed; give clear reasons for; account for
Identify	Ascertain the main feature(s) of
Illustrate	Make clear by the use of concrete examples from a range of sources. Use a figure or diagram to explain or clarify
Indicate	Show; point out; verify
Interpret	Expound the meaning of; make clear and explicit, usually giving your own judgement
Judge	Form an opinion; conclude
Justify	Show adequate grounds for decisions or conclusions; answer the main objections likely to be made to them; make a case for a particular perspective; provide evidence
Outline	Describe the main features, or general principles, of a subject, omitting minor details and emphasising structure and arrangement
Refute	Disprove a statement or argument
Relate	Show how things are connected to each other, and to what extent they are alike or affect each other
Review	Make a survey of, examining the subject carefully
State	Set down the main points; present in a brief, clear form
Summarise	Give a concise account of the main points of a matter, avoiding unnecessary details and examples
Trace	Indicate the development of events or progress of a subject in clear stages

However, until you have acquired advanced essay-writing skills, it is safer to take a fairly conventional approach.

A useful technique is to put the essay title in a circle in the middle of a piece of paper and extend lines out as you think about the title and ideas come to you (a mind map). Some people may prefer to do this in a linear form as a list – choose the method that is best for you. (Chapter 6 provides advice about mind maps.)

Approach (what does the title ask you to do?)

The approach to be taken is indicated by the *instructional* (or directive) word(s) in the essay title, such as 'contrast' 'assess' and 'discuss'. These words reveal how the subject matter should be dealt with. Table 15.1 shows some common instructional words and their definitions.

It is important at this stage that you have a thorough understanding of the essay title. You could compare your understanding with that of a friend to check that you have not misunderstood anything. If there is confusion, ask your tutor for clarification.

Once you have some idea of the scope of the essay, you can establish the main argument (or thesis).

Stop and think

- ○ Do you understand the essay title?
- ○ What are the key words in the essay title?
- ○ How do these relate to the subject matter?
- ○ What initial areas for researching do they suggest?

See
Activity 15.1
FORMAL
LANGUAGE
in the Online
Study Guide.

Exercise 15.1

Key and instructional words

Read the following essay title:

Discuss the proposition that government organisations are subject to more rigorous control and accountability than private organisations.

(a) List the key words.

(b) Outline the approach you would take in completing the essay, paying particular attention to the instructional word(s).

→ Finding your material

After analysing the essay title:

● Highlight the main points and draw up some subheadings. Always keep these in mind.

● Quickly jot down what you know about the question – this will help your subconscious mind to start working on the topic. It may also provide some 'leads' to follow.

- Search initially for information that will provide an overview or a general introduction to the topic, particularly if the topic is new to you. Check if you have already been given any useful sources, such as references supplied by the tutor or module outline, or references and bibliographies in the recommended textbooks.

The most time-consuming part of essay writing is finding and organising relevant material to be included in the essay. Time management is important – make sure you allow sufficient time to read widely about the topic. To find information relating to the topic you will probably need to carry out a search (see Chapter 9). Make a note of the source of any information you intend to use (e.g. the page number, author and title of a book, and the title, author and location of an article). This will be useful when constructing the bibliography for the essay. (See Chapter 9 for information on constructing a bibliography.)

Suggestions when collecting information

- Always keep the essay title in mind.
- Avoid collecting information which, whilst interesting, is irrelevant to the essay. Many students who have difficulty in writing essays introduce information that they are unable to relate to the title. Information is included because they know it rather than know how to use it.
- Use up-to-date material from recent journals and quality newspapers where appropriate. This can add a touch of originality and freshness to the essay, thus helping it to stand out and be more interesting, particularly if a tutor may be marking many essays on the same topic.
- Always make a note of the source of any information, so that you can reference it correctly in your essay.

Organising the material once you have found it can be very difficult. The more ideas you have, the more material you find and the harder this stage becomes. You can have so much material that you feel overwhelmed, and making the decision what to leave out becomes a problem. All the material gathered needs to be worked through in a systematic and purposeful manner. Review it all and determine which parts are relevant to the essay and which are not. This is a time-consuming and very important stage of preparing an essay. Think about the topic over several days and allow your ideas to develop.

Remember...
Your essays cannot be well thought out if everything is left until the last minute, even if you have collected together the relevant material.

Reflect carefully on the information you find before deciding to include it in your essay. This should enable you to formulate the theme or argument that will permeate the essay. The analysis and the way in which you synthesise and present the arguments are your original contribution to the essay.

Once you have most of your material organised and in note form, you can start to plan the essay.

 ## Making an essay plan or outline

The next stage is to construct an essay plan. You may have developed an outline as you have gathered information, but only when you feel you have all the material needed should the plan be written down in a firm and committed manner. However, the plan should never be so rigid that you cannot move away from the original outline – you may have a new idea which means a reorganisation of the material.

Planning is an important part of writing the essay, as it helps to:

- establish your main argument (thesis)
- organise the main ideas and important details into a logical order
- distinguish the main points from the supporting points
- reduce the risk of omitting some important fact
- make the writing of the essay much easier
- make your writing more fluent.

Review your notes to identify the main themes, and separate your rough notes into natural groups that support the different points to be made. You can then consider each of these groups in turn and decide the most logical order in which to put the different elements. When you have worked through each group, you will be in a good position to prepare a rough outline of how your essay will be organised or structured. Try sorting the groups a few times, altering the composition, until a coherent structure begins to emerge.

It is at this planning stage that you need to take into account any word limit set. You may be able to narrow the topic by taking out some of the groups, if you feel that they are not vital in supporting your argument and you may exceed the word limit.

Unfortunately, there are no set rules for what a good essay plan should look like. In many cases it will depend on the particular essay and the style that suits you best. The important thing to remember is that the essay plan should indicate at a glance exactly how you are going to approach the essay and itemise the information you consider relevant.

Suggestions for planning an essay

- Decide the stance you intend to adopt with regard to the topic.
- Decide on the main points.
- Put them in the most logical order - the points should follow a sequence that enables the reader to see how one point connects to the next.
- Set alongside the main points all the supporting evidence, examples, data or illustrations that will be used to substantiate them. The essay will not carry conviction unless the reader believes what is written - this will be achieved by good supporting evidence.

Possible formats for an essay plan

There are a number of different formats that may be used for an essay plan. Three popular ones are outlined below.

Mind maps

Some people use mind maps as a visual plan for an essay. Mind maps can help you to discover the more surprising relationships between the points to be made. After constructing a mind map, a logical plan can then be developed.

Lists

A plan could take the form of a list of headings with all the relevant points itemised under those headings. You could divide the essay into paragraphs and briefly state the content of each one from the beginning to the end of the essay.

Flow charts

A flow chart could be constructed, highlighting the main themes and concepts, and showing how all the points relate to each other using those themes as a link.

Choose whichever method works for you and facilitates your own style of writing essays. The plan is there for you to work from and serves as a constant reminder of what you need to include.

Checklist: what to look for after constructing the essay plan

Is there a theme running through your essay? ☐

Is there a logical progression? ☐

Are the linkages obvious? ☐

Is there sufficient relevant information to answer the question? ☐

Is there any irrelevant information? ☐

Is the balance/emphasis correct? ☐

Is there any repetition? ☐

Does it answer the question? ☐

→ Producing a rough draft

Once you have a plan, you are ready to begin writing the essay. A rough draft is a first attempt at writing the complete essay. It is important to consider how to express yourself – always aim for an appropriate academic style. Remember that an essay is a one-sided conversation. The reader is unable to ask for clarification, so it is important that the essay is presented so that someone else can easily understand it, follow it logically and know how the writer reached their conclusion. Producing a draft is a valuable process because you can begin to see what works and what does not, what satisfies you and what does not, before you totally commit yourself. If possible, ask another person to read through your draft to see if it makes sense to them.

Do not rush into writing the essay. You need to get into the mood to write, otherwise it will be a struggle to find the words to express yourself. It is important that there are no distractions to interrupt your thoughts and writing, so ensure that all the materials you need are present before starting to write.

Stop and think ○ Do you have everything you need to write the essay?

Many people find it difficult to write the first words – even established authors can have this problem. A way of overcoming this is to start with 'Once upon a time . . .' This can help to get the words flowing, but it is essential that these words be changed before the essay is completed! Do not fall into the trap of writing the equivalent of a 'fairy story'. An essay is an academic piece of work and should be researched, referenced and written as such.

Although a rough draft is valuable, on occasions there may not be time to write one. In this case, there is all the more reason to plan the essay very thoroughly. However, do not be tempted to write only a final draft and submit it. This is a sure way to achieve less than you could do with sufficient planning, research, writing, reflection and modification.

The following checklist indicates things you should look for after producing the rough draft for an essay.

See Activity 15.2 PRACTISE FORMAL LANGUAGE in the Online Study Guide.

Checklist: what to look for after producing the rough draft of an essay

Is the emphasis correct? ☐

Do some sections need expanding or contracting? ☐

Are quotations, examples and other illustrative material used in a way that strengthens the arguments presented? ☐

Does the essay flow? ☐

Are there any unsupported personal views and opinions? ☐

Remember...
Leave enough time before the submission date to reflect on the rough draft and make any alterations you feel are beneficial.

Writing the essay

An essay falls into three major parts: introduction, main body and conclusion.

Introduction

A good introduction should set the scene, making it clear what you think the problem or question is, how you are going to approach it and how the essay will develop. It should contain some comment on the topic of the essay – perhaps definitions are needed, or some explanation of what you understand by the title. This section should also state the main issues involved and indicate which aspects of the topic you intend dealing with, and why. The introduction provides the reader with a preview of the stages through which the essay will develop. It usually does not need to be more than a paragraph.

Above all, it is essential that the introduction arouses the reader's interest and gives them reason to continue reading. Spend some time thinking about the first sentence of your essay – it is important that you gain the attention of the reader and make them interested in what you have to say.

Main body

The main body of the essay provides the opportunity to build up explanations and arguments with ideas, opinions and facts. Key points should be presented in a logical order and the linkages between them made explicit. It is vital that the key points are supported by relevant examples and any evidence gathered.

The logic of the paragraphs should reflect the logic of the plan prepared earlier. Each paragraph should raise a central issue, aspect or idea, and include evidence to support it. Ensure that each paragraph has unity and links naturally with the preceding and following paragraphs. Two paragraphs may be on different ideas but linked by that difference: for example, cause and effect, positive and negative aspects of one argument, or a before and after situation. The transition from paragraph to paragraph can often present some difficulty, but it is essential to maintain continuity and to give verbal signposts to your reader showing how you are moving on. This can be achieved by the use of linking words and phrases (see Table 15.2).

Table 15.2 **Common linking words and phrases**

Linking word or phrase	Indicating
but, however, on the other hand, yet, nevertheless, on the contrary	contrast
for example, that is, for instance, in this case	illustration
similarly, moreover, furthermore, in addition, also	extension
therefore, consequently, as a result, thus	conclusion
then, after that, ultimately	the next step

In writing the main body of the essay, ensure that it provides a balanced view and that all aspects are given adequate coverage and supporting evidence.

See Chapter 5 for more linking (transition) words and phrases.

Checklist: writing the main body of an essay

Are key points supported by relevant examples? ☐

Have you made the linkages between key points explicit? ☐

Are the points made in a logical order? ☐

Does it present a balanced view? ☐

Conclusion

When writing the conclusion to the essay, always refer back to the title. The conclusion should show the reader how the discussion in the essay has answered the question or arrived at a point of view.

The conclusion may not involve you in deciding whether or not you support or agree with the topic or concept you have written about, but may simply be a summary of the arguments. However, if the essay requires you to form a conclusion, summarise the main evidence in support of your view, making it clear what conclusions or implications follow from this. Ensure that the arguments presented throughout the essay are consistent with the conclusion.

The conclusion should provide a sense of having reached the end. Both you and the reader should feel that you have arrived somewhere at the end of the essay. It may also be appropriate to suggest to the reader areas worthy of further consideration.

The conclusion is normally about the same length as, or shorter than, the introduction. The introduction and conclusion should agree with each other and must never be contradictory. Avoid the temptation to repeat the introduction – the conclusion should indicate that you have progressed. The conclusion should not introduce new material, but should evolve from the main body of the essay.

Make sure you consider the following points when writing the conclusion for an essay.

> ### Checklist: writing the conclusion for an essay
>
> Have you referred back to the title of the essay? ☐
>
> Are the arguments presented consistent with the conclusion? ☐
>
> Do the introduction and conclusion agree? ☐
>
> Have you avoided introducing new material? ☐

Other points to remember

Subheadings

These tend to split up an essay into separate sections and make it more difficult for the various points to be presented in an integrated way. A good essay is a continuous piece of prose. For the same reason, try to avoid the use of lists in an essay. For example, rather than 'There are three relevant points to consider here: 1, 2, 3, . . .', use whole sentences and paragraphs and say, 'There are three relevant points to consider here. The first of these is that . . . Secondly . . . Finally there is the fact that . . .'

Diagrams or pictures

These may help to get the point across and provide a focus for the discussion. However, like lists, they disrupt the flow of an essay and tend to break it up into sections so that the connections are lost. Thus they should be used only when considered essential to aid the reader's understanding.

Abbreviations

These may be used as long as they are spelt out in full the first time. Similarly, words or phrases that are not in common usage, such as technical terms, should be defined the first time they are used.

References

See Activity 15.3 USING REFERENCES in the Online Study Guide.

If a piece of work completed by someone else or an idea or theory developed by another person is referred to, make it evident that it is not your own original view. This is done by putting the person's name and the date their work was published in the sentence, e.g. Coyle (2004). At the end of the essay, the bibliography should contain a list of all the work referred to, including author, date and title of the book or article where the piece of work can be found. See Chapter 9 for advice on referencing and bibliographies.

Plagiarism

Avoid presenting other people's words or ideas as your own. Plagiarism or using other authors' words or ideas without acknowledgement is not permitted. When making notes from passages in books and articles, put them into your own words; never be tempted to copy them verbatim (word for word), as you could subsequently inadvertently plagiarise, and this could have very serious consequences. Most universities and colleges have strict rules and procedures for dealing with plagiarism.

> **Remember...**
> All work you present during your course of study should be correctly referenced.

See
Activity 15.4
WRITING A
REFERENCE
LIST/
BIBLIOGRAPHY
in the Online
Study Guide.

Quotations

These should be used sparingly. They should support the points or arguments and must be directly relevant to the topic, not used for their own sake. Only use those phrases or sections that are so telling that no paraphrase of the author's idea will be as effective. If you use direct quotations, use quotation marks and acknowledge the author (name and date). The precise source of the quotation should be referenced either in a footnote or in the bibliography. For example:

'Education is what survives when what has been learnt has been forgotten.'*

Skinner (1964)

Stop and think
○ Have you referenced your work correctly?
○ Have you used the Harvard method of referencing?

See
Activity 15.5
PRACTISE
WRITING A
REFERENCE
LIST
in the Online
Study Guide.

Word limit

Many of the essays you write will have word limits, i.e. a maximum number of words that should not be exceeded. If so, it is important not to exceed this. Sometimes you may be asked to write an essay with no word limit. This creates a problem of knowing how much to write and when to stop. There is no clear answer to this, as it depends on the particular approach you decide to adopt when answering the question. Deciding when to stop is part of the learning process and a skill that needs to be developed. It is your decision when to draw the line – a useful exercise is to formulate an explanation of why you stopped where you did.

→ Reviewing the essay

After completing the first draft of the essay, read it through in order to reflect on what is written. Try and do this as though reading it for the first time. This will be easier if you wait for at least a day or two, or preferably a week, after completing the first draft because you will be able to approach it more dispassionately. Reading the essay aloud is a good way to be sure that the language is not awkward and that it flows well.

When reviewing an essay, use the following questions as a guide.

---

*B. F. Skinner, *New Scientist*, 21 May 1964, 'Education in 1984'.

Checklist: reviewing an essay

Coherence
Does it make sense to you? ☐
Will it make sense to the reader? ☐
Is it coherent? ☐

Omissions
Have you included everything necessary? ☐
Are points missed or glossed over? ☐

Logic
Is the material sequenced logically? ☐

Relevance
Is all the content relevant? ☐
Have you included unnecessary padding? ☐

Balance
Is the emphasis correct? ☐
Do some sections need expanding or contracting? ☐

Flow
Does the essay flow? ☐
Are there any repetitions or ambiguities? ☐
Are there any spelling, punctuation or grammatical errors? ☐

Supporting evidence
Is there sufficient supporting evidence to uphold the arguments, views and
opinions presented? ☐
Have you avoided any unsupported personal views and opinions? ☐

Illustrations
Will they aid understanding? ☐
Are they labelled correctly? ☐

Quotations
Are quotations referenced adequately? ☐
Are quotations, examples and other illustrative material used in a way that
strengthens the arguments presented? ☐

Application
Have you answered the question? ☐

Sources
Are all sources referenced correctly throughout the essay? ☐
Is the bibliography complete? ☐

Common criticisms of essays

Table 15.3 indicates some of the common criticisms of essays and suggests some remedies to overcome these.

Table 15.3 **Common criticisms of essays and their remedies**

Criticism	Remedy
Too long or unfocused	Limit your essay plan to what can be included in the word limit. Prune irrelevant information. Keep to the point. Keep referring back to the title.
Too short or lacks sufficient content	Pay more attention to the explanations needed to get your points across. Use more examples. Do more research. Broaden the topic area.
Poor structure, badly organised, rambling	Practise doing essay plans, ensuring logical structure. Check for repetition and unnecessary padding.
Lacks fluency, poor style or presentation	Link your points/paragraphs. Check spelling and grammar. Leave time to review the essay before submitting it for marking.
Unbalanced answer	Check that your answer is not heavily weighted in one direction but gives a well-balanced, fair and objective evaluation of the subject.
Reaching conclusions without good evidence	Ensure you present the evidence for any conclusions you draw – believing it is the case is not sufficient; you must prove it.
Answer too personal	Avoid writing in the first person; use the third person. Do not express your own personal view unless the question specifically asks for it.
Poor conclusion	Ensure you have concluded the essay and indicated how you have answered the question. Do not introduce new information.
Poor introduction	Check you have introduced the topic area and explained to the reader what you are going to do.
Inclusion of irrelevant information	Ensure you understand the question and what it requires you to do. Ensure you answer the question and are not just giving the information you know and are comfortable with.
Boring, lacks originality	Alter your writing style; try and include something novel or take an innovative approach.
Too descriptive	Be more critical and evaluative of the information you have found. Provide a theoretical framework and use your knowledge, experience and examples to support what you are saying.

Table 15.3 **continued**

Criticism	Remedy
Little evidence of background reading	Do more research, widen your reading material.
Atheoretical	Provide more discussion of theoretical approaches.
Taking a chronological approach	If the subject has a historical dimension, beware of taking the easy approach and explaining what happened in the order it happened. Analyse the events and show why they occurred, etc., rather than describing them.
Failure to answer the question	Ensure correct interpretation of the question – look at the instructional words. Keep referring back to the title whilst writing the essay.

Writing essays under examination conditions

When writing essays under examination conditions, similar stages to those outlined above may be followed, although you are obviously unable to leave the examination room to do any research. Examine all the essay titles carefully and select the one(s) you feel most confident about answering. Do not choose a title because you see a topic you recognise and have revised – it is important that you are able to answer the question being asked about the topic.

For more details on essays under examination conditions, see Chapter 18.

Suggestions for writing essays under examination conditions

- Identify the essay you are going to attempt first.
- List the *key words* in the title and identify the *instructional* words.
- Jot down ideas as they come to you.
- Prepare a plan for the essay. Ensure this is legible so that, if you run out of time, the tutor can look at the plan and see how you intended to progress.
- Begin to write the essay. Ensure that you stay within the time you have allocated for the question; it is easy to get carried away when writing an essay.
- If you run out of time, jot down some headings to give an indication of how you would have completed the essay.

Activity 15.2

Dealing with the difficulties of essay writing

Look at the list of problems you identified in Activity 15.1. Devise a strategy that will help you to overcome these problems.

Figure 15.1 **Elements of a good essay**

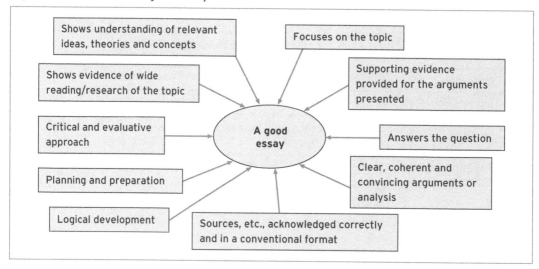

→ Summary

This chapter has outlined that:

- a good essay requires planning and preparation, which take time
- before starting the essay it is necessary to have a full understanding of the title of the essay and the instructional words that indicate how the topic should be treated
- wide reading and research of the topic area are required
- planning and reflection before writing will pay dividends later
- it is always advisable to write a rough draft before writing the final version of an essay
- after writing an essay it is important to read and review it, checking for things such as logical development, grammar, etc.

→ Answer to exercise

15.1

(a) Key words: organisations, government, private organisations, control, accountability.
Other key words that might be appropriate: markets, competition, audit, public sector, government funding, profit/loss.

(b) Outline of one approach:
Examine what government organisations are.
Define public sector.
Define private sector.
Examine and define control and accountability aspects within those organisations.
Present evidence (examples) providing reasons to support and/or refute the proposition argued in the essay.
Conclude.

Report writing

Learning outcomes

After studying this chapter, you should be able to:

- plan the stages and use of time in preparing a report
- use a recognised and logical report structure
- include information appropriate to the purpose of the report
- construct an effective report.

Introduction

Whilst studying at university or college you may be asked to present information for an assessment in a report format. The construction of a report for an assessment allows you to practise presenting information in a format that is very relevant to many forms of employment. Whereas essays tend to be academic and theoretically based, reports are often more action oriented and generally have a wider scope. Report writing will involve using skills of application – applying what has been learned to a particular situation, rather than investigating and discussing theory.

Reports are commonly used for communication within an organisation to present facts or findings about a particular situation for a specific audience. When you join an organisation, it may have its own house style to which all reports are expected to conform. Tutors may also favour a particular style that they require students to adopt.

It is not easy to generalise about reports, as they may take many different forms depending on their purpose and for whom they are written. Whatever the purpose or style of a report, it is crucial that it is objective, accurate and concise, but sufficiently comprehensive for the reader to understand the issues. A well-written report can be a powerful means of persuasion and obtaining agreement or cooperation. Thus, an ability to write effective reports is an important and valuable skill for all students to acquire.

This chapter aims to provide advice on the compilation of reports. The secret of successful report writing is to approach it systematically and present material in a simple, clear and logical way. The preparation of a report divides logically into four stages – preliminary, preparation, writing and review.

Figure 16.1 **Stages of report writing**

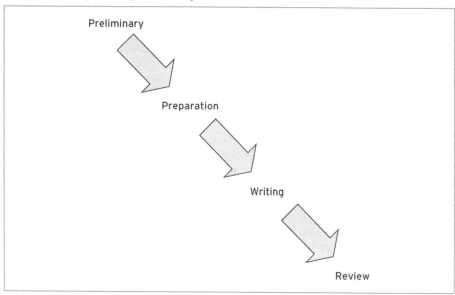

→ Preliminary stage

Before beginning the report, it is important to be clear in your own mind exactly what you have been asked to do. Consider the following.

Objective (why is the report being written?)

The purpose behind the report will influence the way you approach it. A report may be written for a number of different reasons:

- To *provide information*. This may be a straightforward statement of facts or an explanation of events or findings. Examples include an accident report for an organisation's health and safety records; a company's annual report, in which the company's position is summarised for its shareholders and employees, an explanation of a new procedure or a summary of a conference, etc.
- To *make a request*. This type of report aims to persuade or motivate the reader into action – for example, a request to purchase a new piece of equipment, make a donation to a worthy cause, or accept a new procedure.
- To *influence decision making*. An example is a proposal to launch a new product or enter a new market.
- To *solve a problem*. The results of an investigation into a problem are presented within the report and one or more solutions offered based on the findings.

These reasons are not mutually exclusive. You may have to write reports as part of your assessment and they will usually be written from one of the perspectives outlined above. This may involve you adopting a particular role: for example, consultant, manager or trainee. It is important that, before writing a report, you understand from which perspective the report is to be approached and what role, if any, you are to assume. Failure to adopt a particular approach may lose valuable marks.

Stop and think
○ Why is the report being written?
○ From which perspective will you approach the report?

Content (what is the principal subject matter?)

It is important to identify the major subject matter or focus of the report and the themes and issues that will need to be included. This will be helpful when collecting the material and evidence required for the report.

The facts of two different reports may be identical, but the purpose of the report will determine how these facts are presented. For example, pressure groups for and against a bypass around a village may have the same 'facts', but would choose to emphasise different aspects in order to persuade their audience.

Audience (who is the intended reader?)

Remember that the report is being written for the benefit of someone else. To be successful it should be directed to the particular requirements, needs and interests of the reader. Consider who will be reading the report – tutor/lecturer, executives, experts or the ordinary person in the street.

● *What does the reader know about the subject area?* It is important to ensure that you communicate at a level appropriate to the reader and offer enough explanation. If you overestimate their expertise, you may blind them with science, but, on the other hand, if you underestimate it, you may well bore them. As a student, it will be fairly safe to assume that the tutor for whom you are writing the report will be knowledgeable about the subject area.

● *What does the reader want/need to know?* Awareness of this will help you to prepare your case accordingly.

● *What are the reader's opinions of the subject of the report?* Does the reader think the subject is important, and are they likely to support or oppose the recommendations? This may influence how you present your final report.

● *What are the reader's preferences?* Is there a particular format or style they prefer? Do they like to see tables and charts, pictures or statistics? How much detail do they want? You need to tailor the final presentation of the report according to your reader's preferences.

Constraints (what are the limitations?)

What resources are available to you in terms of time (ensure you are certain of the date the report is required), money and information? Is there sufficient published material available to provide the evidence needed? If not, you may need to consider primary sources of information (see Chapter 9).

The answers to these questions will enable you to write the *terms of reference* for your report.

Terms of reference

The *terms of reference* (sometimes called *objectives*) define the scope of the report and indicate how you intend to achieve the aim. They outline the aspects to be considered and indicate the limitations to be observed. It is essential to write feasible terms of reference, as they form the basis of the report, and at university or college you may be graded on whether or not you achieve the terms of reference. If you have any doubts at this stage, seek clarification from your tutor or the person requesting the report. Only when you have determined the terms of reference can you begin to start collecting the data for your report.

Stop and think

○ What are the audience needs for your report?

○ What has already been written about the topic area?

○ What are the terms of reference for your report?

Checklist: the preliminary stage of report writing

Why is the report being written?

What role, if any, do you need to adopt?

What is the subject matter?

Who is your target audience for the report?

What will the reader already know about the subject area?

What does the reader need to know?

What are your reader's opinions of the subject of the report?

How will the principal reader expect the report to be presented?

What, if any, are the limitations to the preparation of the report?

→ Preparation stage

Information gathering

The next stage is to collect the information you need – see Chapter 9 for a more comprehensive approach to gathering the necessary data to complete the report.

What information do you require?

Begin by jotting down your ideas on what could be included in the report – a mind map is a useful tool for this (see Chapter 6). Circle the related ideas and sort them into groups or topics – this will give you an idea of the material you need to collect. Gathering information is very time consuming; only collect material that is relevant to what you are trying to do. Keep focused by continually referring to the terms of reference.

Where from?

Alongside each of the groups or topics identified, list the possible sources of information for it. The sources you need to use will vary depending on the nature of the report.

When collecting information from secondary sources such as books and journals, it is important to note the sources precisely, so that you can refer to them again if necessary. They should also be included in the bibliography. If the collection of primary data is necessary, a section should be included in the report on how this was done (methodology/procedure), unless this is specifically not required. The factual basis of many reports you write will rely mainly, if not entirely, on your own data collection. The reliability of the report depends upon the accurate and honest handling of this data.

Suggestions for the collection of data

- Check the accuracy of the facts.
- Separate facts from opinions and assertions - and assess the merits of these.
- Separate facts from inferences - assess if inferences have a sound base.
- Select information carefully:
  - collect only relevant material;
  - do not exclude relevant information in the interests of brevity.

How much information?

It is difficult to determine how much information is required to write the report. One important rule is that anything irrelevant must be rejected – it may be interesting, but if it does not help to achieve the aim of the report, it is using valuable space and the tutor will not award marks for irrelevancies.

Time may be a factor in how much information is collected, but ensure that sufficient information is provided to allow a complete case to be presented to the reader.

Organisation of material

Once all the material has been gathered, you need to plan carefully the structure of the report. As with any assessment, it is worth spending time in careful planning. This will make the task of writing much easier and will be thoroughly justified by the quality of the final report.

Most subjects can be broken down into major and minor aspects. This is extremely important in report writing, as it helps you to prioritise the material and sort it into manageable sections.

Suggestions for organising material

- List the major points that you wish to make.
- Break these down into smaller or subsidiary points, each with an appropriate heading.
- Under each heading, list the facts, ideas, etc. that logically fit under each heading.
- Alongside these, note the information that will be used to support them.
- Mark the least important points, i.e. ones that the reader may find irrelevant. These will probably be rejected.
- Reread the list to check it is complete. Compare it to the terms of reference, as this will help you to keep focused.
- Once your list is complete, arrange the points in a logical sequence that will enable you to achieve the purpose and lead the reader to the same conclusion as your own.

Following these steps will provide a clear and well-organised structure for the report. It will also help to determine which information should be presented in the main body and which should go in the appendices.

Remember...
Inclusion of unnecessary material will distract the reader.

 # Writing the report

A lengthy report is usually broken down into a number of sections which are standard, recognised parts of a report. The report should be *presented* in the order set out below but may be *written* in a different order. For example, although the summary is one of the first sections to be presented in the report, it would probably be written last.

 ## Title page

The title page is used to identify the report and should contain the following information:

Title of the report

Author's name

Date

Distribution list, if there is one

It is a good idea to keep the layout simple and not to overcrowd the page.

Contents page

The contents page lists the main sections, subsections (if any) and appendices, indicating their page numbers. It can be useful to construct the contents page before beginning to write, as this provides an outline for the report. Most word-processing packages now offer a facility that enables you to construct the contents page automatically.

A list of tables and figures (if used) is usually shown separately.

Summary or abstract

The summary or abstract is a very important part of the report. It provides a brief outline of the major themes or issues covered in the report, so that the reader can gain an appreciation of the whole picture without having to read the full report. The reader may then decide to read the recommendations and only refer to the detail of the report for further information where necessary. The summary must therefore be capable of standing as a complete, accurate and comprehensible item, independent of the main body of the report.

The summary or abstract should contain an overview of the following information:

- the purpose and scope of the report
- background information to set the scene
- what has been done and how
- the main findings
- conclusion
- recommendations (if necessary).

It is no easy task to write this section, so be certain to leave sufficient time to do this.

Introduction

The introduction should provide a broad, general view of the report, indicating what will be covered and why the report was necessary. It should present sufficient background information to enable the reader to understand the context of the report and provide the motivation for them to continue to read.

The best way to tackle the introduction is to be very obvious and state in the first sentence what the report is about. The introduction should supply details about the following:

- *Context.* Provide an indication of the subject of the report, a brief general background and/or history surrounding the report, and who requested it (if relevant). Only sufficient information is needed to enable the reader to understand and follow the report.
- *Purpose.* The aim of the report should be quite clearly and briefiy articulated.
- *Scope.* The terms of reference should be stated, including the limitations of the report.
- *Procedure/method.* Outline briefiy the methods used to gather the information. Sometimes this section appears as a separate section with its own major headings (see below).

Procedure/method

Some reports require a section detailing the method(s) used to gather the information contained in the report. In order for the report to have credibility, the reader must be convinced that the data and information on which the report is based are reliable and valid. This section of the report therefore aims to establish this. It is an opportunity for you to explain which sources of information (books, articles, etc.) were consulted and which methods of investigation (survey, observation, experimentation) were used.

If you experienced difficulties in gathering some of the information, which meant that you were unable to investigate certain aspects, this should be explained in this section. The reader is then able to understand why these aspects were not explored or facts were not given or verified.

The procedure/method section should lead logically to the next section, the main body, which will present the information gathered from each source.

Findings

This section provides the detailed facts and findings of the report and indicates how they were arrived at and the inferences to be drawn from them. It is also important to remember that this section provides the foundation for your conclusions and recommendations. If the report is required to address appropriate academic theory then this section should also contain an analysis of the theory on which the findings of the report are to be based.

There is no specific format for this section, but the facts should be built into a logical and consistent case. Think very carefully about the most logical sequence in which to present the material – always refer back to the terms of reference for the report, as this will prevent you from straying from the topic under scrutiny.

It is helpful to the reader if the main body of the report is divided into major sections which group facts or ideas together under subheadings or numbered points. This creates a logical and persuasive structure and guides the reader smoothly through the report until they reach the point at which the conclusions can be revealed. If there are lengthy sections in this part of the report, it is easier if a brief summary and conclusion is provided at the end of each section. The next section can then restate these and move forward.

This section should be as concise as possible, containing only the essential detail. Any detailed supporting material that may detract the reader from the central theme should be relegated to the appendices.

Suggestions for writing the main body of the report

- Develop ideas logically and as fully as possible (with one main topic or idea per paragraph).
- Consider the different aspects of the problem but keep an appropriate balance - do not develop one section to the exclusion of others.
- Your reasoning should be clear to the reader.
- Explain and justify the points made, presenting supporting evidence where appropriate.
- Keep focused by constantly referring to the terms of reference.

Figure 16.2 **Conclusions**

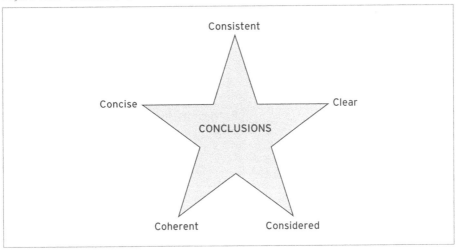

Conclusions

The material presented in the main body of the report should lead the reader logically to the conclusions. The purpose of the conclusions is to summarise the main findings and offer some evaluation and/or opinion of them. The conclusions (see Figure 16.2) should be:

- *Clear* – use simple and direct language. If a number of points are to be made, they should be set out as separate paragraphs with references made back to the main body by page number and paragraph if necessary.
- *Concise* – stick to the point, do not ramble.
- *Consistent* with what has gone before (do *not* introduce any new material at this stage).
- *Considered* – thought through, not superficial suggestions.
- *Coherent* – arguments, themes and issues developed logically.

See Activity 16.2 PRACTISE SUMMARISING in the Online Study Guide.

If the previous parts of the report have been clearly and logically constructed, the conclusions will follow naturally from them. In turn, the conclusions should lead logically to the recommendations (if these are required).

The conclusions are written after the main body of the report has been completed and are the test of a well-written report. They should be brief and the order of presentation should correspond with that of your actual report.

Recommendations

It is not always essential to provide recommendations; this will depend on the terms of reference for the report. If recommendations are required, they should indicate the action needed in order to achieve the aim of the report and follow naturally from, and be based solely on, the material presented in the conclusions. Do not introduce any new issues or arguments that have not been dealt with in the main body of the report or the conclusions.

Figure 16.3 **Presenting recommendations**

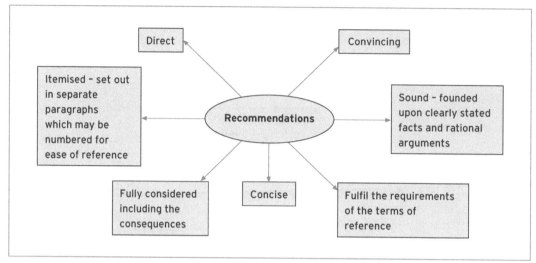

Recommendations are important and influential factors in affecting future action and decision making, so careful thought should be given to them. However, it is important to remember that recommendations are only *advisory* – the decision whether or not to act upon them will be taken by the reader. The tone you use is therefore important – try not to alienate the reader by ordering or threatening, but rather advise, suggest, recommend or urge. This is more effective. For example:

not: The bonus scheme must be introduced immediately.

but: The board should consider the introduction of the bonus scheme as a matter of urgency.

A good report will carry the reader along by the argument, so that by the time they reach the end they will need no further convincing.

References

Whenever you draw from other writers' ideas, provide the reference – an indication of which particular piece of their writing you are drawing from. It is important to use an accepted convention when acknowledging other people's work (for example, the Harvard system) so that the reader may easily identify the item that is being referred to. The Harvard system of citation is simple to use – it requires you to mention only the author and year of publication within the text. The reader may then find a full description of the work that you have cited by referring to the bibliography at the end of your report. For example:

The work of Handy (1993) suggests that . . .

The reader may then turn to the bibliography to determine which of Handy's works is being referred to. It is vitally important that any sources used should be acknowledged and quotations should be attributed correctly to avoid problems with plagiarism.

See
Activity 16.1
SECTIONS OF A
REPORT
in the Online
Study Guide.

Activity 16.1

Referencing

Check with your tutor or librarian which referencing conventions are used in your
university or college – it may be a requirement to use footnotes.

Bibliography

Always provide a bibliography. The bibliography provides a list of materials that have
been consulted as a basis for the report and will therefore provide evidence on the validity of the information presented.

The bibliography should enable the reader to follow up a reference made within the
main body of the work. It is therefore important that the first two elements of the reference (author and date) form the link between the text and the bibliography. Table 16.1
indicates the order in which information should be presented for items appearing in the
bibliography.

It is also important that if information has been retrieved from non-printed sources,
these are also adequately referenced. For example, electronic journal articles retrieved
from the World Wide Web should be referenced in the same way as printed articles, but
include an availability statement and the date they were accessed.

Table 16.1 **Constructing a bibliography**

1 Printed sources		
Books	*Journal articles*	*Newspaper articles*
Author(s), editor(s) or the institution responsible	Author	Author
(indicate editors by ed.)	(Year of publication)	(Year of publication)
(Year of publication)	Title of article	Title of article
Title: Subtitle	*Title of journal*	*Newspaper*
Series and individual volume number	Volume and part number, month or season, page numbers of the article	Date article published
Edition (if not the first)		
Place of publication	Note: Electronic journal articles from the Internet should be referenced in the same way as a printed article, but include an availability statement, i.e. Available from: <http://www...> [Accessed ...]	
Publisher		
Example:	*Example:*	*Example:*
Kotler, P., and Armstrong, G. (2004) *Principles of Marketing*. 10th edition, Upper Saddle River, NJ: Pearson Education.	Capaldi, N. (2005) Corporate social responsibility and the bottom line. *International Journal of Social Economics*, Vol. 32, issue 5, pp. 408-23.	Skapinker, M. (2005) Be cheered: the workplace bully has a soft underbelly. *Financial Times*, 23 March, p. 12.

Table 16.1 **continued**

2 Audio-visual sources		
Videos	*On-line images*	*World Wide Web documents*
Programme title	*Title (or description)*	Author/editor
(Year)	Year	Year
Series title	[online image]	Title
Series number	Available from <www address>	Internet
Place of publication	Filename, including extension	Edition
Publisher	[Date accessed]	Place of publication
Date of transmission/issue		Publisher (if available)
		Available from: <www address>
[Medium: Format]		[Accessed date]
Example:	*Example:*	Example:
How to stop them leaving: Talent management: (2004) London: Video Arts [Video: VHS]	*The Vase of Cornflowers* (1959) [online image]. Available from: <http://www.virtualdali.com/59VaseofCornflowers.html>, [Accessed 24 June 2005].	Gundry, J., and Slater, S. (2005) *Flexible Working: Can Home Workers And Their Managers Make It Work?,* [Internet], Available from: <www.knowab.co.uk/wbwflexwork.html>, [Accessed 11 August 2005].

An example bibliography is shown below:

Campbell, D., Stonehouse, G., and Houston B. (2004) *Business Strategy*. 2nd edition, Oxford: Elsevier Butterworth-Heinemann.

Cannon, H., and Schwaiger, M. (2005) The role of company reputation in business simulations. *Simulation and Gaming*. Vol. 36, no. 2, pp. 188–202.

McKenna. R., and Martin-Smith, B. (2005) Decision making as a simplification process: new conceptual perspectives. *Management Decisions*. Vol. 43, no. 6, June 2005, pp. 821–36(16) [Internet]. Available from: <http://hermia.emeraldinsight.com/vl=19779020/cl=40/fm=html/nw=1/rpsv/cgi-bin/linker?ini=connect&infobike=/mcb/001/2005/00000043/00000006/art00003&infomagic=f7465b9b3ad6be338fab990680f0a60e>, [Accessed 17 August 2005].

Activity 16.2

Bibliography

Check with your tutor or librarian what the conventions are in your university or college.

Select a range of material for a topic you are studying and compile a bibliography according to the convention.

Check with your tutor or librarian that your bibliography is presented correctly.

Appendices

Appendices contain any supplementary material that is needed to support the report but is not essential to the main findings. If they were included in the findings of the report, they would disrupt the flow and detract from the facts and arguments being presented.

For easy reference, appendices should be grouped appropriately and annotated with letters or numbers consecutively as they are mentioned in the main text, e.g. Appendix A1, A2, Appendix B1, B2, B3, etc. It is not a good idea to have too many and those included should be referred to within the main body of the report. Appendices should be presented on the same paper size as the rest of the report. Sometimes the appendices count towards the word limit for the report – check this with your tutor.

Glossary

See
Activity 16.3
FINDING THE
MISTAKES
in the Online
Study Guide.

If technical terms have been used in the construction of the report, you may need to provide an explanation of these terms in a glossary. A glossary provides definitions of terms or acronyms that are technical or difficult because they are specific to the topic area. Glossaries are particularly helpful if the readers include non-experts in the subject area as well as experts.

Acknowledgements

The acknowledgements provide an opportunity to thank the people who have helped in the preparation of the report by providing information or resources. The acknowledgements may be presented either at the beginning or at the end of the report.

→ Presentation

There are a number of different conventions that may be used when compiling reports. If the report is constructed using word-processing software, you may find that the software contains a report-formatting element. Key aspects of report formatting are outlined below, but remember that different organisations, including your university or college, may use, and insist on, their own house style. Check with your tutor to determine if there are any specific rules of presentation that you must follow.

Appearance and layout

However you decide to present your report, it is important to be consistent in the presentation – for example, in the use of underlining and italics, bullet points, font size, line spacing and margins.

Page numbering

Pages of a report are usually numbered consecutively except for the title page. The position of the page numbers (top, bottom, centre, right) should be consistent throughout the report. Appendices are numbered separately on each page.

Figure 16.4 **An example of a report structure**

Report on the ....

1.0 Summary

2.0 Introduction

3.0 Method

    3.1 Limitations

4.0 ....

    4.1

    4.2

        4.2.1

        4.2.2

    4.3

5.0 ....

6.0 Conclusions

7.0 Recommendations

Bibliography

Appendix A ....

Appendix B ....

Headings

These provide a framework within which to construct a well-organised report and act as signposts to the reader. A report could be written without headings, but it would be confusing and thus difficult to read. However, too many headings may interrupt the flow of the text and also make the report difficult to read. It is interesting to note that readers often ignore the headings when reading the text and thus you should treat them as separate from the text and not as part of the structure.

Subheadings

If used, these should be appropriate to the material, guiding the reader through the main sections and providing an immediate outline for reference purposes.

Paragraphs

The first word of the paragraph usually begins at the margin and is not indented. There is no optimum length of paragraph. A paragraph should contain related material and may have to be quite long. However, bear in mind that if paragraphs are too long, the reader may lose the sense before reaching the end. If paragraphs are too short, this may lead to an abrupt style and appearance, and disrupt the reading flow. Single-sentence paragraphs should be avoided.

A new paragraph is usually indicated by additional line spacing. Additional line spacing may also be used above and below each main and group heading to keep it clear of the text. Sub-paragraphs may be used to break up the flow of a very long paragraph or tabulate a number of items or points. If sub-paragraphs are used in the report, they should be indented.

Some reports are written using a classification system for ease of reference. Classification systems use a system of headlines, number or letter sequences and margins to indicate each section or subsection, whose relative importance is indicated by:

- the size of headline
- its number or letter
- the position on the paper.

All classification must be consistent.

Abbreviations

These can be an irritation to the reader if they are unfamiliar with them. The first time an abbreviation is used it should be spelt out in full, with the abbreviation shown in brackets immediately afterwards, e.g. Bachelor of Arts (BA), Institute of Directors (IOD). Future reference to the term may then be shown as an abbreviation. Ensure that any use of abbreviations is consistent.

Graphs, tables, charts

Consider using tables, graphs and bar charts for clarification, not for decoration. They should be used to aid comprehension, provide reinforcement and help the reader to understand relationships. Remember, a picture is said to be worth a thousand words!

Style of writing

See
Activity 16.4
PUTTING IT
ALL TOGETHER
in the Online
Study Guide.

The language and style must be appropriate to the reader and the aim of the report. A report is a formal document and thus you should avoid the use of colloquialisms. Reports should be written in the third person – only use 'I' in an eyewitness report. Try to express yourself in a style that is clear, carries conviction and arouses interest in the reader.

It is a natural tendency to put in additional adjectives, qualifying phrases and explanatory sentences to avoid any misunderstanding, but this is merely padding and slows the reader down so that impact may be lost. The draft report should be pruned ruthlessly to cut out the inessential.

Review

The secret of success in reviewing the completed report, as in writing, is to be systematic. Read the report, not once but several times. Each time you read the report, concentrate on a different aspect – for example, logic, expression, punctuation and grammar (prune out ambiguities, pompous words, spelling and grammatical errors). This list is not exhaustive – there may be other aspects depending on the requirements of the report.

Activity 16.3

Reviewing reports

Find a published report in your library. Assess it according to the checklist in Table 16.2. What are the major omissions?

Table 16.2 **Questions to ask when reviewing a report**

Title page	*Are all the details required present and correct?*
Contents page	Is the list complete and correct?
	Is there a list of tables and charts?
	Are the appendices listed in order and with a page reference?
Summary	Is this understandable on its own if the reader does not wish to read the whole report?
	Is it as concise as possible without any major omissions?
	Is it accurate?
Introduction	Is the background as brief as possible whilst providing sufficient information so that the reader understands the context?
	Are the terms of reference clearly stated?
	Does it motivate the reader to read the whole of the report?
Procedure/ method	Is the method used for gathering the information appropriate?
	Does this section enable the reader to establish the validity of the material?
Main body	Are the findings presented in a logical order?
	Does the text flow naturally?
	Is the language clear and precise?
	Are the facts and figures accurate?
	Are opinions and assertions supported?
	Is the material presented balanced?
	Is each main point well supported?
	Is the content relevant to the terms of reference?
	Are all the main aspects covered in sufficient depth?
	Is all the work correctly referenced?
Conclusions	Do these flow naturally from the main body?
	Has any new information been introduced?
	Are all the conclusions supported?
	Do the conclusions reflect a sound analysis of the material?
Recom- mendations	Is each recommendation listed in an order corresponding to the conclusions?
	Is it clear what action is required?
	Are they relevant to the terms of reference?
	Are they appropriate and practical?
	Do they fulfil the aim of the report?

See downloadable template 16.1 EVALUATING A REPORT for your Personal Development Plan online.

Table 16.2 **continued**

Title page	Are all the details required present and correct?
Appendices	Are there any omissions? Are they in the correct order and numbered accordingly?
Bibliography	Are there any omissions? Is this accurate? Is it presented in the correct format?
References	Are there any omissions? Can the reader trace the references from the information given?
Glossary	Do all the technical terms used appear? Are the terms explained in a way that a non-expert may understand?
Presentation	Is it clearly written and well laid out? Does it meet the needs of the reader? Are the grammar, punctuation and spelling correct?

Types of report

Reports may be written for a variety of purposes. Table 16.3 lists some guidelines for compiling reports for different situations.

Table 16.3 **Guidelines for compiling reports**

Purpose of report	Guidelines
Providing information (good news)	Be direct and present the main idea first. Present all the relevant information.
Providing information (bad news)	Present neutral or positive information first to provide a buffer. When presenting the bad news, provide any reasoning behind it. Avoid using jargon but be logical and clear so that there can be no misunderstanding. Try to be optimistic in concluding, offering a lesser alternative if this is appropriate.
Persuasive request	Get the reader's attention immediately. Present the strongest motivator first. Explain the advantages of accepting the proposal to the reader. Detail the action you want to see and when. If possible, offer some sort of incentive.

See downloadable template 16.2 FEEDBACK ON WRITTEN REPORTS for your Personal Development Plan online.

Table 16.3 **continued**

Purpose of report	Guidelines
Proposal	Provide an outline of the current situation.
	Give a reasoned account of the steps leading to the proposal.
	Outline the advantages and disadvantages of the proposal.
Problem solving	Define the problem clearly and concisely.
	Provide a clear analysis of the problem.
	Indicate the consequences of not addressing the problem.
	Give the possible solutions to the problem.
	Indicate how you are going to evaluate the solutions presented.
	Provide recommendations for dealing with the problem.

→ Group reports

Sometimes an assessment may involve the completion of a group report. One way of approaching this is for each member of the group to look at a different aspect and thus complete a separate section. If this is the case, care must be taken that the finished product is presented as a coherent piece of work, in both content and style. This can take some time, so ensure that there is enough time to do it properly.

In completing a group report, it is essential to hold regular meetings of the group so that progress can be monitored and any problems discussed.

Activity 16.4

Writing reports

1 Identify and examine a problem on campus (e.g. registration, lack of computer facilities) and prepare a report for the appropriate administrator recommending an effective response to the situation.

2 Prepare a report for the university about the cost of studying at university. Outline the methodology used to gather the information about the major expenses that students have to meet, draw conclusions and make recommendations as to how students may reduce their expenses.

Summary

This chapter has explained that:

- writing effective reports is a lengthy process, requiring careful planning and perseverance
- Many organisations have a particular 'house' style, which you may be required to use when constructing a report – if not, it is important to ensure that all the aspects required are covered
- effective reports achieve their purpose, conveying their message authoritatively and convincingly with material presented objectively, accurately and logically
- any opinions or assertions should be supported with facts and any irrelevant material omitted
- reports should be concise but complete and comprehensible.

Presenting to others

Many people are terrified of presenting to a group at first. Most, with practice, come to enjoy it, though usually with an element of nervousness. This chapter looks at the necessary skills and suggests ways in which you can improve your skills as a presenter. You may not become brilliant at it – such people are rare – but you can become good enough to get high marks and impress employers.

Learning outcomes

By the end of this chapter you should:

- be alert to the things that can go wrong with presentations
- have assessed your own strengths and weaknesses in this area
- be able to structure a presentation in a way that is appropriate to your audience
- be developing your delivery technique
- be using visual aids to good effect
- be confident in handling questions from your audience
- be able to control nervousness.

The final face-to-face communication skill you need is that of making a presentation to a group. Poor presentations can be an ordeal for speaker and audience; good ones can be a delight for both. Furthermore, both good and bad presentations are *remembered*. Whether you are presenting your research results to a group of potential collaborators, talking to a group of senior managers in your own organisation, making a pitch to a potential major client or giving an after-dinner speech for a professional association, it is important to make a good impression. You may pay an invisible price for years to come if you do not. On the other hand, if you do well, unexpected opportunities may come your way far into the future. You will also have an immediate feeling of power and euphoria from having had your audience exactly where you want them.

→ Ch 2, 6, 9

This chapter addresses the problem of nervousness and the skills that you need to make a good presentation. Again, these overlap with skills already covered. Being clear about your objectives, understanding your listeners' (albeit now in the plural) needs, expressing yourself appropriately and clearly and checking understanding will be as important as in one-to-one talking or in making a contribution to a group discussion. But additionally you need to know how to ensure that your audience can see and hear you, to gain and hold their attention and to use visual aids to good effect. The bulk of the chapter looks at presenting formally to a captive audience. However, there is a short section on presenting more informally via a poster display with a passing audience.

THE RISKS IN PRESENTATION

Presentations, like written papers or reports, need to be carefully ordered. They need a clear message and should, where possible, use graphs, tables or other illustrations to reinforce the verbal argument. However, the fact that you and your audience are operating in real time makes the risks far greater. If something is difficult to express in writing, you can keep trying until you get it right. If your reader finds that concentration has lapsed, they can go and make a cup of tea, then try reading again from where they 'switched off'. In a live presentation, neither presenter nor audience has a second chance.

There is normally less interchange between speaker and listeners in a formal presentation than in one-to-one or group discussion. Keeping the audience awake, interested and involved is therefore a considerable challenge. You probably know all too well how easy it is to stop concentrating in a lecture and have found sitting still and being 'talked at' a fairly stressful experience. Unfortunately, the older you get, the harder it becomes to be a member of an audience.

As in other areas, the best way to become more aware of what is required is to look at what other people do less than well. You can then look at how those who are more competent do the same thing. Once you are more alert to the different dimensions required, you will be better able to reflect on, and develop, your own skills.

ACTIVITY 11.1

Think of an unsatisfactory presentation that you have attended recently (lectures are fair game here, as well as presentations by fellow students). List all the factors which contributed to your dissatisfaction. Now think of an experience of a good presentation. List any additional features which distinguished this. (You can go on to do this again at the next presentation you attend.)

Good features: _____

_____

Bad features: _____

_____

If your experience is anything like mine, your list of bad practice might include occasions when the speaker did some or even all of the following:

- read a prepared speech in 'written' rather than 'spoken' English
- mumbled, whispered, went too fast or was otherwise inaudible
- used illegible visual aids – perhaps with far too much text in the smallest font
- faced away from you, perhaps while writing on the board or flipchart
- used a hypnotic monotone making sleep irresistible, probably with no visual aids at all
- distributed handouts during the presentation, so that you read these rather than listened
- was muddled incomprehensible, or said nothing you did not already know
- 'lost the thread' by responding at length to barely relevant questions
- went on long beyond the scheduled end
- got into an argument with a single member of the audience.

The remainder of the chapter addresses these common faults as well as covering features which may well have appeared on your list of 'good' points.

→ Ch 1

ACTIVITY 11.2

Did you mention presentation skills as a strength in your SWOT in Chapter 1? If not, use the following questionnaire to assess your skill level (score 5 if the statement is completely true, 4 if mostly true, 3 if it is neither true nor untrue, 2 if it is not very true, and 1 if it is totally untrue)

I have lots of experience in giving presentations _____

The presentations I give are usually very well received _____

I always think carefully about what I need to communicate, and how best to do it to any particular audience _____

I am good at thinking of how to use visual aids to reinforce my message _____

I am confident in using PowerPoint to produce effective overheads _____

I think it is really important to watch the audience, and modify a presentation if it does not seem to be working _____

Total _____

If your score is 25 or above you should not need this chapter – assuming your assessment of your skills is accurate. Below this, you might think about developing an action plan to improve aspects of your skills.

STRUCTURE

The importance of structure was emphasised in the context of written communications, but it is even more important in a presentation. It is very easy for your audience to lose the thread of what you are saying and very hard for them to find it again if they do. They cannot go back and read the difficult bit again. So the classic advice of 'Say what you are going to say, say it, then tell them what you have said' still holds good.

Introduction

You need to settle your audience, so say who you are, what you are aiming to achieve, how long you will be talking and how you plan to operate. Do you want to save all questions except those for clarification to the end, for example, or are you happy to take questions at any point? Will you be handing out copies of your overhead transparencies (OHTs) at the end or do people need to take notes? Once the ground rules have been established, you then need to outline the main points that you will be covering during your presentation. If you can say something that catches your audience's attention at the outset and makes them *want* to hear what follows, then the presentation is likely to go well.

Good presentations:
- have a clear structure
- are clearly signposted
- are clearly delivered
- use varied visual aids
- interest the audience
- do not overrun.

Main presentation

As with a written report, you need to make clear what situation or topic you are addressing and use evidence to support the arguments you are making. Because of the difficulty of following a spoken argument, you need to make your structure absolutely clear and give your audience as much help as possible on this: 'What I have established thus far is . . . (brief summary). The next point I want to make is . . .'. If you give such pointers at regular intervals, perhaps with OHTs to reinforce them, your audience will find it easier to maintain concentration and to stay with your argument.

Conclusion

This is the 'tell them what you have said' section. You need to summarise the points you have made, again using visual aids to reinforce them if possible. If you are making a proposal, then it is worth emphasising the main points of this again. It is also good practice to thank the audience for their patience and to invite questions or discussion.

DELIVERY TECHNIQUE

If you do come across good presenters, study them carefully to see if there are ways in which you could improve your own performance. Even if you are not exposed to skilled practitioners, the following guidelines will give you a good foundation.

Relate to your audience

Talking to a point on the back wall, in an impersonal style, will put an unhelpful distance between you and your audience. Try to sound human in your introduction. Look at people. Say things in the way that they are most likely to understand. Check with them that you are on the right lines: 'Was that point clear?', 'Can you all see this slide?', 'Am I going too fast?'

Make it easy for people to hear

Speak clearly, not too fast, and vary your tone. Use short sentences and straightforward language, avoiding unnecessary jargon. Use 'spoken language' not 'written language'.

If you have ever heard someone (literally) read a paper they have written, you will probably be all too aware of the difference. If not, try reading part of a journal article out loud, then rephrase it using words you would normally use in talking. Avoid turning your back on your audience (whiteboards are a real hazard here) or being hidden by equipment.

Try to be interesting

Vary your pace and use a variety of visual aids if there are appropriate ones. Even something as simple as showing a pile of ten books on a subject can reinforce the point that there has been a lot written on it. Occasional humour can be useful, but don't overdo it (unless you are making an after-dinner speech, when a high proportion of jokes seems to be the norm). Above all, make the relevance of what you are saying clear. It may be less obvious to your audience why something is significant than it is to you: you need to *work* at making sure that they see it too.

Beware of becoming bogged down in detail

It is far harder to absorb detail from a spoken presentation than from a written report. More often, the detail merely obscures the main point. Try to give only as much detail as you need to make your point. If a fine detail is crucial, it is probably better to give this as a handout for later perusal.

Avoid giving handouts while you speak

The distribution of handouts while you are talking distracts people, and you will lose your audience. It doesn't matter how often you say of a handout 'don't read this now' – the temptation to look at it immediately seems universally irresistible. If you distribute handouts before you start, early arrivals will have something to do while they wait. It will also be clear to them how many additional notes (if any) they need to take. Handouts distributed at the end can be a good way of concluding, but you need to tell people at the outset that you are going to do this, otherwise they can feel annoyed if they have taken careful notes which the handout makes superfluous.

Keep your notes brief

Particularly if you are new to giving presentations, you are likely to be tempted to write out the whole thing. Then you know you can avoid grinding to a stop because all you have to do is keep reading. Writing it out can be helpful, and the reassurance of knowing you *could* read it if absolutely necessary is very comforting. But try to keep that as an emergency measure. Even if you do write out a full-text version, you should also write briefer notes from which, barring the onset of total panic, you will actually speak.

These notes should indicate the key points to be made, in order. Such notes are ideally made on index cards. Number them or join them with a treasury tag just in case you drop them. Trying frantically to reorder a hopeless jumble of cards while facing an audience can be deeply embarrassing. Indicate in your notes each point at which you need to use a visual aid. And cross-refer to your transcript so that you can easily switch to that if necessary. (After a few presentations, when you have never used the full notes, you will probably feel confident enough to dispense with them.)

Watch your audience

You need feedback on your delivery and people may not tell you in words. But you will be able to see, if you look, whether a glaze of incomprehension is stealing over your audience. If so, you may need to slow down and explain more, or perhaps check understanding by asking a question. If eyelids are drooping, you may be going too slowly already or have underestimated the prior knowledge of people there. Or you may need to vary your delivery more. If people are tense, tapping feet or fingers with restrained force, you are seriously getting on their nerves and need to find out why. As soon as you pick up signals that all is not well, try to work out why. Unless you are fairly sure what you are doing wrong, *ask* what the problem is – and adapt your presentation in the light of the answers.

Be honest

Trying to fool people seldom works. If there is a weakness in your case, admit it rather than hoping that no one will notice. If they do notice, they will not think well of you for seemingly failing to spot the weakness yourself. But if you admit to it and have formed a good relationship with your audience, they may help you to strengthen the point. Similarly, pretending to know something when in fact you don't may make you look foolish. But admitting your ignorance may allow someone in the audience who does know to contribute their knowledge – to everyone's advantage.

Manage your time

Inexperienced presenters are often surprised at how little it is possible to communicate in a specified time. This is because they do not allow for speech being slower than reading, for questions of clarification, for introductions, for interim summaries or for use of visual aids. It is important to judge how long a presentation will take and adjust it if a dry run shows that your guess is wrong. Aim to undershoot slightly. It is generally better to risk allowing slightly too long for questions than to run out of time, and to finish a little early rather than overrun.

EFFECTIVE VISUAL AIDS

Communication will be far more effective in either writing or speaking if you use images to reinforce your words. Visual aids have already been mentioned several times: this should have indicated that they are essential in formal presentations of any length or complexity. Such aids have three main functions: they can help the audience *understand* a point; they can help the audience *remember* a point; and they can keep your audience *awake*. To make good use of visual aids, you need to think about how each of your points could be reinforced by an action, an object or a picture, and then how best to achieve this reinforcement. The best visual aid to use will depend on both the point you are making and the audience to whom you are making it.

Visual aids can:
- reinforce key points
- clarify meaning
- aid retention
- keep audience awake.

Some things can be conveyed far more effectively by means other than words alone. Relationships are more clearly shown in diagrams, whereas trends are clearly demonstrated in graphs. Other chapters cover representing data visually and diagramming other aspects of a situation, also incorporating the results in written reports. The same principles apply, though within the restrictions of what can be seen from a distance. Revise these principles if you are in doubt. But although you will probably use visual aids similar to those suitable for a report for most of your points, your scope in a spoken presentation is potentially far wider.

Video clips of products, processes, people or places can be hugely effective. Concrete objects can also make a lasting impression. To take an example, when I am running open events to attract potential Open University students, one thing I need to explain is how distance learning works. It is not always obvious that a subject like management can be studied effectively at a distance. So I *show* the audience a course pack, with all the CDs and written units. I *show* them course assignments, covered in teaching comments from the tutor. I may *show* them extracts from teaching videos or a video of a tutorial. This allows me to convey far more about the course than would a mere description. If I wanted to make a point about the volume of reading on a conventional course, I might show the audience a pile of the books on the recommended reading list.

I have seen speakers hold up broken items to make a point about quality, or a new product to make a different point. Cognitive psychologist Stephen Pinker held up a comb to make a point about the innate distastefulness of using a comb to stir coffee. Such images make a lasting impression – though the point they demonstrated is not always clearly remembered. If the image is too strong, then it may overshadow the point (what *was* the significance of this particular distaste?). But this slight caution aside, apart from points which are made better by use of visual aids, people also tend to remember what they see better than what they hear. It is therefore worth using visual aids even to reinforce points which can be made adequately in words in order to aid their retention.

It is also important to incorporate variety to keep people awake and interested. For any presentation longer than, say, half an hour, it is worth using a range of visual aids for this reason alone. You can mix PowerPoint slides (or prepared OHTs) with diagrams you draw on a board or flipchart at an appropriate point (do this quickly and avoid talking while drawing). If appropriate and you have the facilities, video clips and animated PowerPoint slides (used selectively) can help to enliven the presentation.

If your talk is short, you do not need to work so hard at keeping people's attention, and too much variety in visual aids can be counterproductive. It is better to reserve them for points that are best made visually, plus those which you really wish to emphasise. More will be a distraction.

It is now normal to use presentation software: PowerPoint is virtually the standard in management presentations, although other packages are available. This allows far more flexibility than was available before the invention of the laptop. Suppose you are talking with potential clients prior to a presentation and discover that they have concerns that you had not realised when you prepared your presentation. In a couple of minutes you can add a slide or two to address these. You can easily edit the slides you used on one occasion to provide a modified presentation for another occasion. You can easily incorporate charts and graphs from a report into your presentation, or

→ Ch 7, 14 diagrams from your presentation into a report. The use of PowerPoint was discussed in

Chapter 5, and you should aim to become proficient in the use of presentations software if you are not already.

Whatever the kind of visual aid you are using, consider how to maximise its impact and the message it conveys. Your aim is to communicate, and your visual aids are a tool for this, not something to be considered in isolation. Overcomplexity, too many animations and sound effects and too many slides may actually interfere with communication. Fancy backgrounds distract and reduce clarity. Animations may look impressive but are similarly distracting. While it is sometimes extremely useful to build up a picture a bit at a time, you should restrict use of the facility to such times. Words continually flying in from left and right will seldom help your audience to grasp and retain the points you are making. And now that everyone can use PowerPoint, being expert in its use is less impressive than once it might have been. Remember at all times that you are trying to communicate effectively, and use the tools at your disposal to this end alone.

There are less obvious, but perhaps more serious hazards with PowerPoint in terms of the way that it can easily constrain your presentation to an endless series of bullet points. As Naughton (2003) pointed out, PowerPoint was conceived in a software sales environment, so it tends to turn everything into a sales pitch. There was a version of the Gettysburg address doing the email rounds a while ago that demonstrated this limitation (see **www.norvig.com/Gettysburg** for some light relief on this topic). But Tufte, a Yale professor and expert on visual communication, goes further in his criticism, arguing that PowerPoint's ready-made templates tend to weaken verbal and spatial reasoning and corrupt statistical analysis. He attributes the Columbia space shuttle disaster to a slide that led Nasa to overlook the destructive potential of the crucial loose tile (see 'PowerPoint does rocket science', on Tuft's website **www.edwardtufte.com**). His analysis may also add to your understanding of the idea of argument mapping outlined in Chapter 4.

→ Ch 4

General requirements for visual aids

It may sound blindingly obvious, but many people ignore the requirement for an audience to be able to *see* visual aids if they are to be of use. Even experienced speakers have been known to show slides which reproduce a full-page table from a book, with perhaps 200 numbers in invisibly small type. The amount of effective information you can convey on a slide is surprisingly small. Before finalising your visual aids, check that they will be visible to the normal eye from the same distance as the back of the room in which you will make your presentation. A good rule of thumb is to aim at no more than four points per slide.

Colour can either enhance or hinder clarity. Think about how you use it. I have seen tasteful but totally useless slides in shades of blue on blue, the words invisible from more than three paces. Use both colour and light/dark contrast to enhance legibility and emphasise key points. And be careful about fancy backgrounds: they may look good in themselves but they obscure your message.

For 'transient' presentations, for example on group work, where all you are seeking is to convey your thought processes to fellow students, it is fine to use flip charts or acetates. But it is still important that you manage the amount of information per chart, and ensure that charts will be legible from the farthest seat. (Avoid using red pen, or any light colour, as these are not easily visible at a distance.) You can prepare flipchart sheets in the same way as slides and ask a fellow student to be responsible for displaying the right one on cue. (Trying to talk and manage a flipchart is possible but not easy. It helps considerably to split the responsibility.)

If you are still using OHTs, another obvious point (well, I wish it *were* obvious) is always to use photocopying, not write-on, acetate in a copier. Photocopier acetate is firmer and the box should be clearly labelled as suitable for copying. The write-on sort melts in the machine, making a mess which only the engineer can sort out, and which will make you unpopular all round.

ACTIVITY 11.3

You can easily assemble an exhibit for your portfolio that addresses both your ability to use images and your ability to read and respond to materials. Take as the basis for this a presentation you make in class, perhaps summarising something you have studied. Your presentation needs to include appropriate visual aids. You also need a way of obtaining feedback from your tutor and/or those present. The exhibit should include the notes for your talk and copies of the images used, together with a description of how you selected both content and images, feedback on their effectiveness and what you would do differently next time in the light of this feedback.

HANDLING QUESTIONS

Sometimes questions are helpful, but I have seen them wreck a presentation completely. Until you are fairly experienced, and feel confident that you can handle questions during your talk, it is safer to take substantive questions at the end. Make it clear at the outset that during your presentation you will deal only with requests for clarification and that there will be time for questions at the end. Otherwise, you risk being completely sidetracked from your main argument or disconcerted by challenges to what you are saying before you have completed your case. If you want to postpone a question, either take a note of it so that you do not forget or, better still, ask the questioner to ask it again at the end. This means that your brain is not distracted by trying to remember the question while giving the talk.

When you do accept a question, your listening skills will be important. It is hard to listen carefully when you are nervous, particularly if someone is asking a complex multiple question. If this happens, jot down the key parts of the question, otherwise it is easy to answer the first part and forget all the rest. If you are at all uncertain what the question means, clarify this with the questioner. You may feel that it makes you look stupid if you don't understand. But if the questioner is far from clear it is sensible to pick up on this. You may tie yourself in knots if you try to answer a question that you have only partially understood: this does not look all that impressive either.

If a question challenges what you have said, resist the temptation to become either defensive or aggressive. Take the contrasting view seriously, looking for ways to develop your position in the light of it, unless you are convinced that the questioner really has missed the point of what you were saying or is misinformed. If the point has been missed by the questioner, it is possible that others missed it too, and finding another way of making it may be helpful. But if you cannot quickly satisfy the questioner, it is usually better to suggest that you discuss it after the presentation is finished, rather than get into an argument that will be of little interest to most of the audience.

People ask questions for many reasons. In work presentations, there will be some who are trying to make an impression on the audience, perhaps with a view to establishing themselves as a rival expert or advertising their own business. Or they may simply like being the centre of attention. Where questions are clearly being asked in the questioner's personal interest, it is simplest to thank them for raising their point, agree with as much of the point as you can, perhaps suggest a discussion outside the meeting and move on to the next question.

If questions reveal a genuine weakness in your presentation, it is usually better to accept this and ask for suggestions from the questioner and the audience for ways around the difficulty. You may find that someone can suggest a way forward. If, however, the difficulty seems to you to be much less significant than the questioner is suggesting, you will need to make sure that the audience does not end up devaluing the bulk of what you have said.

POSTER PRESENTATIONS

Thus far the chapter has addressed formal presentations to a (normally) seated audience. At conferences it is common to supplement the formal presentation programme with less formal poster presentations. A large space will be made available, and each presenter will be allocated wall space for a poster. The audience will wander round the room, looking at the various displays and stopping to discuss those of particular interest with the 'presenter', who will be standing by the poster ready to answer questions.

This allows participants access to a much greater number of presenters than would otherwise be the case, and is often used to allow students to present their research. If you are doing a dissertation you may have the opportunity to take part in a poster session within the university or at a larger conference. This sort of presentation is also sometimes used in organisational contexts, at meetings between members of different project groups, so it is worth extending your presentation skills to include this format. In either case the poster presentation tends to be aimed primarily at peers and/or colleagues.

Poster presentations present different communication challenges to the presenter. The 'talking' part tends to be less intimidating: you are talking to people individually or in very small groups. On the other hand, these conversations are equivalent to the 'questions' part of a formal presentation, which is in many respects the most challenging part as much of the control passes to the questioner.

The real challenge for most, however, is in poster design. Typically you will have a space 1 metre high, and 1.5–1.75 metres wide. This space has to work hard for you. As with any communication, your first task is to clarify your objectives. What do you want the poster to achieve? Clearly this will depend on what you are presenting upon and the context in which you are presenting. Are you simply aiming to inform as many participants as possible? If so, what are the key points you are trying to get across? Are you trying to sell yourself or your research, and if so, to whom? Are you aiming to engage colleagues in conversation? If so, what would you particularly like to talk with them about? Are you seeking like-minded people from other universities with whom to network? If so, what would be most likely to interest such people? This is not an exhaustive list. It merely indicates the sort of objectives you might have. You need to be absolutely clear of your objectives on each occasion.

Posters aim to:
- attract
- inform
- start conversations
- advertise your work
- summarise achievements.

Clarity is paramount because 1.5 square metres is not very big, and anything within this space has to be visible from around 1.5 metres away. So every word needs to count, and you need to use pictures (or graphs or whatever) as much as possible. Aim to 'show' rather than 'tell'. A good rule of thumb is 20 per cent text, 40 per cent graphics and 40 per cent space. This last 40 per cent is not a 'waste of precious space'. You could cram more into it, but the overall effect would be far less than the impact of what you can communicate via the 60 per cent if it is well laid out.

Given this limitation on what you can effectively include, there are some important questions to answer.

- What are your (very few) key points?
- How can you convey these graphically?
- How can you lay these out on a poster so that they will communicate to someone walking past at a distance of up to 2 metres?

Remember, you may be in competition with dozens of other posters, and participants will not look in any detail at more than a small proportion of these. You will not have time to talk to everybody even if you attract them. So how can you ensure that you engage those people with whom you are likely to have the most profitable conversations, prime them to ask the most useful questions, and leave a favourable impression both of you personally and of the work that you have done?

If you Google 'poster presentations' you will find a wealth of information on how to lay out posters for maximum impact. The essential messages are:

- You need to say who you are, where you come from and the topic covered by your poster – IN VERY LARGE WRITING.
- You need to have a clear 'path' through the poster so that people can follow the narrative easily.
- You cannot afford to waste a single word – 'Findings' or 'methodology' do not convey information by themselves. Something like '80% misunderstand age

legislation' carries a message. Think newspaper headlines here. Writ large, and with bar charts or other simple graphics to support them.

▪ You need a way of continuing the exchange when you have 'engaged' someone's interest. At the very least show your email address clearly on the poster. But it is even better to have a handout expanding on key points, with your email address on it. Safest of all, particularly if your key aim is to network, is to have people write *their* email address (or write it for them) and email a more substantial document – the text behind the headlines – a couple of days later, with a note saying how much you enjoyed talking to them.

Figure 11.1 shows two possible layouts for poster presentations for a standard research presentation. You may be able to be far more creative – but do remember the need for clarity from 2 metres distance. Messy and cluttered do not, on the whole, attract.

CONTROLLING YOUR NERVES

It is natural to be nervous when standing up in front of a group of people, whether in formal presentation or in a poster display. The adrenaline it generates can give your performance an excitement that it would otherwise lack, so do not aim to become totally blasé about it. But excess nerves can be a liability, drying your throat and making you physically and verbally clumsy. If you think that you are worrying more than is reasonable, there are several things that can help considerably: get as much practice as you can; concentrate on exposing yourself to similar situations; practise deliberate relaxation; and prepare for each specific presentation.

Increase your confidence in presenting by:
▪ frequent practice
▪ relaxation techniques
▪ thorough preparation.

If you *are* over-nervous, you probably avoid all situations where you need to talk in front of people, or to strangers one to one. But the best way to reduce nervousness is to seek out such situations and force yourself to talk. Find the least threatening situations first – talking to a small group of students before addressing the whole class, getting used to the class before giving a paper at a conference. But *do* it. Each time you will feel less nervous.

This is one form of practice which 'desensitises' you to the general trauma of the situation. Another form is to have one or more 'practice runs' of a specific presentation. This will mean that you are confident about the structure of the talk, have practised some of the phrases you will use, know where to use your OHTs or other visual aids and have checked how long it takes, so that you are not worried about having too much or too little material.

→ Ch 2 Relaxation techniques, discussed as part of stress management in Chapter 2, can help reduce this sort of stress too, though you need to be familiar with the techniques for best effect. If you have not yet practised them, a short period of deep breathing will help. And a *small* alcoholic drink can sometimes be useful.

But your best weapon against nerves is the knowledge that you have done everything possible to prepare for the event, that you have carefully researched your subject and audience, your talk (or poster) is well structured and your notes are well organised,

Sheila Cameron The Open University	LEADERSHIP: THE ANSWER TO EVERYTHING?

| Introduction
xxxxxxxxxxxx
xxxxxxxxxxxx
xxxxxxxxxxxx
xxxxxxxxxxxx
xxxxxxxxxxxx
xxxxxxxxxxxx |  | Title C
xxxxxxxxxxxx
xxxxxxxxxxxx
xxxxxxxxxxxx
xxxxxxxxxxxx
xxxxxxxxxxxx
xxxxxxxxxxxx |

| Title A
xxxxxxxxxxxx
xxxxxxxxxxxx
xxxxxxxxxxxx
xxxxxxxxxxxx
xxxxxxxxxxxx
xxxxxxxxxxxx | Title B
xxxxxxxxxxxxxxxxxxxxxxxxxxx
xxxxxxxxxxxxxxxxxxxxxxxxxxx
xxxxxxxxxxxxxxxxxxxxxxxxxxx
xxxxxxxxxxxxxxxxxxxxxxxxxxx
xxxxxxxxxxxxxxxxxxxxxxxxxxx
xxxxxxxxxxxxxxxxxxxxxxxxxxx | Conclusion
xxxxxxxxxxxx
xxxxxxxxxxxx
xxxxxxxxxxxx
xxxxxxxxxxxx
xxxxxxxxxxxx
xxxxxxxxxxxx |

Sheila Cameron The Open University	LEADERSHIP: THE ANSWER TO EVERYTHING?

| Context
xxxxxxxxxxxxxx
xxxxxxxxxxxxxx
xxxxxxxxxxxxxx
xxxxxxxxxxxxxx
xxxxxxxxxxxxxx | 2
xxxxxxxxxxxxxx
xxxxxxxxxxxxxx
xxxxxxxxxxxxxx
xxxxxxxxxxxxxx
xxxxxxxxxxxxxx
xxxxxxxxxxxxxx
xxxxxxxxxxxxxx
xxxxxxxxxxxxxx | 4
xxxxxxxxxxxxxx
xxxxxxxxxxxxxx
xxxxxxxxxxxxxx
xxxxxxxxxxxxxx
xxxxxxxxxxxxxx
xxxxxxxxxxxxxx
xxxxxxxxxxxxxx
xxxxxxxxxxxxxx
xxxxxxxxxxxxxx |

| 1
xxxxxxxxxxxxxx
xxxxxxxxxxxxxx
xxxxxxxxxxxxxx
xxxxxxxxxxxxxx
xxxxxxxxxxxxxx
xxxxxxxxxxxxxx | 3 | 5
xxxxxxxxxxxxxx
xxxxxxxxxxxxxx |

Fig 11.1 Possible layouts for poster presentations

your visual aids well chosen and you have at your fingertips supporting evidence and examples. Dry runs, described above, can be part of your preparation. Remember, a presentation is a challenge, but it can be exciting and rewarding, and can provoke interesting discussion on a subject dear to your heart. Preparation is so important that more detail is given below.

Even if you have prepared, you may well experience an initial onrush of nerves when you stand up to make a formal presentation. To get you over this, make sure that you have your introductory remarks written out in full, preferably learned by heart. Take a sip of water and a deep breath, go over your introduction and by then you will have calmed down enough to enjoy yourself.

PREPARATION

Preparation is the key to successful presentation and you cannot afford to cut corners if you want to do well. You need to have thought carefully about what to communicate, how to structure it and how to add impact to your arguments by examples and visual aids. For important presentations, you will want to rehearse your arguments several times. Much of this can be done piecemeal, for example while exercising or in a waiting room, *sotto voce*. But you will need one full-scale, real-time rehearsal to check timing, use of aids and flow of arguments – or responses to a poster and likely questions. Ideally, find colleagues or friends to act as an audience and ask them to give you feedback afterwards. If this is impossible, then, for a formal presentation, tape yourself and replay the tape after a decent interval, listening critically and noting points where you need to change something. For a poster, come back to it a few days later and try to pretend that you know nothing about the topic.

If you are giving a presentation at work, to clients or potential customers, or a paper at a conference, your preparation needs to extend to ensuring that the location is set up as you want it, temperature is appropriate and equipment working properly. You do not want to be hunting for porters or chasing around for a fresh bulb for the projector while half the audience has arrived and is watching your increasing panic. So arrive early and make all the necessary checks.

Preparation for your *next* presentation should be informed by feedback from the last, so it is important to capture as much feedback as possible. Make a note of your immediate reactions in the light of audience response. Do this as soon as possible after the event, noting in your learning journal your feelings and points for future action. If possible, have a friend in the audience charged with giving you their reactions and suggestions. You may even be able to design and distribute a short questionnaire for the audience to complete on leaving. If the presentation is one of a series, this can be extremely useful in helping you to adjust future events to meet audience needs more effectively. If you are likely to have the chance to participate in more than one poster display, feedback may have the same benefits. If you are preparing an exhibit on your presentation skills, it will be important to include all such feedback.

SUMMARY

This chapter has argued the following:

- Presentation skills are an important part of communication in the work context and may indeed be tested during selection procedures.

- During your studies you will have many opportunities to develop these skills and they may even influence some of your marks.

- Successful presentation depends on adequate preparation. You need to be clear on your objectives and those of your audience, and structure is even more important here than with written communications.

- Good visual aids help audience concentration, comprehension and retention. Using PowerPoint or a similar package to project slides from your PC is flexible and looks professional.

- Audibility, visibility and ability to pace your delivery to suit your audience and your content are essential.

- Questions can be an asset or a disruption. Substantive ones are probably best taken at the end.

- Poster displays present major challenges of distilling the core message into words and graphics visible from 1.5–2 metres away.

- Extreme nervousness can be disabling but lower levels can help. Practice, relaxation and preparation will help you to reduce excessive nerves.

Further information

- Bradley, A. (2006) *Successful Presentation Skills*, 3rd edn, Kogan Page.
- Collins, J./Video Arts (1998) *Making Effective Presentations*, Kogan Page.
- Conradi, M. and Hall, R. (2001) *That Presentation Sensation*, Financial Times Prentice Hall.
- Leech, T. (2001) *Say it like Shakespeare*, McGraw-Hil. This gives an interestingly different slant on presenting.
- Manchester Open Learning (1993) *Making Effective Presentations*, Kogan Page.
- Williams, J.S. (1995) *The Right Way to Make Effective Presentations*, Elliot Right Way Books.
- **http://www.ncsu.edu/project/posters/NewSite/** – there are many useful websites but try this one.

Index

Tax S

WOKING

Made Ea

Stefan Bernstein

The author is a qualified tax consultant with practices in London and Wiltshire. He advises corporations and individuals on their financial planning strategies. In addition, is a registered representative of the Stock Exchange and founder member of the Institute of Financial Planning.

TAKE THAT LTD.

Take That Ltd.
P.O.Box 200
Harrogate
HG1 2YR

By Stefan Bernstein

10 9 8 7 6 5 4 3 2 1

ISBN 1-873668-09-0

Printed and bound in Great Britain.

Contents

Appendices

Preface

"Like it or not, a knowledge of self-assessment will be vital if you are to avoid the pitfalls which await you"

When Tax Self-assessment was first discussed, like many people, I didn't take it particularly seriously. Even as a practitioner, it seemed like it would be nothing more than another technical change, the like of which we are used to dealing with on a very frequent basis. However, there is a great deal more to self-assessment than that. For a start, the Inland Revenue tell us that 9,000,000 people are affected, but I suspect that there will actually be more.

The Inland Revenue invested a small fortune in a massive training programme, not only for their own staff, but for accountants and lawyers. They clearly recognised the changes they made were far reaching and could be complicated. In fact, self-assessment used to be called 'a simplified assessment'. They soon dropped 'simplified' in favour of 'self'.

Like it or not, a knowledge of self-assessment will be vital if you are to avoid the pitfalls which await you, and the sometimes severe penalties which can be levied. There is no question about it, self-assessment is to be taken very seriously. The Inland Revenue are bound to take a dim view of anyone who simply tries to ignore what, for many tax professionals, is the most significant set of changes seen in their career.

Quoting directly from the Revenue's own publications, "Tax is your responsibility .... There may be penalties if you fail to comply." You have been warned!

Introduction

"Self-assessment is not a new tax. It is simply the system of collection and the obligations of the various parties which have changed."

Self-assessment has been called a major overhaul of the U.K. tax system, and in many ways it is. However, there is a great deal that remains unchanged, and which will be familiar to those of you who have a working knowledge of the outgoing system.

For many people, for example, employees paid by PAYE or those who are retired, the changes may not be that significant, although they should be understood because of the potential penalties for non-compliance. For others, however, notably company directors, the self-employed and so on, the changes are fundamental and considerable attention will need to be paid to the new dates for paying tax, the new dates for filing a tax return, the need to keep all sorts of records, and the various different penalties which can be levied if you fail.

But, self-assessment is not a new tax. All the old taxes with which you are familiar, Income tax, Capital Gains tax, National Insurance, Inheritance tax, VAT and so on, remain unchanged. It is simply the system of collection and the obligations of the various parties which have changed.

This book is intended to take you, step by step, through the various different alterations which have taken place. It is not a heavily technical manual, because until you understand the ground rules and have an overview, it is pointless to complicate matters with tax computations or statutory references. For the self-employed, the production of certain figures and schedules is unavoidable, but wherever possible anything that might slow your reading of the text, and your assimilation of the key information, has been placed in appendices at the back of the book. Once you have understood the basics, then it should be relatively simple for you to find out any depth of further detail that you require.

The Inland Revenue do have a support line which you can telephone, and many local offices have a counter that you can visit in order to have more difficult questions addressed. But, fundamentally, you simply need to adhere to the rules as they are briefly set out in this book. **So long as you are keeping your records, submitting accurate returns on time, and paying your tax without missing the relevant deadlines, then you will have reduced the likelihood of facing penalties or difficulties with the Inland Revenue.**

The structure of the book is intended to make clear what hasn't changed, so that you can understand the basics, and then, what has changed. Clearly, the focus at The Revenue is likely to be on the major changes they have brought about, but you will be unable to judge those changes without reminding yourself of how things used to work. The first chapter, therefore, is designed to confirm what remains in place.

Chapter One

The Survivors

"The basics of U.K. taxation remain broadly the same"

A great deal has survived the advent of self-assessment; this should not be overlooked. The basic rules which have been in place for decades remain so, and there will be very little defence if you try claiming that you have made mistakes because of the introduction of a new system. This section deals with the major concepts with which you should refresh your memory.

Tax Rates

The rates of tax have not changed. Accordingly, we still have Lower, Basic and Higher rates of income tax. The same applies to Capital Gains. National Insurance rates for employees, and indeed the self-employed, have also remained constant. Finally, stamp duty remains unaffected. All other things being equal, you should not find yourself paying more tax under self-assessment.

You should be aware, of course, that tax rates are liable to change in the Budget each year. Once announced, those tax rates should be brought in the following April. This has little to do with self-assessment which is concerned with how that tax is collected.

Tax Allowances

We are all entitled to some form of Income Tax Allowance. Usually referred to as our Personal Allowance. Once again, not only has the level of these allowances not changed, but the criteria for becoming entitled to them also remain the same. Accordingly, if you previously received the Single Person's Allowance as well as the Married Couple's Allowance, then nothing should change in that regard, and you will still have all your options regarding the transfer of unused allowances and so on.

PAYE

Millions of people are employed in jobs where they are required to pay tax under the "Pay as You Earn" system. What this means, is that individuals are given a tax code which approximates to the allowances to which they are entitled. Pay in excess of this tax code is then taxed at the Lower, Basic and Higher rates as appropriate, based on weekly or monthly entitlements. This system remains unaltered in concept by self-assessment. There are certain minor changes to Form P11D requirements which govern expenses and benefits such as motor cars, but generally speaking, the same system will continue to apply. You should still receive net pay based on your tax code allocated before the tax year begins. Self-assessment has the odd change to how over or under-payments are sorted out, but they should not have a significant effect.

This should come as quite a relief to millions of tax payers in the PAYE whose burden would have been enormous had that system changed. Incidentally, it is an extremely effective system raising billions of pounds for the Exchequer by using employers as collecting agencies. Being so efficient, the system did not require change!

The Tax Return

You will still be required to complete a tax return, although its format is fairly different, and the date for its submission is different. Nonetheless, the general requirement to report sources of income and gains remains with the taxpayer, and one could argue that it has been slightly extended (see later).

Liability to Tax

We are liable to tax, based on our residence status and where the income arises. Accordingly, non-residents earning money in Japan are unlikely to pay any U.K. Income Tax. Joe Bloggs, born and bred in Yorkshire, and working there, will. Self-assessment has not changed this in any way. Once again, certain reporting requirements have changed, and these are explained later.

Investment and Tax

You may still be liable to pay tax on your investments and the way each type of investment is taxed has not changed. As a handy reference *Appendix One* details various different types of investment and how they are taxed.

Chapter Two

The Most Significant Changes

"The variety of records which you might need to keep is very considerable."

This chapter is intended to consider fundamental changes and those changes most likely to catch out the ordinary taxpayer. Subsequent chapters give greater detail for the self-employed company director, investors, trustees and the retired. The following pages are the areas in which most difficulties are likely to arise.

Keeping Records

It has always been prudent to keep records, but those which were compulsory, and the number of taxpayers who had a mandatory requirement to keep them, was relatively small.

Now, all tax-payers will have to keep some form of record in order to substantiate their tax position.

Records Worth Keeping

- P60 • P45 • P11D
- Expenses Vouchers
- Share Dividend Slips
- Unit/Investment Trust Statements
- Building Societies Statements
- Bank Statements
- Life Assurance Proceeds
- Capital Assets

You might decide that keeping records is more bother than it is worth, but the penalties are serious, and can be as much as £3,000 for each incident of not keeping records, or keeping inadequate records.

The variety of records which you might need to keep is very considerable. The Inland Revenue, in their basic publications have listed over **100 different types of voucher or paperwork which you need to keep**. They have also made clear that certain types of electronic records will be acceptable.

As well as the tax forms that we perhaps have all kept in the past, such as P60s, P45s and P11Ds, you may now be required to keep more detailed records, for example, business journeys in a company car, or in a car relieved against your self-employed profits. You will need to retain vouchers and dividends slips from your investments, along with interest statements from Building Societies and bank accounts. Keeping your bank statements would also be prudent, and you may even need to keep a record of proceeds from Life Assurance policies which you have sold or surrendered, or any capital assets.

The simple fact of the matter is that the onus is now on you.

You need to keep records to enable you to complete your tax return. Generally speaking, you will need to keep them for some 22 months after the end of the tax year to which they relate. Accordingly, the records to the year April 5th 1998 will need to be kept until January 2000.

For the self-employed, the requirement is even greater. They will need to keep records for five years after their fixed filing date. Some more details of these are in the next chapter.

All in all, this is one entirely new aspect of self-assessment which you must approach with due care and diligence.

Tax Return

Under the new rules, if you need a tax return for any reason, *and the tax man hasn't sent you one*, then the obligation rests with you to request one.

You might, for example, have received some sort of income or gains of which the Inland Revenue may not be aware. Perhaps you have sold some investments or a second home. Perhaps you received a small amount of one-off consultancy income. Maybe you have inherited some funds and invested them in the bank which now pays you interest. **In any of these circumstances, the obligation rests with the taxpayer to request, complete and submit the relevant tax return.**

Under the old system, you were obliged to notify income and gains to the Inland Revenue, but now the obligation is to do so within six months of the end of the tax year in which you received the relevant income or capital gains.

Completing your Return

You have three basic choices when you come to submit your return.

1. You can fill in the forms yourself and provide schedules, then send them to the Inland Revenue and ask them to calculate any tax that may be due.
2. You can fill in the forms yourself, and calculate the tax due.
3. You can approach an accountant or other qualified adviser in order to guide you.

The new tax return requires actual figures to be entered for your income or gains, and any deductions or reliefs which you may be claiming. You cannot leave items blank for the Inland Revenue to complete, as their only obligation is to calculate the tax for you if you choose that particular route.

The Submission of your Return

Let us use the first full year in which self-assessment applies as an example - the tax year 1997/98, i.e. the one that runs from 6th April 1997 to 5th April 1998.

If you want the Inland Revenue to calculate your tax, then you must submit your return with the supporting schedules (called **Supplementary Pages** by the Revenue) by 30th September 1998. You should note that this is one month earlier than under the old arrangement. The idea of this is to give the Inland Revenue sufficient time to calculate the tax that you owe so payment can be made by 31st January 1999.

If you decide that you are going to calculate the tax yourself, then you must submit your return with the relevant calculations and payment by 31st January 1999.

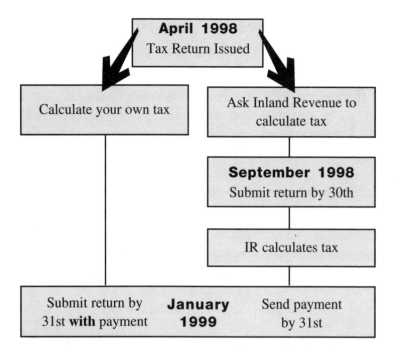

At first sight it may seem that, if we are talking about the year 1997/98, the tax is not really due until 31st January 1999, and so you will have a great deal of time. However, in practice, this will not be so. You will have to wait until 5th April 1998 before you know what your liabilities to income or gains tax might be. You will then have the summer to complete your return and send it in to the Revenue for them to calculate the tax.

If you are doing it yourself, then you also have most of the winter. But, beware, the summer contains the school holidays and the period up to 30th January will include Christmas - one thing the Inland Revenue could not change!

Crucial Dates

So, the crucial dates are 30th September, 31st January. The earlier date, if you want the tax man to do the maths, and the later date if you are confident to do your own.

PAYE

One important exception is that if you are taxed under the PAYE system, then any underpayment of tax will be collected through that system under the following year as long as your return is in by 30th September. If not, then the Inland Revenue cannot guarantee to collect it through the PAYE system, and will therefore have to raise an assessment on you.

Late Return

Under the old system, there were penalties for late returns, and this has not changed. However, the new system is rather clearer.

The 31st January date is absolutely clear, and you must abide by it. If you do not, then you will be subject to a fixed penalty which is at no-one's discretion. The fixed penalty is £100 if you have not sent in your return by 31st January in the tax year following the tax year to which it relates. Should you fail to have sent it in by the end of July in that same year, then a further £100 will be levied.

Many wealthy tax payers may consider one or two hundred pounds to be of no consequence. However, the Inland Revenue have further powers - if they think that the penalty is not likely to make you produce a tax return, then they may ask the Commissioners of Inland Revenue to apply further penalties -

and these penalties can be up to £60 a day! That's £420 a week, or more than £10,000 in six months!

In practice, such a severe penalty would only be levied at a persistent offender. Nonetheless, the facility is there, and you have been warned.

The Payment of Tax

Once again, this is an area in which a fundamental change has taken place. A brand new system of "payments on account" has been introduced. This is rather like the system which has been in place for the self-employed for many years. It is slightly difficult to grasp at first, but once you have understood it, should be fairly simple.

If you are required to make a payment on account, then you will make payments on:

- 31st January in the tax year, and
- 31st July following the end of the tax year.

If the two payments you have made amount to less, or more, than the amount which you should have paid, then a balancing payment, or repayments, will be made on the following 31st January.

Imagine therefore that you pay £5,000 on 31st January 1998, and £5,000 on 31st July 1998, but that your total tax due is only £8,000. On 31st January the following year, 1999, you will be due for a repayment of £2,000. (In practise, this will be offset against the payments which you are likely to be making in any event, so that the whole system should square itself up at that point.)

Calculating How Much To Pay

If you have decided to calculate your own tax, (and you recall this means that your tax return needs to be in by 31st January), then you will also calculate your own account payments. The process is as follows:

1. Take the figure for the tax you paid in the previous year. (This does not include Capital Gains tax and tax deducted at source).
2. Pay one half of this figure on the first date (31st January).
3. Pay the other half of the tax on the second (31st July).

One advantage of asking the Revenue to calculate your tax, is that they will also tell you if you have to make these payments on account, and they will tell you how much they are.

Please note that you will not have to make these payments on account for Capital Gains tax, or where your self-assessment represents a small proportion of your overall income - for example, if you earn £100,000 a year, but only have £500 of self-assessed income. The tax return explains this as you are completing it.

Paying Tax Late

You may decide to use the tax man as a bank, and either pay your tax late or deliberately underpay. If you do so, then you will be charged interest, just as you are under the present system. To be fair, if the figures fall the other way, then the Inland Revenue will pay you interest on any overpayments you may have made.

Very Late Payments

If you leave tax outstanding after the final payment date of the 31st January, then you may be subject to surcharges.

A 5% surcharge can be levied on any tax unpaid by 28th February after the end of the tax year. Moreover, a further 5% surcharge will be due on any amount you have still not paid by 31st July.

In their publications, the Inland Revenue point out that where such late payments are due to the inefficiencies of your accountant, you will still be liable, and not him.

Payments on Account Statements

The Inland Revenue are trying to be as user friendly as possible, and produce an account statement which resembles a credit card statement. This should enable you to keep track of your current position.

Chapter Three

The
Self-Employed

"You can expect the Inland Revenue to concentrate heavily on the self-employed."

Given that most employees are taxed under PAYE, and a great many investments are subject to deduction at source, then one of the major areas for the Inland Revenue's attention will be the self-employed. On the one hand, it should not be too difficult because the self-employed are already used to complying with a great many rules in respect of their tax affairs. On the other hand, being pressed for time in their work, they may have little spare time to devote to learning tax changes.

Whilst many self-employed people have some sort of professional advice, be it from a bookkeeper or accountant, there will still be obligations which ultimately fall to the self-employed individual to sort out. **The Revenue have made it clear in their publications that where an accountant makes an error, perhaps filing papers late or paying insufficient amounts of tax, the penalty will, of course, rest with the taxpayer.** For the self-employed, therefore, self-assessment is of considerable significance.

Who is Self-Employed?

There is some confusion as to the precise meaning of self-employed. Often, people work in a fairly self-sufficient role but they have only one "customer". It is quite possible that they would be construed as employed in those circumstances.

There are some important tax cases which have been decided over the years which seek to qualify whether or not certain individuals are employed or self-employed. For example, if you have a contract for service with an organisation, you are more likely to be employed than if you have a contract of services, (the difference is subtle but significant).

Another indication is whether or not you are taking financial risk in your endeavours, and whether or not you are using your own tools or premises.

The point behind this is that, under self-assessment, you have an obligation to inform the Inland Revenue within six months of the end of a tax year of any income or gains you may have had. It is crucial that you report such information in the correct format, stating whether or not you are self-employed or merely employed. There is also considerable obligation on your employer/customer to ensure they understand whether or not they are dealing with an employed or self-employed person. It is recommended that anyone who is in doubt clarifies this situation immediately. The consequences are considerable. For example, if you are deemed to be employing somebody, but have not deducted any tax simply because you thought they were self-employed, then you could suddenly find yourself with a considerable financial obligation of paying all the PAYE and National Insurance to which you previously thought you were not subject.

Similarly, for the individual employees/self-employed, there are very considerable difference in rules for what is a deductible expense and so on. In short, you must clarify your status.

Calculation of Tax

Self-employed people generally have a wider variation in their earnings than those people in regular employment. This is brought about by cyclical trading conditions, or it may be as a result of investment within the business. Additionally, there can be certain deductions, for example, new equipment or other charges, that can alter the level of profit declared. Accordingly, while self-employed people are calculating their own tax, there will be a good deal of work to do.

Alternatively, the self-employed can have the figures in early and allow the Revenue to calculate the tax. But it may be that cash flow considerations mean the self-employed must know what their tax liability is as soon as possible, so they can ensure they have enough funds.

Payment of Tax

Under the old rules, tax was due on 1st January in the particular tax year, and the 1st July following this. These dates are now synchronised with the other main self-assessment dates, and have become 31st January and 31st July.

However, the system has changed. Under the old system, you might receive a tax assessment based on the information you have provided. This assessment is then split in two, with half being payable on 1st January and the other half on 1st July. Because of the complexity of many self-employed people's circumstances, and the speed at which they can change, it frequently became necessary to alter the assessment before 1st January, or alter it subsequent to 1st January so that the July payment would be reduced.

For example, an assessment might be raised in the sum of £10,000, with £5,000 being payable on 1st January 1994 and £5,000 payable on 1st July 1994. This assessment might be issued in November 1993. However, a large pension payment might be made which would affect the amount of tax payable and it was possible to reduce the January and July payments to reflect this.

Alternatively, the large pension payment might be made in March 1994, after the first self-employed payment in January had been made. It would then be possible, in certain circumstances, to have the whole of the deduction against the July 1994 tax payment.

Under self-assessment, this situation would be different because you will either calculate your own tax, paying half on

31st January and half on 31st July, or the Revenue will calculate it for you, with payments on the same dates. If the two payments you make on account come to more than the tax which actually becomes due for that tax year, then the balancing payment will not be made to you until the following 31st January. This is an important cash flow consideration and a significant change for many people in the way tax is collected.

Tax Return

The general rules for completing and submitting tax returns will apply to the self-employed. That is to say, if you want your tax calculated, you will need to have the return in by the end of September following the tax year. If you are calculating your own tax, then you have until 31st January. In a sense, this is something of a relaxation because previously, tax returns had to be in by 30th October. However, a word of warning is needed.

Many accountancy firms have a cyclical business and become extremely busy towards the end of October. Following that, they were always busy towards the end of the tax year - the first quarter of the calendar year. What they may now find is that they will be just as busy around September, trying to make the end of September deadline. And they will be even busier trying to make the 31st January deadline and deal with end of year tax planning issues.

The self-employed should therefore discuss with their advisors how, and in what form, they would like information in order to avoid being stuck in some peak of activity with which small firms sometimes find it hard to deal.

Penalties

Once again, there are fixed penalties for late returns, and these are automatic. If your return is not sent in by 31st January in the year following the year to which it relates, there will be a £100 penalty. Should it still be outstanding six months later, then there will be a further penalty.

You will still face the late payment charges, being a 5% surcharge on any tax unpaid by 28th February after the end of the tax year, and a further 5% surcharge on any amounts still unpaid by 31st July following the relevant tax year.

More significantly, if the Revenue decide to do so, they can simply determine the amount of tax they think is payable, along with penalties and surcharges. **They will then be authorised to collect that tax even if it is way above your actual liability.** So, you could find yourself having the Collector knocking on your door and seizing your assets for an amount of tax that is well in excess of anything you actually owe. It is therefore in your interests to ensure that your affairs are in order as soon as possible.

If the Inland Revenue collect an inappropriate amount of tax, they will of course pay it back once you have got your affairs up to date. However, the cash flow problems could be severe, and the only way out is to keep up to date.

Basis of Assessment

One of the most fundamental changes for the self-employed, and which has now been in operation for some time, applies to the basis of assessment.

Under the old system, self-employed people making up accounts to, say, the end of July in a particular tax year, would be assessed on those accounts for the tax year following the year in which those accounts ended. So, if your accounts were to the end of July 1987, that would be in the tax year 1987/88. You would then be assessed in 1988/89. This gave you a considerable time between the end of your period of account and your actual assessment.

However, this has now all changed. We have moved to what is called the *current year basis of assessment*. What this means is, for the example above, the assessment would have been in 1987/88 rather than the next one.

This system has applied to all new self-employed businesses which started after April 1994. But now it is being applied to all the existing self-employed businesses, who will no longer have the benefit of the long time lapse between the end of their year of assessment and the taxation of the relevant profits.

This is a relatively simple concept, but it is complicated for several reasons. First of all, there have to be transitional provisions for the old self-employed to the new self-employed. Secondly, when there are losses, or changes in accounting dates, or other complications, the calculations can become very difficult indeed. *Appendix Two* outlines the basics; first for those who have started a new business since the current year basis started to apply, and secondly for those who have been running a continuous business since prior to that date.

Record Keeping

All tax payers are under an obligation to maintain and retain records for tax purposes. Perhaps the hardest hit will be the self-employed, because not only are their records likely to be more complex than the average employed tax payer, but they need to be kept for a longer period.

The law says that the records that shall be "kept and preserved" shall include records of the following:

"All amounts received and expended in the course of .... business .... and .... in the case of a trade involved in the dealing of goods, all sales and purchases of goods made in the course of that trade ...."

This is a very wide requirement and you can expect the Inland Revenue to apply it seriously.

You should maintain the following records:

1. Information on all your sales and business receipts.

2. The supporting records, for example, your paying in slips, bank statements, invoices, and so on.

3. A record of all purchases and other expenses and the relevant back-up documents such as invoices.

4. You should make a note of any amount taken from your business bank account or diverted from your receipts in cash.

5. You should note any amount you have paid into the business personally, for example, the introduction of capital.

---

6. You must keep a records of any purchases or sales of assets used in the business, for example, fixtures and fittings, furniture or motor cars.

7. You should keep a record of personal drawings whether this is in cash or cheque form.

8. If you have any employees, you will need to keep adequate records of payments to them, including casual workers. Any benefits you may provide must also be adequately recorded.

Appendix Three gives an idea of how a sub-contractor should keep records, along with a retail shop, being two common types of self-employment.

Computer Records

In this day and age, many self-employed people find it impossible to run a business without some sort of computerised bookkeeping records. Not only is this efficient in terms of time, but it can keep down accountancy and audit fees by the information being provided in a legible comprehensible form. Moreover, it is far easier to post your accountant a computer disk update than have a member of staff deliver books for inspection. (The books will still need to be inspected, but many people have moved as far as they can towards computer records).

Unfortunately, the Inland Revenue require that you still keep the original paper records of your sales, purchases, or other transactions, and it will only allow you to use microfilm or an optical imaging system. Hence, it is no use sending the Tax man a floppy disc through the post which records all your entries throughout the year. You will still have to maintain and retain paper records.

Conclusion

There are many self-employed people working within the U.K. economy and self-assessment will affect every one of them. The Inland Revenue is also quite aware that there is a great deal of tax uncollected as a result of the diversity of self-employed activity, and the scope for petty fraud, such as cash deals.

You can therefore expect the Inland Revenue to concentrate heavily on the self-employed, and the best way to keep out of trouble is to understand and comply with the rules.

Chapter Four

Penalties

"There may be penalties
if you fail to comply."

This is the chilling statement taken from a Revenue publication. There is no doubt that these penalties have been introduced with a view to their being levied. One could be charitable and say that they are there to encourage us to comply, but one could also be cynical and say that the chances of many people complying correctly first time is rather remote, and penalties are bound to be levied. This chapter therefore pulls together the various penalties and tells you how to avoid them.

Late Returns

You should, by now, have understood that the 31st January date is critical. If you have not produced your tax return (and, in some cases, your own calculation of the tax due) by this date then you will face an automatic fixed penalty. This is currently £100. Further, if you fail to produce your return six months after that, by 31st July, then you will face a further £100 penalty.

If the Inland Revenue judge that the fixed penalty is not sufficient to make you act, then they have the option of charging you £60 a day.

Interest and Surcharges

In the past it has always been possible to pay your tax late because systems usually lag behind, and there is always the exercise of trying to catch up. The new system, however, has interest charges and surcharges.

If you pay insufficient tax when you are making your payments on account or any balancing payments, then you will be charged interest. This is broadly the same as the current system. The official rate of interest is declared in advance and so you will know the amount which you will face.

To be fair, if you have made overpayments of tax, then the Inland Revenue will pay you.

If your tax is still outstanding after the final payment date (31st January), then you will pay surcharges. There is a 5% surcharge on any tax which is unpaid by 28th February - only a month after the tax was due.

There is a further 5% surcharge if any of that amount is still unpaid by 31st July, which is six months after the tax was due.

Please be aware of the Revenue's power to determine the amount of tax on your behalf and start to levy the penalties and surcharges, and then collect that tax. Whilst you will be able to get it back if it turns out to be too much, you nonetheless fact the prospect of "investing" in the Inland Revenue whilst you are sorting matters out.

Record Keeping Penalties

You have already seen the need to keep records for all taxpayers. In order to encourage you to do so, there are some fairly stiff penalties.

The Inland Revenue have said they will take a "common sense view" if they discover a taxpayer has failed to keep adequate records. However, as their brief is to collect the correct amount of tax, they will find that difficult if they do not have the supporting documentation. The warning they issue is, *"you could end up paying more tax than necessary, simply because you are unable to provide adequate supporting records"*.

This is very serious. On the one hand we know what penalties we will be paying for other offences. A 5% surcharge is fairly comprehensible, as is a £60 a day late filing penalty. But, the threat that you will "pay more tax" because your records were "inadequate" is very worrying. It would seem to suggest that the onus of proof will always lie with the taxpayer. If the Inland Revenue can construct an argument for a higher amount of tax, but you do not have the evidence to disprove it, then you might end up having to pay that tax. Amounts in this respect could make automatic penalties pale into insignificance.

Not only that, but there is a further penalty of up to £3,000 that can be charged for any year of assessment where there has been "failure to maintain adequate records".

In practice, the major financial penalties will probably only be applied to persistent offenders or people who have been treated sympathetically once, told exactly what records they should keep, and who have then failed.

Conclusion

Automatic penalties, and surcharges, can only be avoided by complying with the law. This is why they have been designed, and so you can be certain that they will be levied if you fail to meet the relevant requirements. Moreover, the option for the Taxman to determine the amount of tax he feels appropriate if your records are weak or incomplete will probably be the major area of dispute under the new system.

Summary of Penalties

Return not sent back by 31st January	£100
Return still not sent after six months	+£100
Further delay	up to £60/day
Tax outstanding after 31st January	5%
Tax outstanding after six months	+5%
Failure to maintain "adequate" records	£3,000 +unspecified "More Tax"

Chapter Five

Capital Gains Tax

"Few people end up having to pay Capital Gains Tax. But for those who do, it is often a nasty surprise."

Can you imagine, therefore, if, in addition to being found liable for tax, you are penalised for paying it late (because you were unaware of the liability), and penalised for not reporting it in the first place. It is worthwhile, therefore, that every taxpayer understands the basics of Capital Gains Tax.

Who is Liable ?

Any U.K. resident can be liable on world wide gains, whether or not the proceeds are brought back to the U.K.

What is a Gain?

If you purchase or acquire by other means a "chargeable asset" (see below), and sell it on at a profit, you have made a chargeable gain.

Chargeable Asset

A chargeable asset is, for example, a share, a unit trust, a second home, your share in a business, or certain personal items.

You cannot make a capital gain on cash, or currency for your own use. There is no Capital Gains Tax on gilts, nor are such things as lottery or pools winnings treated as a Capital Gain. *Appendix Six* give further details on what specific exclusions there are from chargeable assets.

Inflation

You will not generally pay tax on inflationary gains because there is a special relief known as "indexation relief". So, if you buy shares in ABC Ltd for £1, and sell them for £2, if there has been inflation in the intervening period of, say, 50 pence in the pound, then you will be assessed to tax only on the balance.

Exempt Amount

Each individual is allowed an amount, set at budget time, which is entirely tax free. That is to say you can make gains of that amount every year, after your indexation allowance, without paying any tax.

What hasn't changed

The basic concept of Capital Gains Tax remains unchanged. The allowance is still available and the main rates of tax remain applicable (although both subject to change by Budgets). The methods of calculation, the offset of gains or losses, the concepts of selling at under value and so on, all remain intact. The major change is in record keeping.

Record Keeping

Imagine you sell a small plot of land which you bought many years ago. If the sale proceeds are £20,000, then you may well have a Capital Gains Tax liability. Whatever happens, you will be obliged to report it on your tax return which must be submitted no later than six months after the year of assessment in which the gain took place. Once you have done so, the Inland Revenue will want to compute your tax and will ask for further information.

Imagine however, that you do not have any proof of the amount which you paid for the land. You might have paid £20,000 and, therefore, made no gains. Alternatively, you may have made enormous gains, but the onus of proof will always be on you. So, you might find yourself paying more tax than is absolutely necessary, and being penalised for not having kept adequate records.

Moreover, you may have losses which you made in times gone by, and which you will like to relieve against the gains. If you cannot substantiate those losses, then the tax man may disallow them. Every £1 of losses he disallows could be worth 40 pence to you. It will be most important, therefore, to keep these records.

Time Limits

Whilst the statutory time limits for keeping records are notionally 22 months or so, the records that you will be keeping may relate to an earlier period. Imagine you bought the land in question in the early 1980s. You will need to keep proof of purchase and any expenditure you have made in the meantime, otherwise you may face penalties in the form of an increased tax charge.

Allowable Losses

One problem arises with allowable losses. Imagine you have losses from years gone by which you have not yet used because you have not had the capital gains against which to offset them. It may well be that you entered these losses in your tax return at the time. But, if not, you still have five years and ten months from the end of the year of assessment in which the losses originally arose to inform the Inland Revenue about those losses. This will then give you the option of setting them off against future capital gains.

Time passes quickly and it may well be that the losses which you would like to set off could be, say, ten or more years old. If so, you may not still have the relevant records. However, as long as you notified the Inland Revenue on your tax return within the five years and ten months deadline, then those losses should still be available for offset, and you should not face any penalties for failing to keep records for that length of time.

Types of Records

You would be well advised to keep the following:

1. Any contract notes or conveyance notes for assets you have bought, leased or exchanged.
2. Details of any assets which you have given away to family members, charities, or placed into trusts.
3. Copies of any professional valuations you have obtained, for example, antiques or land, and the time when the transaction took place.
4. Details of any assets of which you have no acquisition costs, that is to say, those which you may have been given.
5. Details of any expenditure at the time of sale, perhaps on legal fees or stamp duty and so on.

Payments on Account

Thankfully, with Capital Gains Tax you will not have to make the twice yearly payments on account. The process will be much the same as it is now, with you reporting your gains, agreeing them with the Inland Revenue, and then paying the tax which is requested.

Conclusion

Currently, much about Capital Gains remains the same, but you should be aware that keeping records has become more complicated.

Chapter Six

Record Keeping

"You should note that this is a legal obligation, and is not optional."

Perhaps the area in which most individual taxpayers will fall down, is that of record keeping. The need for tax returns and the timely payments of tax will be quite clear. However, the adequacy of records, or inadequacy, may not become apparent until such time as there is a form of Inland Revenue Investigation.

Only once the records are requested will you truly know whether they are deemed acceptable by the Authorities. Accordingly, you will need perhaps to overcompensate by making yourself aware of every type of record that you could be likely to need. This chapter, therefore, deals with the types of record which it seems prudent to keep, along with those the Inland Revenue have already made clear will be more or less mandatory, it further tells you how to keep them, and for how long.

Obligations

The Inland Revenue have made it clear that from 1996 the keeping of records by all taxpayers will be obligatory under the law. The basic requirement is to keep adequate records to enable you to complete a tax return. You should note that this is a legal obligation, and is not optional. As for excuses, you will have to see how matters develop, but you can be certain that even if you do manage to get away with inadequate records once, you are unlikely to be able to do so twice.

What to keep

The phrase "any records necessary to complete a tax return", could be very wide indeed. For those in business, or those with more complicated affairs, including more than one source of income, for example, investments, then in order to produce an honest tax return, you will certainly need to do so from primary records. The following sections deal with the type of records you might want to keep.

Employed People

The list below includes those records which relate to your employment. Clearly, if you have a self-employment, a pension or some investments, you will need to pay attention to those sections as well.

Generally speaking, the employed should keep the following:

1. The form P60: This is the certificate you get from your employer at the end of every tax year which tells you how much you have earned, and what tax and National Insurance was deducted. This is a primary record of which the Inland Revenue PAYE division also receive a copy.

2. Any form P45: This is the form received when you leave an employment. It details how much tax and National Insurance has been deducted, and what your gross pay has been. It is possible to have more than one P45 in any year.

3. Form P160: This is a form which your employer gives you when you retire or start to draw a pension.

4. Form P11D: This form is intended to show all the benefits in kind you may have received during the year, such as private medical insurance, or the use of a company car.

5. It will be wise to retain your payslips and ensure that they accord with your P60 at the end of the year.

6. If you are in any sort of share option scheme, then you should keep all of the supporting information that you can. Generally, such schemes will be either tax free or liable to Income Tax or Capital Gains Tax. Accordingly, keeping every shred of evidence will make life easier.

7. Any other type of receipt you have had from your employer, such as training awards or incentives and so on, would also be worth keeping.

8. Finally, if you leave an employment and receive any form of ex-gratia, redundancy, or severance payment, you should keep the surrounding documentation and correspondence, as it will often dictate how the payment should be taxed.

Self-Employed

See Chapter Three & Appendix Three.

Pensioners

You should keep the following:

1. Any P60 which is produced by your former employer, or any other occupational pension scheme which pays you a pension. Additionally, such certificates may be produced by third parties such as insurance companies.

2. Any analysis you receive from the DSS in respect of your State Pension, where it is broken down into various components.

3. Details of any disability or mobility allowance or other state benefits to which you may be entitled.

Investors

Often, the Inland Revenue's first warning bell into investigating anyone is when they discover undeclared investment income. You should keep records of this type very carefully.

1. All dividend mandates showing the dividend you receive and the tax deducted. This applies to shares as well as unit and investment trusts.

2. Any bank and Building Society statements or tax certificates which are produced at the end of the tax year, or on closure of the account.

3. Any bank statements which show tax deducted from the account as you go along, and the amount that has been credited net.

4. Any details of gross interest you have received, for example, National Savings, or offshore accounts.

5. Details of any Purchased Life Annuities or other similar investments.
6. Details of any Chargeable Events certificates relating to Life Assurance Policies or Investment Bonds.
7. Any distributions you may receive from a Trust, and the supporting correspondence.

For the avoidance of doubt, you might like to keep documents which prove the source of any funds, for example, if your investment income should double one year, then the Inland Revenue may want to know where the capital came from. You should, therefore, save anything that you consider relevant in this regard, perhaps proof of winning a cash prize or an inheritance under a will.

Capital Gains

The section on Capital Gains lists items which it might be useful to keep, and some of this will cross refer to the income produced by such assets. For example, Unit Trusts and shares will not only be chargeable assets, but they will probably have produced an income stream during the period for which they have been held.

Overseas Investments

Just because your investments are overseas does not mean that you will not have to keep records. You should keep all the same records which you keep for U.K. investments, along with details of any currency transactions you might have made, for example, in converting your US gains from dollars to sterling, or your original investments from sterling to dollars.

Computer Records

Many people these days run their family money on some sort of computer programme on a PC. However, this does not free you from the requirement to keep the necessary paperwork for Inland Revenue inspection. Accordingly, all the requirements listed above must be complied with, even if you have a sophisticated computer record to back them up.

Special Situations

Some employed people incur expenditure on behalf of their company, and then claim it back regularly. Perhaps they are running up hotel bills or spending money on fuel for their motor car. Whatever the purpose, these expense claims will need to be very detailed. Not only will you have to keep records of all your purchases and receipts, along with a copy of whatever you submit to your employer, but you should also keep a detailed mileage log. This is because if you have a company car, the amount of tax you pay can be reduced based on the amount of business mileage you do. It is important to keep a record, therefore, to prove that you have actually incurred business mileage, rather than personal mileage.

Similarly, the self-employed might keep a record so that when the private use element of their motor car is challenged, they will be able to substantiate it.

Remember, the Inland Revenue have said that the keeping of records may save you from paying tax unnecessarily. The inference is, of course, that *without the records, you will simply pay the tax.*

Penalties

Of course, in order to encourage you to keep records, there are penalties as detailed above in other chapters. The major penalty is £3,000 for serious and repeated offences, but you should be aware of the implicit penalty of paying more tax when you have insufficient records to prove a lower liability. This in itself is such a open-ended feature of the tax system, that it will, undoubtedly trap many unwary taxpayers.

Chapter Seven

Company Requirements

"There could be a greater administrative requirement for complying with the Inland Revenue's demands"

Major national organisations should clearly have clued up finance directors and advisers to ensure that they are able to comply with the law. But, there are also a great many smaller companies, perhaps they are simply husband and wife partnerships which have incorporated. Alternatively, they might simply be smaller concerns. It is important that the individuals in these companies understand the sort of requirements with which they will have to comply.

The Collection of Tax

The pay and file system was introduced some time ago, and most companies will be familiar with it. Companies will not be paying tax on the two operative dates for individuals and so self-assessment is unlikely to affect them in this way.

Record Keeping

What will undoubtedly affect the smaller company is the need for the keeping of records. Of course, most small companies already do keep records, but you should note that the £3,000 penalty can equally well be applied to a corporation as to an individual. Hence, if you think that any paperwork might be relevant, then you should ensure that you keep it for at least 22 months, and if longer, until the relevant year of account has been settled with the Inland Revenue.

Employee Requirements

Of course, one of the major effects for a company may well be that the individuals that work within it suddenly have a much more diligent attitude to record keeping. They are likely to be asking for more information from you. For example, they may well want a copy of their P11D and supporting schedules in case such is requested when they submit their own tax returns.

You may well find that copy P60s and the like are more frequently requested. Further, you may find those people with company vehicles are keen to have some sort of evidence as to what constituted a company journey, rather than simply travelling to work. Also, those people with "pool cars", may well require a note from the company to the effect that any vehicle used was a pool car and did not constitute a taxable benefit.

All in all, there could be a greater administrative requirement that you comply with the Inland Revenue's demands, as channelled through individual taxpayers.

New Rules

There are new rules of which all employers should be aware. For example, there is now a time limit for which a P60 must be given to an employee. This will be 31st May in each year, and applies for the first time in 1997.

There is now a new P45 form which has four parts rather than the old three. Part 1 should be sent to the tax office as it currently is. Part 1A, 2 and 3 should be given to the employee who will then detach part 1A for his or her own retention, giving only parts 2 and 3 to the employer. There is also a little extra information required on the new style form.

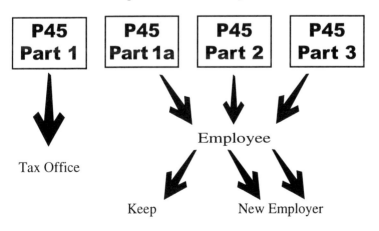

There is now a time limit for giving form P11D to employees. For the tax year 1996/97 and thereafter, this date will be 6th July.

P11D forms have also changed and it is recommended that employers obtain a stock of new forms in order to see what extra information is required. The Inland Revenue is offering information packs and seminars for employers as well as the usual local tax office help, either in person or on the telephone.

Penalties

The law allows for a penalty of up to £3,000 for each incorrect or incomplete P11D form.

There are further penalties of up to £300 per form for every form which fails to comply with the Revenue's requirements in respect of P11Ds and P60s. Moreover, if the failure continues, then a further £60 per form can be levied for every day that the failure continues.

Clearly, although the changes are relatively minor, there is no doubt that the Inland Revenue intends to apply them and that any employer would be well advised to obtain the new forms and a statement of the new requirements.

Chapter Eight

Completing Your Tax Return

"It is quite feasible for an individual to complete and submit their own Tax Return."

You will not be able to deal with the implications of the self-assessment regime unless you are clear about your responsibility regarding the Tax Return and its completion. These issues need to be looked at in detail because millions of people will be receiving Tax Returns, or be liable to request one.

Even those people who have previously had the old style Tax Return will be receiving the new style Return for the first time and there are some very significant differences, not only in the format of the Return, but in your own obligations for completion of the main section and the supplementary schedules.

The experience in other countries where similar self-assessment systems have been introduced, has been that the need for accountants has risen four-fold, although, hopefully, this chapter will relieve you of the need to employ one in most circumstances.

The Tax Return Itself

The previous Tax Return had many pages, and taxpayers, or their advisers would complete those sections which were relevant, leaving blank, or crossing out, those which were not.

The new style Tax Return is quite different. It has only eight pages, and it is then up to you to request those schedules (supplementary pages) which relate to your different sources of income.

For example, on the second and last pages of the Tax Return, there are nine colour-coded boxes referring to different sources of income. One of these, Land and Property Income, perhaps from renting a room in your house or a second property, is coded red, whilst Capital Gains is coded blue. The Revenue should send the ones they think you'll need, but you may need to request others depending on your circumstances. The back of the Tax Return allows you to indicate which supplementary pages you are enclosing.

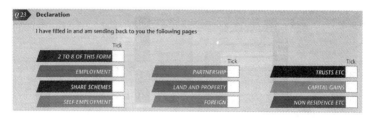

The Schedules

The *Supplementary Pages* are as follows:
Employment - Magenta
Share Schemes - Purple
Self-Employment - Orange
Partnership Income - Turquoise
Land and Property - Red
Foreign Income - Deep Yellow
Trust Income and Receipts - Brown
Capital Gains - Blue
Non-Residence - Green

Thankfully, as you will see from the above, there is no specific schedule for income from savings and investments which is still included on page three of the Tax Return.

Completing the Return

The Inland Revenue have tried to make matters as simple as they can, although taxation is inherently complicated. By colour coding and using a series of different steps, it is hoped that most people will understand the system, and that the various helplines and offices will not be inundated with requests for help.

Step 1 The first step is to answer all the questions on page two of the return which will determine which schedules you actually need. If the answer to question four "Were you in partnership", is "yes", then you will need to tick the box marked "yes" and request the turquoise partnership schedule.

Inland Revenue

INCOME AND CAPITAL GAINS *for the year ended 5 April 1997*

Step 1

Answer Questions 1 to 9 below to find out if you have the right supplementary pages.
Please read pages 4 and 5 of your Tax Return Guide if you need help. The Questions are
colour coded to help you identify the supplementary pages and their guidance notes.
If you answer 'No', go to the next question. If you answer 'Yes', you must complete the
relevant supplementary pages. Turn to the back of the Tax Return to see if you have the
right ones and look at the back of the Tax Return Guide to see if you have the right notes.
Ring the Orderline on 0000 0000 between 8 am and 10pm for any you need.
If I have sent you any you do not need, ignore them.

*Check to make sure you have the
right supplementary pages and
then tick the box below.*

Q1 Were you an employee, or office holder, or director, or agency worker in the year ended 5 April 1997? | NO | YES | EMPLOYMENT YES

Q2 Did you have any taxable income from share options or share related benefits in the year?
(Dividends from shareholdings are to be included at Question 10) | NO | YES | SHARE SCHEMES YES

Q3 Were you self-employed (but not in partnership)? | NO | YES | SELF-EMPLOYMENT YES

Q4 Were you in partnership? | NO | YES | PARTNERSHIP YES

Q5 Did you receive any rent or other income from land and property in the UK? | NO | YES | LAND & PROPERTY YES

Q6 Did you have any taxable income from overseas pensions or benefits, or foreign companies or savings institutions, offshore funds or trusts abroad, or from land and property abroad or gains on foreign life insurance policies? | NO | YES

Do you want to claim tax credit relief for foreign tax paid on foreign income or gains? | NO | YES | FOREIGN YES

Q7 Did you receive any income from trusts, settlements or estates of deceased persons? | NO | YES | TRUSTS ETC YES

Q8 Capital gains
- have you disposed of your exempt only or main residence? | NO | YES
  If 'Yes', read page 5 of your Tax Return Guide.
- did you dispose of other chargeable assets worth more than £12,600 in total? | NO | YES
- were your total chargeable gains more than £6,300? | NO | YES | CAPITAL GAINS YES
  You may also need to fill in the Capital gains pages if you made a capital loss.

Q9 Are you claiming that you were not resident, or not ordinarily resident, or not domiciled, in the UK for all or part of the year? | NO | YES | NON RESIDENCE ETC YES

Step 2
Fill in your supplementary pages now BEFORE going on to Step 3.
Please use blue or black ink and ignore pence.
Tick this box when you have filled in your supplementary pages

Step 3
Now fill in Questions 10 to 23. If you answer 'No' to a question, go straight to
the next one. If you answer 'Yes', fill in the relevant boxes.

Remember
- You do not have to calculate your tax - I will do it for you if you send your Tax Return to me by 30 September. This will save you time.
- The Tax Calculation Guide I have sent you will help if you decide to calculate the tax yourself.
- You do not have to wait until 30 September 1997, or 31 January 1998, to send me your Tax Return.

Step 2

Once you have obtained the right supplementary pages, complete them (see later) before moving on because you'll need their results in subsequent steps.

Step 3 Go through the rest of the Return, completing questions 10 to 23 - basically the rest of the form. Some of these questions are split into a variety of sub-questions, and you will need to read every single one. For example, in the question of interest you receive, you will need to distinguish between that on which tax has been deducted (for example, a UK Building Society or bank) and that from which tax may not have been deducted, such as that from an overseas bank. The questions are specific and comprehensive and you will see that they cover a wide variety of sources of income.

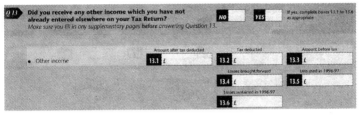

Taxpayers should pay particular attention to question 13 which is a catch-all, asking for details of any income or gains not covered elsewhere. So, you will not be able to say that any non-declaration on your part was down to the design of the form.

Questions 14, 15 and 16 allow you to claim the various reliefs to which you may be entitled.

Question 18 is significant because it asks whether or not you want the Inland Revenue to calculate your tax. If you do, then you will need to have the Return in by the end of September,

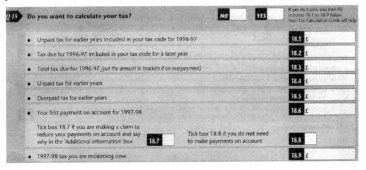

whereas if you are calculating your own tax, you have until the following 31st January.

Question 19 is also important because you might want to claim a repayment of tax. For example, you may have suffered tax at source on all your investment income, and taking no account of your personal allowance. This section should help resolve that.

Questions 20 and 21 are simply your personal details, whilst question 22 covers a few odd situations such as post-cessation business receipts or spreading of royalty income.

Finally, question 23 simply requires your signature, having ticked the right boxes for your supporting schedules. Taxpayers will not fail to read the warning "If you give false information or conceal any part of your income or chargeable gains, you can be prosecuted. You may also have to pay substantial financial penalties". You have been warned.

Completing the Schedules

It could be argued that dividing the various types of income into (mostly) one-page schedules makes the whole thing more comprehensible. This modular approach should break the job down for you, but does create the risk of your overlooking something. You should, therefore, continue to refer to page two of the main Tax Return to ensure that you are not failing to complete a particular schedule.

Employment Schedule (Magenta)

The employment schedule is the one which most people will come across, and you will see from question 1.8 through to question 1.11 how important it is that you have kept your P60 or P45.

Section 1.12 to 1.23 covers any expenses you may have, and it is important that you have kept strict records, for example, in respect of a company car.

Revenue   *EMPLOYMENT*

If you have answered 'Yes' to Question 1, fill in pages E1 and E2. If you want help, look up the box numbers in the notes on employment at the back of your Tax Return Guide. They are colour-coded to match the form.

FINAL DRAFT

Fill in a separate copy of these pages for each employment.

Details of employer

Employer's PAYE reference
1.1

Employer's name
1.2

Date employment started
(only if between 6 April 1996 and 5 April 1997)
1.3 / /

Employer's address
1.5

Date finished
1.4 / /

Postcode

Tick box 1.6 if you were
a director of the company
1.6

and tick box 1.7 if it
was a close company
1.7

Income from employment

■ *Money - see Notes on page E2*

- payments from P60 (or P45 or pay slips)   Before tax **1.8** £

- payments not on P60 etc   - tips   **1.9** £

     - other payments (excluding expenses shown below and lump sums
and compensation payments or benefits shown overleaf) **1.10** £

- tax deducted from payments in boxes 1.8 to 1.10   Tax deducted **1.11** £

Benefits and expenses - see Notes on pages E2 to E6

	Amount			Amount
• assets transferred/ payments made for you	**1.12** £		• vans	**1.18** £
• vouchers/credit cards	**1.13** £		• interest free and low interest loans	**1.19** £
• living accommodation	**1.14** £		• mobile telephones	**1.20** £
• mileage allowance	**1.15** £		• private medical or dental insurance	**1.21** £
• company cars	**1.16** £		• other benefits	**1.22** £
• fuel for company cars	**1.17** £		• expenses payments received and balancing charges	**1.23** £

Completing Your Tax Return

Self Employed (Orange)

Those who are self-employed will receive a further four-page schedule (or will have to ask for one), although this is relatively simple if your *annual* turnover is below

Income and expenses.

You must fill in this page if your annual turnover is £15,000 or more

If you were registered for VAT, do the figures in boxes 3.16 to 3.51 include VAT? **3.14** or exclude VAT? **3.15**

Sales/business income (turnover) **3.16** £

	Any disallowable expenses included in boxes 3.33 to 3.50	Total expenses
● Cost of sales	**3.17** £	**3.33** £
● Construction industry subcontractor costs	**3.18** £	**3.34** £
● Other direct costs	**3.19** £	**3.35** £

box 3.16 less (box 3.33 + box 3.34 + box 3.35)

Gross profit/(loss) **3.36** £

Other income/profits **3.37** £

● Employee costs	**3.20** £	**3.38** £
● Premises costs	**3.21** £	**3.39** £
● Repairs	**3.22** £	**3.40** £
● General administrative expenses	**3.23** £	**3.41** £
● Motor expenses	**3.24** £	**3.42** £
● Travel and subsistence	**3.25** £	**3.43** £
● Advertising, promotion and entertainment	**3.26** £	**3.44** £
● Legal and professional costs	**3.27** £	**3.45** £
● Bad debts	**3.28** £	**3.46** £
● Interest	**3.29** £	**3.47** £
● Other finance charges	**3.30** £	**3.48** £
● Depreciation and loss/ (profit) on sale	**3.31** £	**3.49** £
● Other expenses	**3.32** £	**3.50** £

Put the total of boxes 3.17 to 3.32 in box 3.53 below

total boxes 3.38 to 3.50

Total expenses **3.51** £

boxes 3.36 + 3.37 less box 3.51

Net profit/(loss) **3.52** £

Tax adjustments to net profit or loss

boxes 3.17 to 3.32

● Disallowable expenses **3.53** £

● Goods etc. taken for personal use and other adjustments (apart from disallowable expenses) which increase profits **3.54** £

box 3.53 + box 3.54

Total additions to net profit (deduct from net loss) **3.55** £

● Deductions from net profit (add to net loss) **3.56** £

boxes 3.52 plus 3.55 less box 3.56

Net business profit for tax purposes (put figure in brackets if a loss) **3.57** £

£15,000. If not, you will need to fill in pages 2-4, and it is likely you will need some form of professional help in this regard because you will have to distinguish between allowable and disallowable expenses within your business, which is often a matter of experience (see example of page two, opposite).

On page three you will need to provide the results of your capital allowance computation, with which you are also likely to require some form of professional help. The rest of the boxes on that page are fairly straightforward, and the last page of the self-employment schedule asks for a balance sheet. Once again, it may be that professional help is required if you are producing your own accounts.

Trust Schedule (Brown)

The brown Trust Schedule, is fairly straightforward, simply asking for the income receivable and the tax paid. You do need to split this up into the different types of income you have had, but there should be a managing trustee who can take responsibility for this. If not, you will be wise to run the form past a local accountant.

Land and Property Schedule (Red)

Rather like the Self-employment and Partnership Schedules, the Land and Property Schedule asks for information to be extracted from your accounts, and copied over to the return. If you have someone producing your accounts, it would be wise to have them complete the schedule on your behalf. If you produce your own accounts, then you will simply need to take great care that you copy over the right figures.

Shares Schemes (Purple)

There is a further purple form for those people who are employed and who benefit from share schemes. This is an extremely complicated area and I would imagine that the 'Payroll' section of a company would be responsible for helping you to complete the information.

The grant and exercise of share options can be particularly complicated and you will need to know what type of scheme you have, and whether or not the proceeds should be entered onto the purple Share Schemes form or the blue Capital Gains Tax form. You will have to refer to your employer in this regard, otherwise establishing the correct answers to the questions could be expensive and would certainly be time consuming.

Capital Gains Schedule (Blue)

The Capital Gains Tax schedule, once again, requires you to compute your own chargeable gains. If gains are significant, then you would be wise to seek professional help because there is a considerable variety of different reliefs and allowances, and you will need to ensure that you have claimed the right ones. This is a one-page schedule, but there is room for you to give details of up to 22 assets of which you have disposed!

There are two further schedules, one relating to non-residents, and one to foreign income, and both are rather specialised.

Non-Residence Schedule (Green)

The Non-Residence schedule asks you to complete a series of questions asking very specific details on your citizenship and the days spent in the UK. There are also questions about your intentions when you came to the UK or when you left the UK, and as there is likely to be a reasonable amount of tax at stake, you will be advised to, once again, confirm the details with a local accountant.

Foreign Income and Gains (Yellow)

The Foreign Income and Gains schedule simply requires you to enter the county of origin and the amount of tax deducted on any overseas gains, so that you can receive your foreign income tax credit if appropriate, or pay more tax should the foreign rate have been lower than the UK. You should note that you are required to enter income from foreign property on this form rather than the red form which covers the UK Land and Property. It is likely that you will have some sort of collection agent for foreign property, and they should be able to assist you in providing the relevant figures for repairs, maintenance, finance charges and so on.

Partnership Schedule (Turquoise)

If you are trading in partnership, you will need the turquoise schedule, which comes in two forms, long and short. The latter is simple, and those who require the former will, undoubtedly, need professional help with sections on 'overlap relief' and other complex issues.

Conclusion

In conclusion then, it is quite feasible for an individual with relatively simple circumstances requesting one or two of the simpler schedules to complete and submit their own Tax Return. However, those people who have trading income, overseas income, or any unusual chargeable gains, may find that their only option is to use a professional until they become used to the Tax Return and its schedules. (This is really little different to the current system).

The Inland Revenue is providing a helpline, and is ready for the simpler queries, but they will not be giving advice (for example, on what expenses you might claim), nor will they be producing accounts for you. The result is, therefore, that you should **request a Tax Return as soon as possible and try to complete it as soon as you receive it.** This will give you the time to make mistakes and come across points you do not understand which you might then be able to resolve before you pass any deadlines.

Chapter Nine

Calculating Your Own Tax

"For many people, it will be important to know exactly how much they owe"

The Inland Revenue will be issuing a tax calculation guide for those people who wish to calculate their own tax liabilities. This is a particularly complicated form and requires nearly two dozen pages of explanation in the manual which the tax man issues to accountants and other professional advisors! Nonetheless, it may be worth having a go yourself, because if your affairs are relatively simple, and you are reasonably numerate, you may find it feasible to work out your own tax.

The first thing to do is to decide which of the various tax calculation guides you will need. One is for all your income, another is for capital gains only, and a third is for lump sum receipts. The former is the one which most people will probably require and, although it has 114 separate boxes, so long as you follow the instructions to the letter (to the number and colour also), then you should be able to complete it.

The first calcualtion page (page five of the form) essentially gets you to copy figures over from the various schedules you'll have completed, plus deductions you might have, such as personal pension relief, or maintenance payments.

Page six covers the allowances you are claiming and the arrows show where the various totals need to be entered. The next page organises the totals and gets you to perform the basic calculations mostly by adding and subtracting.

Finally, this all comes to resolution on the back page (page eight) where sources of income, the income tax deducted at source, and any further tax due, should become apparent. The very last section allows you to work out what your payment on account should be for the subsequent 31st January.

Remember that you do not have to calculate your own tax, you can simply submit your return and wait for the Inland Revenue to do it. However, for many people, it will be important to know exactly how much they owe, or may expect as a rebate, because if the Inland Revenue is pressed (and it undoubtedly will be), then **it may be some time before you know exactly how much you owe and you will then have to get the money together very quickly** because of the automatic penalties which can apply.

A Case Study

Perhaps the easiest way to understand the Inland Revenue forms is to see how they would be completed in a fictitious case. Accordingly, this section deals with a set of reasonably ordinary circumstances and indicates how the various forms would need to be completed.

Because of the nature of the new forms there are a lot of references to numbered boxes, so you may find it helpful to obtain a full set of forms from your local tax office before working through the example.

Imagine Mr and Mrs Green have the following circumstances. John is employed, earning £30,000 per year, and he has a company car. He has a Building Society account that paid him £1,140 last year. He also has a PEP and has sold some shares which he inherited from his mother with a value of £6,000 two years ago, for £8,000 this year. John pays a pension premium of £2,000 p.a.

His wife Ulrika is a part time teacher earning £6,000. She has sold shares for £30,000 which she bought three years earlier for £5,000. Moreover, she lets out the flat which she owned before she married John, with a gross rental of £10,000 p.a before expenses. There is also a small mortgage on that flat. Ulrika also has an income from a trust set up by her grandmother many years ago, and she receives £760. John and Ulrika have three children, and they wonder what to do about their tax affairs.

Basic Action

The first thing that each must do is request a Tax Return. Once received, John will require the magenta Employment Schedule (see page 55), but he will not require any other schedules. His Building Society income will be completed under question 10 of the ordinary Return, (as will any dividends on the shares he inherited), and his pension relief will be claimed under question 14.

According to the notes alongside question 8 on capital gains, (page 52) he has neither made more chargeable gains than £6,300 nor disposed of any chargeable asset exceeding £12,600. Beyond this, therefore, John will have no further forms to request.

Ulrika must also request a Tax Return, and she will require the magenta Employment form for her work as a teacher, she will also require the red Land and Property form because she lets out the flat which she still owns. She will also require a Capital Gains blue schedule because her gains have been more than £6,300 and her disposals more than £12,600 (question eight again). Finally, she will require the Brown Trust schedule in order to report that income.

Completing the Tax Return in Detail

You will probably need to obtain a copy to follow this example

John

John will need to complete his Tax Return paying extra attention to question 10, where he will need to complete boxes 10.2, 10.3 and 10.4 with the figures £1,140, £360 and £1,500.

His PEP does not need to be reported, nor do his chargeable gains. However, he will want to claim relief for his pension contribution at box 14.11 and 14.15.

John will have to include the Employment schedule, and, like his wife, copy the details from his P60. However, he will also need to include at 1.16 the taxable amount of his company car and at 1.17 any fuel he may have.

Those schedules will then need to be attached to his Tax Return and sent in to the Revenue for calculation before the end of September following the relevant tax year. If Ulrika and John are happy to work out their own tax, then they may wait until 31st January before submitting their Returns.

Ulrika

Ulrika will need to tick "yes" to question 1 on page 2 of the Tax Return, as well as question 5, question 7, and question 8. She will not need to complete question 10, nor question 11 or

12, nor 13, as she is reporting all her income under the right section. (Note that if her shares paid dividends, then Ulrika would need to complete sections 10.15 to 10.17 on page 3). She will ignore the third section of question 15 (15.3), because she will be claiming the interest on her mortgage under her red supporting schedule.

Ulrika will need to complete section 16 to indicate that she is married and question 18 if she wants her tax to be calculated (*an example for self-calculation follows*). It might also be wise to complete question 20 and 21 so that the Inland Revenue have the correct information and question 22.2 will probably result in a more rapid repayment of any tax she may be due.

Before sending it in, she will have to sign the declaration on question 23, and indicate that she has completed the Employment, Land and Property, Trust, and Capital Gains schedules. Turning to these specific schedules, the Brown Trust section is relatively simple. She should enter the figure £770 in box 7.1, £230 in box 7.2, and £1,000 in box 7.3. As long as she is satisfied that the family trust is operating correctly, there will be no need to provide additional information.

The Land and Property schedule will take a little more time. She may ignore box 5.1 through to 5.18, but will need to include the £10,000 in box 5.20.

Her expenses will need to be detailed in box 5.24 to 5.29, and totalled in box 5.30. Her net profit will be included in box 5.31.

If she is claiming any tax adjustments, then these will need to be detailed in box 5.32 to 5.38 and totalled in box 5.39. If she is happy with the mathematics, then the profit for the year can simply be detailed in box 5.43.

The blue Capital Gains schedule will need to report her total chargeable capital gains in box 8.8, but on the reverse of the form she will need to record the assets she has sold, the disposal proceeds (£30,000), the gain she is reporting (£25,000) and the date at which she held it. The total chargeable gain of £25,000 will be entered in box 8.1, and, in Ulrika's case, box 8.7. Box 8.8 will then be box 8.7 less her allowance of £6,500.

Finally, Ulrika will need to include the Employment schedule and copy the details from her P60 into boxes 1.8 to 1.11, and, as she has no further benefit, there will be no need to complete that schedule any further.

Back to the Tax Return; this will then have to be submitted along with the supporting schedules.

Calculating Ulrika's Tax Liability

Many people will need to know how much extra tax they are likely to have to pay and will therefore want to calculate their liability. Let's see how this works in practice by completing a tax calculation working sheet for Ulrika.

We will need to assume that Ulrika has £2,000 of allowable expenses on her rental income and that she has paid a certain amount of income tax via the PAYE system, in order to make the forms make sense.

Note the Tax Calculation Guide contains a few pages of pre-amble. So the calculations actually start on page five.

The first box will show the total earned income from the first page of the tax return along with any other income, in this case the rental and trust income. Any deductions will be dealt with in boxes W13 to W19 so that the last box on this first page should be the total of Ulrika's taxable income. This then is copied to the top of the seventh page of the working sheet.

Tax calculation working sheet

Total income from

- **Employment** *including benefits and less* expenses for **each** employment
  Add income in boxes 1.8 to 1.10, 1.12 to 1.23 and 1.27 to 1.29

  First employment £ 6,000   Other employments £

  Deduct any figures in boxes 1.31 to 1.38   £   £

  Total taxable income   £   + £   = W1 £ 6,000

- **Share Schemes** (from box 2.31)   W2 £

- **Self-employment** (from box 3.89)   W3 £

- **Partnerships** (from boxes 4.32, 4.65 and 4.68)   W4 £

- **Land and property** (from box 5.43)   W5 £ 8,000

- **Foreign income** (from boxes 6.2, 6.4, 6.5 and 6.8)   W6 £

- **Trusts, settlements or estates of deceased persons** (add together any figures in taxable amount column and deduct any figure in box 7.19)   W7 £ 1,000

- **UK savings and investments** (total any figures in taxable amount column on page 3 of your Tax Return)   W8 £

- **UK pensions, retirement annuities and benefits** (add together any figures in 'taxable amount' column on page 4 of your Tax Return and deduct any exemption in box 11.13)   W9 £

- **Maintenance and alimony received** (from box 12.3)   W10 £

- **Other income** (copy the figure in box 13.3 less any figure in box 13.5)   W11 £

  Total   Total column above   W12 £ 15,000

Deductions for

- **Personal pension** (add together any figures in boxes 14.5, 14.10, 14.15, 14.16 and 14.17)   W13 £

- **Vocational training** (multiply any figure in box 15.1 by $^{100}/_{76}$)   W14 £

- **Interest on qualifying loans** (from box 15.3)   W15 £

- **Maintenance or alimony paid** (see notes page 2)   W16 £

- **Charitable covenants, annuities and Gift Aid payments** (multiply any figures in boxes 15.9 and 15.10 by $^{100}/_{76}$)   W17 £

- **Losses and post-cessation expenses** (from boxes 3.82, 4.12, 4.58, 5.16, 5.44, 8.16 and 15.11)   W18 £

- **Trade union and friendly society death benefit payments** (from box 15.12)   W19 £

  Total   Total boxes W13 to W19   W20 £

  Total income less deductions   box W12 less W20   W21 £ 15,000

CCO (Draft 96/97)   ■ TAX CALCULATION GUIDE: PAGE 5   now copy the figure in box W21 to box W22 on page 7

(Note that we are not talking about deductions within the rental accounts as these have already been claimed the on red rental income sheet.)

Tax calculation working sheet continued

Reliefs
- you get basic rate relief automatically - further relief will be due if you are liable to higher rate tax.

- **Pension payments**
(from boxes 14.15 and 14.17) W23.1 £

- **Vocational training**
(from box W14) W23.2 £

Total W23.3 £

Copy to W23

Allowances given as a deduction from your income
- you may need to check your entitlement - see notes page 3.

- **Personal allowance**
- normally £4045 unless you are non-resident and not claiming allowances W25.1 £ **4045**

- **Age related personal allowance**
- see notes page 3 W25.2 £

Savings income taxed at the lower (20%) rate.

- **Partnership savings**
(from boxes 4.32 and 4.65) W28.1 £

- **UK savings**
(from box W8) W28.2 £

- **Foreign savings**
(from box 6.2) W28.3 £

- **Trusts, settlements and estate income**
(from boxes 7.6, 7.12 and 7.15) W28.4 £

Total W28.5 £

- **Blind person's allowance**
- £1280 W25.3 £

- **Transitional allowance**
(from box 16.4) W25.4 £

- **Blind person's surplus allowance from your spouse**
(from box 16.27) W25.5 £

Total W25.6 £ **4045**

Copy to W28

Allowances and reliefs given in terms of tax
these reduce your tax bill - you may need to use the Question 16 Notes on pages 23 to 26 of the Tax Return Guide and on pages 3 and 4 of this guide.

- **Married couple's allowance**
- see notes on pages 3 and 4 W42.1 £

- **Married couple's surplus allowance**
(from box 16.28) W42.2 £

Notional tax is not repayable and so has to be calculated as an allowance given in terms of tax rather than being regarded as tax deducted at source. It is treated as paid on:

- **Partnership notional tax**
(from boxes 4.73 and 4.74) W44.1 £

- **UK scrip dividends**
(from boxes 10.22, 10.25, 10.28 and 10.31) W44.2 £

- **Trusts, settlements and estate income** (from box 7.14) W44.3 £ **1000**

Total W44.4 £

- **Additional personal allowance**
- usually £1,790, may be split with another person - see the notes W42.3 £

- **Widow's bereavement allowance** -
(if your husband died this year or last year and you have not remarried) W42.4 £

- **Interest on loans**
(from box 15.2) W42.5 £

- **Maintenance and alimony**
(boxes 15.4 and 15.5 and the notes for box W16) W42.6 £

Total W42.7 £

Copy to W44

CCO (Draft 96/97) ■ TAX CALCULATION GUIDE: PAGE 6

Page six has boxes for taxed income including Ulrika's trust income, and a series of boxes (W25.1 - W25.5 and W42.1 - W42.6) for the various allowances. Page three then seeks to ensure that income is taxed, and allowances given

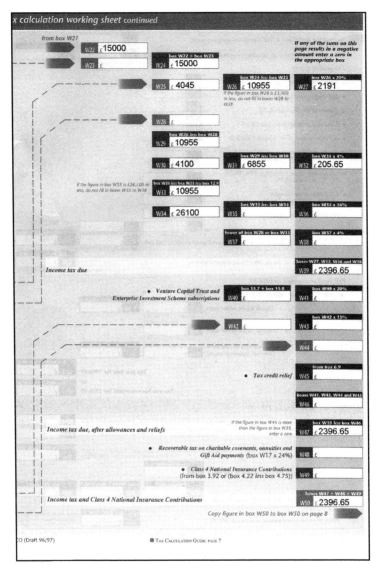

x calculation working sheet continued

from box W21

W22 £ 15000

W23 £

box W22 + box W23
W24 £ 15000

If any of the sums on this page results in a negative amount enter a zero in the appropriate box

W25 £ 4045

box W24 less box W25
W26 £ 10955
If the figure in box W26 is £3,900 or less, do not fill in boxes W28 to W38

box W26 x 20%
W27 £ 2191

W28 £

box W26 less box W28
W29 £ 10955

W30 £ 4100

box W29 less box W30
W31 £ 6855

box W31 x 4%
W32 £ 205.65

If the figure in box W33 is £26,100 or less, do not fill in boxes W35 to W38

box W26 less box W23 less box 12.9
W33 £ 10955

W34 £ 26100

box W33 less box W34
W35 £

box W35 x 16%
W36 £

lower of box W28 or box W35
W37 £

box W37 x 4%
W38 £

Income tax due

boxes W27, W32, W36 and W38
W39 £ 2396.65

● *Venture Capital Trust and Enterprise Investment Scheme subscriptions*
W40 £

box 15.7 + box 15.8

box W40 x 20%
W41 £

W42 £

box W42 x 15%
W43 £

W44 £

● *Tax credit relief*
W45 £

from box 6.9

boxes W41, W43, W44 and W45
W46 £

Income tax due, after allowances and reliefs

If the figure in box W46 is more than the figure in box W39, enter a zero
box W39 less box W46
W47 £ 2396.65

● *Recoverable tax on charitable covenants, annuities and Gift Aid payments (box W17 x 24%)*
W48 £

● *Class 4 National Insurance Contributions (from box 3.92 or (box 4.22 less box 4.75))*
W49 £

Income tax and Class 4 National Insurance Contributions

boxes W47 + W48 + W49
W50 £ 2396.65

Copy figure in box W50 to box W50 on page 8

at the appropriate rate, either 20%, 23%, or 40%. Like most people, Ulrika will claim her personal allowance in box W25.1 and will be credited with the 20% rate of tax by the pre-printed box W30. On the far right of the form the

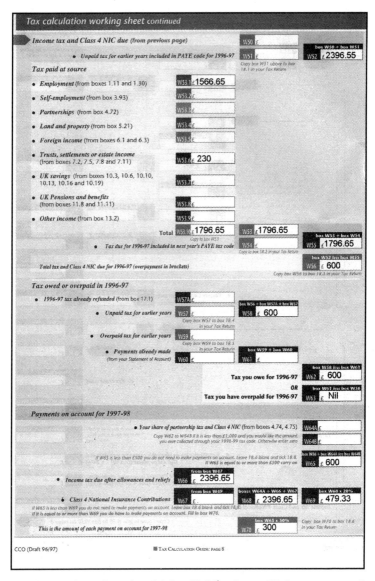

Tax calculation working sheet continued

Income tax and Class 4 NIC due *(from previous page)* — W50 £

• *Unpaid tax for earlier years included in PAYE code for 1996-97* — W51 £

box W50 + box W51 — W52 £ **2396.55**
Copy box W51 above to box 18.1 in your Tax Return

Tax paid at source

• *Employment* (from boxes 1.11 and 1.30) — W53.1 £ **1566.65**

• *Self-employment* (from box 3.93) — W53.2 £

• *Partnerships* (from box 4.72) — W53.3 £

• *Land and property* (from box 5.21) — W53.4 £

• *Foreign income* (from boxes 6.1 and 6.3) — W53.5 £

• *Trusts, settlements or estate income* (from boxes 7.2, 7.5, 7.8 and 7.11) — W53.6 £ **230**

• *UK savings* (from boxes 10.3, 10.6, 10.10, 10.13, 10.16 and 10.19) — W53.7 £

• *UK Pensions and benefits* (from boxes 11.8 and 11.11) — W53.8 £

• *Other income* (from box 13.2) — W53.9 £

Total — W53.10 £ **1796.65**
Copy to box W53

W53 £ **1796.65**

• *Tax due for 1996-97 included in next year's PAYE tax code* — W54 £
Copy to box 18.2 in your Tax Return

box W53 + box W54 — W55 £ **1796.65**

Total tax and Class 4 NIC due for 1996-97 *(overpayment in brackets)* — W56 £ **600**
box W52 less box W55
Copy box W56 to box 18.3 in your Tax Return

Tax owed or overpaid in 1996-97

• *1996-97 tax already refunded* (from box 17.1) — W57A £

• *Unpaid tax for earlier years* — W57 £
Copy box W57 to box 18.4 in your Tax Return

box W56 + box W57A + box W57 — W58 £ **600**

• *Overpaid tax for earlier years* — W59 £
Copy box W59 to box 18.5 in your Tax Return

• *Payments already made* (from your Statement of Account) — W60 £

box W59 + box W60 — W61 £

Tax you owe for 1996-97 — box W58 less box W61 — W62 £ **600**

OR

Tax you have overpaid for 1996-97 — box W61 less box W58 — W63 £ **Nil**

Payments on account for 1997-98

• *Your share of partnership tax and Class 4 NIC* (from boxes 4.74, 4.75) — W64A £

Copy W62 to W64B if it is less than £1,000 and you would like the amount you owe collected through your 1998-99 tax code. Otherwise enter zero — W64B £

box W56 + box W64A less box W64B — W65 £ **600**

If W65 is less than £500 you do not need to make payments on account. Leave 18.6 blank and tick 18.8. If W65 is equal to or more than £500 carry on

• *Income tax due after allowances and reliefs* — from box W47 — W66 £ **2396.65**

• *Class 4 National Insurance Contributions* — from box W49 — W67 £

boxes W64A + W66 + W67 — W68 £ **2396.65**

box W68 x 20% — W69 £ **479.33**

If W65 is less than W69 you do not need to make payments on account. Leave 18.6 blank and tick 18.8. If it is equal to or more than W69 you do have to make payments on account. Fill in box W70.

This is the amount of each payment on account for 1997-98 — box W65 x 50% — W70 £ **300**
Copy Box W70 to box 18.6 in your Tax Return

CCO (Draft 96/97) — ■ TAX CALCULATION GUIDE: PAGE 8

total tax that she should be liable for will be computed simply by following the instructions and simple maths.

The back page (eight) is important because although we have computed that Ulrika will be liable to pay £2396.65 on her income for the tax year, she has already paid tax via her employer and on the trust income. So the back page allows credit for this tax and seeks to establish what the outstanding amount is by deducting the tax already paid, (£1796.65) from the total liability, there is a balance of £600 to be collected in two equal instalments of £300 each. The statement of account which Ulrika receives will show an outstanding balance of £600, and request two payments on 31st January and 31st July.

You'll see from this example, it is likely that the first run through will be a little difficult, and it might be wise to work on a copy of the form rather than make mistakes on the original.

Conclusion

Completing your Tax Return is unlikely to be a simple or easy task. **Moreover, as there will be inevitable delays with the sheer weight of difficulties faced by ordinary individuals, then you will be wise to send in your Returns early.** Because, if you do not, and the Return is wrong, or your calculation is wrong and the Return has to be sent back to you for correction, then the automatic penalties and interest will run from the 1st February following the tax year.

So, if you submit your Return on 31st January, and it is not accepted as correct, then interest runs immediately, during all the time in which your Return is being rejected, sent back to you, corrected and re-submitted. This contrasts with the old system whereby interest did not necessarily run, and was dependant upon the type of income to which it referred.

Chapter Ten

Conclusion

"It is difficult to imagine which taxpayers will genuinely remain unaffected."

S elf-assessment is, without doubt, going to affect a wide variety of people. It is difficult to imagine which taxpayers will genuinely remain unaffected. The new requirements for the submission of returns, the new dates for the payment of tax, the major and wide ranging requirements for records to be kept, along with the variety of stiff penalties that can be applied for non-compliance, will surely prove to be a very considerable burden for the tax payer.

"Simplified Assessment" changed into "Self-Assessment" with very little in the way of fuss. But, it is quite clear now that tax payers themselves have a greater and more explicit responsibility to manage their tax affairs competently and efficiently.

The Inland Revenue has recently recognised its function as public servant, and the publication of many useful leaflets, the introduction of help lines, and the Taxpayers Charter, all give the taxpayer the opportunity for some sort of relaxed dialogue without confrontation. Nonetheless, it is clear that the system may take a while to become efficient. After that, I cannot see that a tax payer will have any defence at all for ignorance of the law.

This is quite clear in record keeping penalties where the Revenue say that they will not apply them except in repeated cases of non-compliance. If the self-assessment regime is to work, then it must raise taxes efficiently and effectively. To do this, tax payers will certainly be pursued and penalties applied. The situation should be clear from this book. Start to organise NOW, and don't throw anything away.

The approach must be as follows:

1. Get organised.

2. Act fast.

3. Get help if you need it.

Appendix One
Investment Matrix

Investment Type	Nil	Income tax Basic	Higher	Capital Gains Tax
Cash	Reclaim	No further	Further	No Tax
Nat.Savings Account	No Tax	No Tax	No Tax	No Tax
Nat. Savings Inc.Bonds	No Tax	Basic Rate to pay	Basic and higher to pay	No Tax
Gilts/ Corporate Bonds	Reclaim	No Further	Further	No Tax
National Savings Certificates	No Tax	No Tax	No Tax	No Tax
Shares	Reclaim	No Further	Further	Yes
Unit Trusts	Reclaim	No Further	Further	Yes
Investment Trusts	Reclaim	No Further	Further	Yes

Investment				
Insurance Bonds	No Tax / No Reclaim	No Tax	Further	No Tax
Offshore Ins. Bonds	No Tax	Basic Rate to pay	Basic and higher to pay	No Tax
PEPs	No Tax	No Tax	No Tax	No Tax
Venture Capital Trusts	No Tax	No Tax	No Tax	No Tax
Offshore Roll-up Funds	No Tax	Basic rate to pay	Basic and higher to pay	No Tax
Purchased Life Annuities	Reclaim	Basic rate to pay	Further	No Tax
Pension Income	Reclaim	No Further	Further	No Tax
2nd Hand Life Policies	No Tax	No Tax	No Tax	Yes
Qualifying Life Policies	No Tax	No Tax	No Tax	No Tax
Guaranteed Income Bonds	No Tax	No Further	Further	No Tax

Investment Matrix

Appendix Two

Basis of Assessment for New Businesses

In Chapter Two, on the major self-assessment changes, we mentioned the fundamental change in the basis of assessment. This section in intended to outline the situation for new businesses, and the transitional provisions for existing businesses.

The example below is as simple as they come, and your own circumstances may be much more complicated, particularly if you have changed your accounting date. However, you will, hopefully, be able to recognise the basic principles.

Imagine that, under the old system, a new business began in June 1987. The profits were as follows:

To May 31st 1988	£10,000
To May 31st 1989	£12,000
To May 31st 1990	£14,000
To May 31st 1991	£15,000

The assessments would have been:

1987-88	£ 8,333
1988-89	£10,000
1989-90	£10,000
1990-91	£12,000

The previous year basis would apply whereby the accounts relevant to a tax year of assessment would be those ending in the **previous** tax year. So, for 1990-91, the accounts to May 1989 are used. A period ending 10 months before the start of the tax year!

Under the new system, calculations are different and the preceding year basis disappears. Imagine in the example above that the start date of the business had been June 1995 and that the results were identical. The assessments become:

1995-96	£ 8,333
1996-97	£10,000
1997-98	£12,000
1998-99	£14,000

See how the third year of assessment changes to a current year basis and the ten month gap no longer applies.

The arrangement applying to those people who were self-employed before April 1994, who now need transitional rules, is more complicated.

The tax year 1995-96 will be the last to use the old basis and this means that 1996-97 will be a transitional year. The result is that self-employed businesses will be taxed on the average profit for two consecutive trading periods, so that from 1997-98 onwards, the current year basis will apply.

The example below sets this out.

Profits

To May 31st 1994	£10,000
To May 31st 1995	£12,000
To May 31st 1996	£14,000
To May 31st 1997	£15,000

Assessments

1995-96	£10,000
1996-97 (£12,000 + £14,000) x 50%	£13,000
1997-98	£15,000

As you can see, the two years to 31st May 1996 are averaged so that the previous year basis can die out and the current year basis can become fully operational. This really does mean that a year's profits escape tax!

Beyond this simple example you are likely to need the guidance of an accountant because there are increasingly complicated calculations where losses are involved, changes of accounting date or partnerships.

Appendix Three

Record Keeping Requirements

It is easy to get worked up about the new record keeping requirements. However, a great deal is basic common sense.
Many well managed businesses will, in any event, have always kept the type of records which the tax man is looking
for. Others, however, may not have, and this will not be a result of anyone wishing to hoodwink the Inland Revenue, but
simply a question of habit. Well, habits will have to change if
you wish to keep on the right side of the authorities.

This section gives two examples of the types of records
which might need to be kept. It has been constructed from
a combination of the Revenue's own publications on the issue, along with professional comment in journals and
magazines. It cannot guarantee to be absolutely exhaustive, but, it will give you a very thorough indication of the
information likely to be needed.

The Retail Shop

You should retain the following:

1. Any till rolls or other electronic records of sale,
    perhaps you have a sophisticated sales system
    with down-loaded stock control system.

2. Details of any other income which your shop might receive. For example, you might be a National Lottery agent and be paid commission.

3. Bills for purchases and expenses.

4. A record of your stock on hand at the end of the relevant year.

5. All invoices that you have received or raised.

6. All your banking books and Building Society statements, any pass-books, cheques stubs and paying in slips relevant to the business.

7. A cash book.

8. Details of any capital you may have introduced.

9. Any funds you have taken out of the business, either in the form of a cheque or cash from the till for your personal use.

10. Details of any assets which are used for both business and private purposes, most obviously, a motor car.

11. You should also keep a record of any goods taken for your own use.

12. If you should take cash from the till in order to pay small expenses, for example, the window cleaner, then you ought to report this.

Generally, of course, you must keep all records which can substantiate your tax return.

Sub-Contractors

Despite the housing recession, there are still a great many sub-contractors working in the domestic and commercial construction industries. This has always been an area of Inland Revenue interest because the scope for fraud is considerable, and the records of some contractors and sub-contractors, are not particularly good.

The records you should keep are as follows:

1. You should keep a record of all funds which are due to you for work you are doing, whether they are from private individuals or contractors.

2. You should keep a record of all invoices which you raise.

3. If you are using a 714, then each time you give a voucher to a contractor, the Inland Revenue suggests that you write your record on the stubs in the book of vouchers. In the absence of a 714, then form SC60 should serve the same purpose.

4. If you have any items you are claiming as a business expenditure, for example, tools and work clothes and so on, then you should keep all the bills.

5. If you are running a vehicle as part of the business, then, once again, you need to keep all the relevant

bills for maintenance and fuel, along with a mileage log to substantiate your business use.

6.   It would also be useful to keep a records of all private funds you pay into bank or Building Society accounts, as well as any cash you take out for your own personal use.

Conclusion

The above are just two examples which demonstrate that there are certain vital primary records such as money in and money out, and all the supporting documentation.

Appendix Four

Tax Office Enquiry

The Inland Revenue recently issued a booklet concerning enquiries (investigations or checks) into self-assessment tax returns issued after April 1997. Their aims in making enquiries are as follows:

1.   To ensure that you pay the right amount of tax "no more, no less."

2.   To ensure that everyone else is also paying the right amount of tax, which has an indirect effect on you.

3.   To discourage tax evasion.

The point is that the 'enquiries' will be random. This means that anyone, from the most complicated self-employed business person to the old lady in Brighton, can suddenly be investigated by the Inland Revenue.

It has been made clear that tax returns containing mistakes are more likely to be looked at more thoroughly than those that do not, although there is still the random element of even the best presented paperwork.

The Process

You will be told in writing that the Inland Revenue will be starting enquiries. You will be told what your rights are. There is a time limit of 12 months from the filing date during which the Revenue must tell you that they are to start their enquiry. Of course, if you submit your tax return late, then this period will be extended.

Professional Advisor

You are allowed to use an accountant or tax specialist who will represent you, and it may well be worth contacting someone in your local area who has dealt with simple enquiries and who is able to give you an inside track. There is some division within the profession, **there are those that argue that engaging an advisor might make the Inland Revenue unsympathetic and there are those that say that it is the best form of protection.** You will need to make up your own mind.

Extent of the Enquiry

You may find that the enquiry simply deals with one or two issues on your Return. At this stage, you might well be asked to produce records. Alternatively, you could be the subject of a complete and thorough examination of all your tax affairs. Whilst the tax man will request only "relevant records", we have already seen how extensive this can be.

Penalties

The Inland Revenue have stated that, "If you provide information you know to be false, you could be liable to prosecution".

Findings

Of course, if there is nothing wrong, then the tax man will say so and tell you the enquiry is over.

If there is something wrong, then you may well be asked to pay tax on account towards any additional tax which the Revenue thinks is due from you. New figures will be put forward and you will have to agree these (or disagree) and then amend your self-assessment. The time limit for doing this will be 30 days.

Appeal

You can, of course, appeal to the Commissioners of the Inland Revenue as you can now. The aim, however, will be to agree most situations without the need for that process.

Further Penalties

In addition to the interest you will have to pay on any late paid tax (because you did not say it was due when you first submitted your Return), you may also have to pay the surcharge. In addition to this, there are penalties for incorrect Returns, but only if the error was due to negligent or fraudulent conduct.

Expenses

If you have to provide information for the Inland Revenue and discuss it with them, and particularly if you engage a personal advisor, you will incur expenses. However, the Inland Revenue's obligation is nothing more than to treat you fairly and relatively efficiently. The costs you run up in defending yourself are down to you. If the Revenue made a genuine mistake, then you may get financial redress.

Conclusion

All taxpayers should be aware that, in addition to the already comprehensive requirements to comply with the rules, there is the threat of a random audit. I have no doubt that, as the years go by, more people will be subjected to such audits based on their success in raising extra tax. I am sure it will become common to meet these people and hear their distressing stories of how Big Brother treated them. Of course, there is one way out of this - make sure your affairs are absolutely straight.

There is no doubt that the time spent in getting your affairs in good order will be far less than proving that a sloppily rendered Tax Return is correct, and paying any penalties that arise.

Appendix Five
Main Self-Assessment Penalties

Offence	Penalty
Failing to submit a return by 31st January	£100 fixed
Failing to submit a return by 31st July	£100 fixed
Continued failure	£60 per day
Late payment of tax (one month)	5% surcharge
Late payment of tax (six months) N.B. Interest will also be charged.	5% surcharge
Failure to maintain and retain adequate records	up to £3000

Appendix Six

Capital Gains Tax

M any taxpayers find Capital Gains tax difficult to handle because its payment is a relatively rare occurrence. This section sets out an example of how Capital Gains Tax works, along with various useful details as to what might constitute a chargeable asset in the first place.

There are many significant assets which are not chargeable to Capital Gains at all. For example, your principal private residence (the home in which you live most of the time) will not be subject to Capital Gains tax in most circumstances. There are also useful exclusions for second properties which have been provided for dependent relatives. There is no Capital Gains Tax on Gilts, nor on cash which has gone up in value. Cars are also free of Capital Gains Tax, the point being that very few of them ever go up in value.

The most significant class of assets generally liable to Capital Gains Tax will be second and subsequent properties, Unit Trusts and shares. Whilst many businesses are also chargeable assets for Capital Gains Tax, there are significant reliefs which operate to reduce or eliminate the Capital Gain in most cases.

The example below shows how the whole process works. Basically, an asset is sold and, from the sale proceeds, you are allowed to deduct any costs, such as stamp duty or legal fees. This is then compared with the original purchase price to which indexation relief is added. This then leaves you with a net chargeable gain from which you take your personal allowance. The balance is then taxable at 20% and 40% depending on your overall position.

Imagine you bought a second home in 1982 for £50,000 and now sell it for £120,000. The calculation should look like this:

	£
Sale Proceeds	120,000
Less allowable costs of sale	2,000
Less original cost	50,000
Gross gain	68,000
Less indexation (Inflation relief), say	45,000
Net gain	23,000
Personal exempt limit(97/98)	(6,500)
Taxable gain	16,500
Tax at 23%	3,795
or 40%	6,600

You should be able to use this as a template for any gains which you think you might have. There are very complicated provisions concerning assets owned before 1965, or acquired before 1982. Additionally, where you have bought and sold holdings in the same share over a prolonged period, then there are complicated rules as to which shares are deemed to be sold, and when. These "pooling provisions" are beyond the scope of this appendix and you will need further advice. Hopefully, however, this section simply allows you to identify when a capital gain may be an issue.

Appendix Seven

Glossary

Age Allowance   An increased personal allowance for those people aged over 6 at the beginning of the tax year.

Anti-Avoidance   Specific legislation introduced by the Inland Revenue to combat avoidance schemes.

Avoidance   The use of legitimate means to reduce one tax bill.

Bed & Breakfast   A system of selling and immediately re-acquiring assets in order to realise a chargeable gain, or allowable loss.

Benefits in Kind/ Fringe Benefits   Benefits provided by an employer for which the employee does not usually have to pay. For example, company cars or company accommodation.

Commissioners   Either special Commissioners who are full time professionals, or general Commissioners who are unpaid local people. Each is intended to adjudicate where there is a dispute between the taxpayer and the Inland Revenue.

Chargeable Gains (allowable losses)   When a chargeable asset is sold, there will either be a profit or a loss.

Domicile   The country you regard as your normal home.

Earnings Cap — A level of earnings beyond which pension contributions cannot be relieved.

Evasion — The use of illegal methods to avoid paying tax.

Estate — The total of an individual's property world-wide.

Furniss v Dawson — A fundamental tax case which sets out the Inland Revenue outlook on certain types of complicated tax avoidance schemes.

Gifts with Reservations — Gifts made to avoid inheritance tax, but which fail to do so because a benefit is reserved for the donor.

Intestate — A description whereby an individual has died without making a will, so that certain fall back provisions apply.

Interest in Possessions — An individual's entitlement to the income of a trust.

Indexation Allowance — A means of allowing for inflation on chargeable gains.

Independent Taxation — A system whereby a husband and wife can be treated as entirely separate individuals for income tax purposes, and C.G.T.

Ordinary Residence — Refers to your status as a taxpayer in the country in which you ordinarily live.

Personal Allowances — A set level of deduction from income before income tax is applied.

Residence — A term used specifically in taxation to denote an individual's temporary home for the purposes of taxation.

Schedules   Additional modules (usually two pages long) used in conjunction with the main tax return to calculate your income and capital gains.

Spouse Exemption This refers to the facility of passing unlimited assets between UK domiciled spouses without inheritance tax charges.

Supplementary Pages   See Schedules

Taper Relief   A system whereby the tax charged on chargeable transfers is reduced to reflect the number of years since that transfer between 3 and 7.

TESSA   The Tax Exempt Special Savings Arrangement, whereby the income from a deposit account may be credited without income tax deductions, subject to a 5 year holding period.

Trust   A mechanism where one party (the Trustee), hold assets for another party (the Beneficiaries), usually at the request of the Settlor (the one who introduced the assets in the first place).

Tax Payer's Charter   A statement of Revenue policy as to how they will deal with the public.

Widows' Bereavement Allowance   A specific allowance which may be claimed by a widow in the year of her husband's death and the following year.

Year of Assessment   The tax year which runs from April 6th through to April 5th.

Appendix Eight

Further Information

The Inland Revenue publish a variety of useful leaflets and reportlets. Here is a list of the most important.

Leaflet	Topic
I.R. (insert)	Shows all tax rates and allowances for current year. (see also I.R.90)
I.R.34	Covers P.A.Y.E.(see I.R.69)
I.R.58	Covers working abroad.
I.R.60	This covers income tax and students.
I.R.91	Allowances for widows.
I.R.121	Income tax and pensioners.
I.R.92	One parent families.
I.R.93	Separation, divorce, maintenance.
I.R.78	Personal pensions and SERPS.
I.R.89	P.E.P.S.
I.R.110	Savings and investments.(see also I.R.127)
I.R.123	Mortgage relief.
I.R.83	Independent Taxation. (see CGT 15)
C.G.T.14	Basic introduction to C.G.T.
C.G.T.4	Rules on letting part of your home. (see also I.R.87)
C.G.T.13	Indexation relief.
I.H.T.3	An introduction to inheritance tax. (also I.H.T.1)
I.R.45	What happens when someone dies with income tax, C.G.T. and I.H.T.
I.R.120	Taxpayers charter and how to get information from the Revenue.
I.R.37	How to appeal against the decisions reached by the Revenue.
SA/BK1	Self Assessment general guide.
SA/BK2	Self Assessment guide for self employed.
SA/BK3	A guide to record keeping.
SA/BK4	A general guide to record keeping.
SAT3	Self Assessment - what it will mean for employers.

Appendix Nine

Important Dates

January 31st	Returns must be in.
February 28th	Automatic penalty surcharge.
April 6th	Tax Returns sent out.
May 31st	P60s to be handed to employees.
July 6th	P11Ds due from employer.
July 31st	Second payment on account.
September 30th	Send in your Return if you want the Inland Revenue to calculate your tax.

Understand Bonds and Gilts in a Day   £5.99

This handy title shows potential investors, and those with an interest
in the bond markets, how to assess the potential risks and rewards,
giving a simple to follow set of criteria on which to base investment
decisions. Having shown the inexperienced investor how to go
about buying bonds, it also teaches even the most arithmetically shy
how to calculate the yield on a bond and plan an income based
portfolio. The confusing terminology used in the bond market is
clearly explained with working definitions of many terms and a
comprehensive glossary.

For the more seasoned bond and gilt investor there are sets of bond
strategies laid out so the reader can evaluate their holdings and pick
a course of investment which best suits their needs.

Using illustrations and examples *Understand Bonds and Gilts in a
Day* shows how investors can ❑guard against default by the issuer,
❑diversify a portfolio to smooth delayed payments of interest
❑determine which bonds and gilts are carrying a premium and
which a discount ❑avoid the liquidity risk of rising interest rates

Tax Loopholes for the Ordinary Taxpayer   £4.99

This book could save you a fortune. You don't have to be rich to
take advantage of tax loopholes which could save you hundreds and
even thousands of pounds. By Stefan Bernstein.

The Complete Beginner's Guide to The Internet   £4.95

Everywhere you turn these days, it's Internet this, Cyberspace that and
Superhighway the other. Indeed, hardly a day goes by without us being
bombarded with information and reasons why you should be on the Net.
But none of that is of much help in making an informed decision about
joining and using the Internet.

What exactly is The Internet? Where did it come from and where is it
going? And, more importantly, how can everybody take their place in
this new community?

The Complete Beginner's Guide to The Internet answers all of those
questions and more. On top of being an indispensable guide to the basics
of Cyberspace, it is the lowest priced introduction on the market by a long
way at a *surfer-friendly £4.95* (alternative books cost around £30).

Complete Beginner's Guide to Buying & Using a Computer   £3.95

Complete Beginner's Guide to Making Money on the Internet   £3.95

Understand Derivatives in a Day   £5.99

By understanding how derivatives affect apparently safe investments, such as pensions, endowment mortgages and equity plans,
you can make sure your own cash is in good hands.

Nick Leeson and Co.'s dealings in the derivatives market ruined a
well-respected bank. How could this possibly happen? How could a
teenager run up a several hundred thousand pound debt by trading in
options? And, perhaps more importantly, how do derivative traders
earn their huge bonuses?

Learn...❏How private investors get started... ❏To Hedge, Straddle and
control Risk... ❏   Ways to limit the downside but *not* the upside...
❏About *risk free* derivative strategies... ❏Trading Psychology - Fear,
Hope and Greed...   ❏Also, the History of Derivatives; Currency
Speculation; Long and Short puts; Tarantula Trading; and much more.

Understand Financial Risk in a Day   £5.99

Risk management is all about minimising risks and maximising
opportunities. Those who understand what they should be doing,
as a result of their risk calculations, will usually come out as
winners. Those who flail around in the dark will, more often
than not, be the losers.

Understand Financial Risk in a Day is a perfect introduction to the
subject. Light on detailed formulae and heavy on easy-to-follow
examples it will lead the reader to a greater awareness of how to
evaluate the risks they are facing and adapt a strategy to create the
best possible outcome. All of the latest risk management techniques
are discussed and the best tools selected for dealing with each aspect.